FROM THE COWSHED TO THE KOP

FROM THE COWSHED TO THE KOP

MY AUTOBIOGRAPHY

PETER CORMACK

WITH BRIAN WEDDELL

BLACK & WHITE PUBLISHING

First published 2012
by Black & White Publishing Ltd
29 Ocean Drive, Edinburgh EH6 6JL

1 3 5 7 9 10 8 6 4 2   12 13 14 15

ISBN: 978 1 84502 422 2

Typeset by Ellipsis Digital Ltd, Glasgow
Printed and bound by Scandbook AB, Sweden

To my family who have been a constant source of support,
encouragement and inspiration throughout

CONTENTS

TESTIMONIALS

'My main memory of Peter was when he played for Hibernian and I played for Dunfermline Athletic and Rangers, and at that time games were very competitive.

Peter of course was a very skilful and talented player and always looked to express himself that way. I can always remember his performance against Real Madrid, and being there to witness his Man of the Match performance was a privilege and still remains in the memory bank to this day.

All in all, he had a wonderful career which puts him in the pantheon of other Scottish players of his time.'

— Sir Alex Ferguson

'As well as being a good player Peter was also a good mate, not just with me. He was popular with all the players when he was at Liverpool Football Club.'

— Tommy Smith

'Before I teamed up with Peter at Bristol I regarded him as a good player, who had bags of energy and a decent touch. But playing with him in the same side I realised that Peter was a much better player than I had previously appreciated. He was also a great guy, good friend, with a funny sense of humour and he was a great asset to the teams he played for throughout his very successful career.'

— Joe Royle

'Peter was not only a very talented midfield player, he was a fun character to be around. He always had a smile on his face and a funny story to tell in the dressing room. Football-wise he worked extremely hard in the midfield and was capable of supplying match-winning passes, and also very good in the air for not the tallest of players.

To this day he and his family are delightful, he comes to my charity golf tournament each year and delights the players with his stories, and of course, his dress sense.'

— Ray Clemence

'Peter was a very good coach and a true "Boot Room" disciple. Everyday at training he would remind the players that the game is about footballers and not tactics. He was a very good man-manager and I learnt a lot from him that stood me in good stead both as a player and in my own coaching career.'

— Michael Weir

'In my opinion Peter was one of the best players to grace Scottish football in the 1960s. He was 100 per cent committed on the park, had two good feet and was very good in the air. The fact that he went on to play in Bill Shankly's great Liverpool side of the 1970s is testament to Peter's football ability, determination and dedication. Peter and his wife Marion were also great company, and Liz and I particularly enjoyed meeting up with them during the 1982 World Cup in Spain.'

— Billy McNeill

'Peter is not a big lad but on the football park he was very brave and strong, never giving defenders a moment's peace. I enjoyed playing alongside him at Bristol City as he added a competitive edge to the team and, like me, had a tremendous desire to win. He also livened up the dressing room with his dry sense of humour and mischievous fun.'

— Norman Hunter

CO-AUTHOR'S NOTE AND
ACKNOWLEDGEMENTS
BY BRIAN WEDDELL

As a football-mad youngster growing up in Lochend, only a centre half's blooter from Easter Road, most of my youth was spent playing with my younger brother Stevie in the shadow of the Hibs ground and watching the men in green and white on a Saturday afternoon. Despite this early introduction to the Hibees my mum had been a lifelong Hearts supporter and Mother's milk must have indoctrinated me to the Jambos from a very early age. So whilst I spent most of my formative years watching Hibernian, my football loyalties have always been with the 'boys in maroon'.

My dad had been smitten by the great Hibs Famous Five side of the 1950s, but Smith, Ormond, Reilly, Johnstone and Turnbull had long departed Easter Road when I started paying my sixpence at the boys' gate in the mid-1960s.

From my regular vantage point way up on the east terracing, the first Hibs player to catch my attention was the high-stepping number ten, Peter Cormack.

When the north terracing at Easter Road was covered in the mid-1960s I still preferred the panoramic views of the pitch from the 'extension', and anyway 'The Cowshed' ended up becoming popular territory for pitched battles between Hibs and opposing fans.

My interest in Peter coincided with my own football development in the Hermitage Park Primary School football team and the local eleventh Boys' Brigade. For me, Peter embodied everything required of a good inside forward – non-stop running, hard tackling, creative passing and lethal finishing with either foot or with his head.

Like nearly every schoolboy growing up dreaming of life as a football pro I sought out my dad's advice on players to study and he was in no doubt that the Hibs inside left 'was a very good footballer'.

To me, my dad was a cross between Jock Stein and Bill Shankly and his opinion that Peter Cormack was a good player and worth watching made my trips to Easter Road all the more worthwhile.

I marvelled at Peter's work rate and, for one so slight, his ability to win fifty-fifty tackles with opponents twice his size. But most of all it was Peter's uncanny knack of popping up to score important goals time and time again that convinced me I was watching a midfield maestro at work.

When Peter left Hibs for Nottingham Forest in 1970 my interest in his career did not end there. Coverage of English football was not as easily accessible then as it is these days, but I kept up with Forest results in his first two seasons down south through my weekly *Shoot* football magazine. Then when he signed for Liverpool, for the only time in my life, I changed my football allegiances.

Prior to July 1972 my 'English' team was Chelsea but Peter's move to Anfield saw me dumping the men at 'The Bridge' for Liverpool Football Club. I spent the next four years following Peter's and Liverpool's fortunes when highlights of their games were shown on *Sportscene* on a Saturday night, and they were never far from the top of my *Shoot* cardboard league table.

That is why researching and putting together the story of Peter's career in football has been a labour of love for me.

Peter's story couldn't have been told without the help of the man himself and Marion, his good lady for over forty years. They were always on hand with some golden nuggets of information and endless cups of tea whilst we chewed the fat on his time in the game. The task was also made easier by having access to the volumes of newspaper cuttings initially collected by Peter's mum that Marion and he added to over the years.

I would like to give special thanks to the following and acknowledge use of material from: *Bristol News Green 'Un*, *Daily Record*, *Derby Evening Telegraph*, *Edinburgh Evening News*, *Liverpool Echo*, *Nottingham Post*, *The Scotsman*, *Scottish Daily Express*, *Yorkshire Post*, the Cowdenbeath FC website, Mark Rowantree, Hugh Taylor, Tim Taylor and Jimmy Wardhaugh.

I am also grateful to wee Peter for helping to fill in some of the blanks on their time at Anorthosis in Cyprus, and when he played for Morton when his dad was first team coach. Son-in-law Lee also deserves a special mention for his help and support.

Thanks are also due to Kevin Keegan who, when invited to contribute the book's foreword, reacted even quicker than he did in his prime with half-chances in the penalty box.

I was also struck at the eagerness of other former team-mates who were only too happy to get in their 'tuppenceworth' when asked to contribute to Peter's autobiography.

This account of Peter's career has been enhanced through the contributions of Tommy Smith and Ray Clemence of Liverpool, Norman Hunter & Joe Royle at Bristol City, Billy McNeill of Celtic, Michael Weir who played under Peter at Hibs and, last but not least, Sir Alex Ferguson, who recalled playing against Peter in the 1960s.

I am also indebted to Nottingham Forest and Bristol City for providing details of Peter's playing career at the City Ground and Ashton Gate. The Liverpool Football Club, Hibernian FC and *iHibs* websites were also treasure troves of information.

Thanks are also due to the many staff at the National Library of Scotland who helped me research press articles on Peter's playing and managerial days.

Robert Reid, the Partick Thistle secretary, and a few other jobs besides at The Jags, was extremely generous with his time and provided a wealth of information on Peter's first managerial job at Firhill, and a special thanks is also due to Sue Griffiths who looks after the ex-Liverpool players and organises their annual get-together.

I am also grateful to Terry 'the Hibee' Rudden, Mark 'the Red' Bellamy, David 'the Professor' Begg and Don 'the other Hibee' Morrison for the additional invaluable research they provided to help ensure the accuracy of the statistical information on Peter's playing career.

Thank you to everyone at Black & White Publishing for their support and professional input which has greatly enhanced the quality of the finished article.

Last but not least, this labour of love would not have come about without the patience and understanding of my wife Kerri and our daughter Ellie – their devotion to *Emmerdale, Corrie* and *Eastenders* gave me the peace and quiet I needed to document Peter's considerable time in football.

I hope this team effort has done Peter's career justice and, like me all those years ago, you will also appreciate just how good a footballer Peter Barr Cormack was. I hope you will also see what every one of his former team-mates told me, that most of all, he is a really good guy.

Brian Weddell

FOREWORD
BY KEVIN KEEGAN

It is both a pleasure and a privilege to contribute the foreword to the autobiography of Peter Cormack, who was not only a great footballer but also a really good friend and team-mate at Liverpool.

I first met Peter a year before he signed at Anfield, when I made my Liverpool debut against Nottingham Forest in August 1971. Peter and his Forest team-mates could not prevent me scoring in my very first game for Liverpool nor do anything to stop us winning the match 3–1. Little did I think that the following season Peter would be switching red allegiances and gracing our Liverpool team with his elegant touch, powerful running and clinical finishing.

Liverpool was a dream signing for me when I joined from Scunthorpe in May 1971 and I know Peter felt exactly the same when Shanks signed him the following year.

Many of the English lads at Liverpool used to joke that the only reason Bill Shankly signed Peter was to have a Scot in the squad who could help translate some of Shanks' utterances. But Peter proved, with his contributions on the football park and the vital goals he scored for us, that he was much more than a mere translator of Bill Shankly's broad Scots accent.

When Peter got his chance in the first team he grabbed it with both hands. Like me, he scored on his home debut and the Liverpool fans took him to their hearts in his first appearance at Anfield.

The 'Kopites' loved Peter's style of play. One minute he would be breaking up an opposition attack and seconds later he would appear in our opponent's penalty box having a pop at goal.

Shanks devised his own special methods of motivating Liverpool players and boosting their confidence. With me he'd regularly say, 'Eh son, just go out there and drop hand grenades.' With Peter he would constantly tell him that 'he was the final piece of the jigsaw' for our side – and he was absolutely right. Peter's signing added a touch of class to our midfield and it was no accident that in his four years at Anfield Liverpool won two League Championships, the FA Cup and the UEFA Cup twice.

I have no doubt that if Peter had managed to avoid the knee injuries that eventually cost him a regular place in the side he would have been part of the squad that went to Rome and won Liverpool's first European Cup in May 1977.

Peter and I quickly became good friends rooming together at away games, where we would spend hours discussing team tactics and analysing our opponent's strengths and weaknesses. That was where our interest in coaching and football management began to take root.

Time and time again, Peter proved his loyalty and friendship on and off the football pitch. In 1974 Liverpool played a pre-season game against Kaiserslautern in Germany. I was sent off after I waded into one of their players who went right over the ball on Ray Kennedy, who had just signed from Arsenal. To be honest, I happened to be first in a queue of several Liverpool players who rushed to exact retribution, and following the subsequent melee the referee sent me off.

Liverpool were keen not to see me suspended and after the match club officials claimed it was a case of mistaken identity. Peter Cormack came forward and suggested that because we were similar in height, build and had the same hairstyle that Liverpool say it was him who flattened the German. Peter had previously told me about his brushes with officialdom in Scotland, 'And anyway, I'd have been proud of that punch, Kev,' he said, smiling mischievously.

Peter did me a favour that time, but no one could help me four days later when I got sent off at Wembley in the Charity Shield for fighting with Billy Bremner of Leeds.

Peter and I did enjoy one healthy rivalry – in the fashion stakes. The mid-70s was not a memorable period for men's fashion and my flared trousers were so wide they completely covered my platform shoes. A blessing I didn't fully appreciate at the time.

Peter got so caught up in the fashion bug that for a time he was designing and modelling his own 'creations'. As far as I am aware he didn't end up as Merseyside's answer to Yves St Laurent, but perhaps some Cormack 'exclusives' are still gracing the Kop.

One of Bill Shankly's favourite sayings was that 'a man should always do his best whatever he attempted. If you're going to sweep the street then make sure that your street is always the cleanest in town'. No matter which position or role Peter Cormack was asked to play throughout his football career he epitomised that philosophy, always giving 100 per cent and making a valuable contribution for his side. You only have to look at his record where he played in far more winning than losing sides, scoring his fair share of goals into the bargain.

Over the intervening years Jean and I have always enjoyed catching up with Marion and Peter, reliving our great days in Liverpool. Peter Cormack enjoyed a very successful football career, and I am delighted that his achievements are being recognised at long last.

Peter Cormack is a great role model for any young people setting out on a career in professional football, and I am sure you will see this for yourself in the following pages.

Peter was a consummate football professional and a credit to the game. One of life's genuinely nice guys and someone whose friendship I have always valued.

Kevin Keegan

1

SHANKS TO THE RESCUE

It had been a long hard season. My tenth in top-flight football, my third year as a professional in the English First Division and my first season at Liverpool Football Club.

On that sunny Saturday afternoon at the end of April 1973 the Reds took to the pitch at Anfield as soon-to-be-crowned English First Division Champions.

Five days earlier I had made my fiftieth first-team appearance of the season and scored Liverpool's first goal in a 2–0 defeat against our biggest rivals Leeds United. That victory may have guaranteed us the title but before our final league match against Leicester City, Liverpool's manager, the legendary Bill Shankly, was lecturing and winding up the players as if the next ninety minutes were the most important they had ever played.

Shanks was a perfectionist and his dedication, desire and infectious enthusiasm rubbed off on everyone at Liverpool Football Club.

The players idolised Shanks and Liverpool fans worshipped him. That Saturday seemed a lifetime away from my Liverpool debut seven games into the season against the reigning title holders Derby County at the Baseball Ground. Little did I think, following the 2–1 defeat by Brian Clough's team, that eight months later I would be ninety minutes away from picking up a League Championship winners' medal.

*

At the end of the previous season I was plying my football trade with a Nottingham Forest team that was relegated from the First Division. Finishing second-bottom of English football's top flight meant automatic demotion, which was a body blow to Forest's loyal fans and shattered team morale in the dressing room.

I had heard it said many times previously that a person's character is determined by how they deal with adversity, and for the first time in my football career I had to face up to failure and it did not sit comfortably on my slender shoulders.

I was approaching my twenty-sixth birthday and reaching the peak of my game and did not want to waste my talents in the lower echelons of English football. I was not looking forward to the start of the season and my first week of pre-season training at the City Ground was a real chore.

I think it is fair to say my mood was that of a bear with a very sore head but that was when the hand of fate once again came to my rescue and my saviour was a living football legend.

When I got the call from Liverpool manager Bill Shankly I would have willingly run all the way from Nottingham to Anfield to meet him.

I had known Bill's brother from his time as manager at Hibs, but Bob Shankly was a quiet, shy and retiring man, most of the time. In fact, he was the exact opposite of everything I had seen, heard and read about Bill. Shanks was a shrewd, experienced 'old school' Scot who lived and breathed football. He had played all his professional football in England with almost 300 appearances for Preston North End. But the Second World War arrived just as he was reaching his peak and he retired from playing in 1949, four years after the end of hostilities.

After hanging up his boots Shanks went straight into football management with Carlisle United and after spells at Grimsby

Town, Workington and Huddersfield he was appointed manager of Liverpool in 1959.

When he arrived on Merseyside, Liverpool were languishing in the Second Division, the stadium at Anfield was in a state of disrepair and training facilities at Melwood were overgrown with only one mains water tap. By the time I arrived at Anfield, thirteen years after Shanks, this articulate, no-nonsense, working-class Scot had transformed the club and its facilities and taken Liverpool from the Second Division to the top of English football. He had done all this by turning adversity to his advantage. Anfield stadium and the team's training facilities were completely overhauled. He brought in new training methods, taking into account players' diet as well as fitness. Shanks also introduced an all-red playing strip and placed the 'This is Anfield' sign above the entrance to the tunnel.

Oh, and he also created 'The Boot Room', which was to be Shanks' legacy for Liverpool's subsequent domination of English and European football for more than twenty years.

Bill Shankly was a football visionary years ahead of his time, respected and revered wherever he went.

His most famous remark constantly quoted in the media was 'Football's not like life and death. It's more important than that'. People laughed at the comment but Bill really did believe it. It's an old cliché but he ate, lived and breathed football twenty-four hours a day, seven days a week.

The Liverpool fans worshipped him, opposition fans respected him, other managers genuinely liked him and players were in awe of him. When Shanks spoke everyone listened.

In my life I have met a few people whose personality could dominate a room full of people. Bill Shankly's persona was so large he not only dominated dressing rooms but his personality dominated the football-mad city of Liverpool and the whole football world.

*

I am not the least bit embarrassed to admit that when I got the call to an audience with the Liverpool manager I was shitting myself through both fear and excitement – a strange sensation I agree.

Confidence and pre-match nerves had never been a problem for me but that July morning in 1972 I sat nervously, twitching like a wet-behind-the-ears teenager about to set out on his football career, nothing like the battle-hardened pro with ten years' first team experience and several Scotland caps that I was.

When the time came to meet the great man face-to-face, Shanks greeted me like a long-lost prodigal son. Now, thinking back to that day forty years ago, my palms start to sweat, my heart is racing and the hairs on the back of my neck are standing on end just like they were then.

'Aye, Peter son, great to meet you at last. You're going to win lots of medals here at Liverpool. You are joining a great club and you'll be part of a great team,' he enthused.

Without pausing for breath Shanks asked me what I had been doing in the close season.

I realised this was my chance to impress on him how dedicated I was to my craft. I sat forward in my chair, puffed out my chest and after a couple of deep breaths I said, 'Well, Mr Shankly, I've been training hard over the summer. I go for a cross-country run every day to build up my stamina and do sit-ups and press-ups to tone my stomach muscles.'

I sat back contentedly, waiting to hear fulsome praise for my professionalism and dedication. But instead of admiration the great man shook his head and said, 'Naw, naw son. You're a professional footballer, no' Brendan Foster. Do you think the World Snooker Champions practice by going for a swim every day? Here at Liverpool Football Club fitness is important but oor training is done with the ball, laddie.'

As I was to quickly learn, that was all part of the Shankly

psychology, kidology, man-management approach – call it what you like – but at that moment his answer totally wrong-footed me.

He then slid the contract in front of me and I couldn't put pen to paper quickly enough and get out of the office in case Shanks was having second thoughts about signing me.

It wasn't until I was sitting down on the train out of Lime Street Station on my way back to Nottingham to tell Marion the good news that it dawned on me: I had no idea what the terms of the contract that I had just signed at Anfield were. I hadn't a clue if I had signed for one, two, three or four years nor how much I was going to be paid.

Thankfully my wife was very understanding when I arrived home still in a state of excited shock. In any event, we had nothing to worry about. Signing for Liverpool was the best move of my football-playing career, both professionally and financially.

My contract details couldn't have been further from my mind as I sat next to Shanks in the Liverpool dug-out on a sunny late-April afternoon at Anfield. I had been injured in the match with Leeds earlier that week and the boss wanted to rest me to ensure I was fit in time for the first leg of the UEFA Cup Final taking place eleven days later. The minutes slowly ticked away as the game against Leicester headed for a 0-0 draw. Not the result Shanks wanted or the performance he had demanded but as he constantly said, 'A Football League Championship is a marathon not a sprint and it is the team that lasts the season stronger that comes out on top.'

That season Liverpool had proved that they were the best team in the English First Division and the Liverpool fans who packed into the stadium long before kick-off were enjoying every minute of the celebrations.

After ten years as a professional footballer I was about to

realise one of my boyhood ambitions of winning a League Championship medal. Little did my Liverpool employers know that I would have paid them a small fortune for the privilege of being part of the squad of players out on the pitch that day – a bit-part player in a scene that was to become one of English football's iconic images of the twentieth century.

Playing in front of the famous Kop was always a great experience, especially when we were on form and winning matches in style as we had done for most of that season. But that April Saturday in 1973 was extra, extra special.

As the game was nearing its conclusion the noise levels in the stadium gradually increased until it reached a deafening crescendo. Midway through the second half the fans that were packed into the Kop started singing, 'Ee aye adio we've won the League, we've won the League. Ee aye adio we've won the League.'

They continued chanting non-stop for the remainder of the match.

When the referee blew his whistle to signal full-time, mayhem broke out on the pitch, in the stands and on the Kop – it was utterly chaotic. Players ran around ecstatically embracing one another, and although he was more than twice my age Shanks beat me in the sprint to join the joyous scene.

After congratulating every single player the manager ran to the Kop to salute his adoring fans.

He was wearing his 'lucky' grey suit with his deep red shirt, standing out like he was a well-dressed fan watching his favourite team. When Shanks saluted the cheers of the Kop it was like a messiah acknowledging the worshipping faithful. Some of the Kopites ran onto the pitch and for a while he was engulfed in a sea of supporters decked in red-and-white scarves. When he eventually emerged several minutes later he had a Liverpool scarf draped around his neck and a smile of satisfaction as wide as the river Mersey.

As I watched the scene unfold it was hard for me to believe that I had become an integral part of the team that had just won the English First Division title.

My feelings of joy and elation were a total contrast to the empty feeling of despair I endured twelve months earlier at Nottingham Forest after our final league game, ironically only a few hundred yards from Anfield at the ground of Liverpool's neighbours Everton.

The football gods had indeed been kind to me, but that Saturday afternoon was not all down to Lady Luck. I felt I had earned my right to be at the top of the football mountain, drinking in the success.

I had worked bloody hard at my craft and my all-round foot-balling abilities, dedication, determination with a wee bit rub-of-the-green thrown in for good measure helped me realise my boyhood ambitions.

But doesn't everyone enjoy their share of good and bad luck as they travel through life?

I have always been the first to acknowledge that the dice had been rolling in my favour from the day I was born. If it wasn't for the skills of the doctors, dedication of the nurses and my mum's fighting spirit, my match might have been over before the ref had even blown his whistle to start the game of life.

During childbirth my mum's heart stopped beating and it was thanks to the medical professionals that my mum and I survived. I guess you could say that even in my first match I was deter-mined to play the ninety minutes and still be on the pitch for any extra-time and penalties.

That Saturday evening following my first League Championship success, the city of Liverpool was just one big party (well, at least it was for the Red half).

The players celebrated with their wives and girlfriends, and the atmosphere was that of one big happy family enjoying a very special occasion together.

I was so high on adrenalin that I didn't need any alcohol to get a buzz, and anyway our season was not yet over. We still had the small matter of two legs of the UEFA Cup Final against Borussia Moenchengladbach to look forward to, and all the players were up for doing the 'double' and winning Liverpool's first European trophy.

It wasn't until the next day that the magnitude of my first season at Liverpool really sank in. I sat for several hours and reflected on the previous twelve months where I had gone from the depths of footballing despair to the pinnacle of my career. I thought about the great players Bill Shankly had brought together with the stated aim of creating a Liverpool team that would not only win trophies but take English football to a new level. Experienced professionals like Tommy Smith, Chris Lawler, Ian Callaghan and Peter Thompson and young, hungry men setting out on their football careers such as Kevin Keegan, Emlyn Hughes, Steve Heighway and Brian Hall. And behind those outfield players the best goalkeeper in England, Ray Clemence, signed five years earlier for £18,000.

I'd regularly pinch myself going off to training every morning knowing that I was part of a team of professionals that I liked, admired and respected. But I didn't have an inferiority complex – far from it. My ego was constantly massaged by Shanks, who would remind me, my team-mates and the fans that he regarded my signing as 'the final piece of the jigsaw' of that great Liverpool team.

When I looked around the dressing room at the array of great players I had as team-mates, the boss made me feel ten feet tall, comfortable in the knowledge that I was an integral part of the setup. But that was Shanks; like all great managers he knew how to get the best out of each individual and how to blend that into a successful football team on the park.

That Sunday after the Leicester game, relaxing at home with Marion and our young daughter Donna Lee, my mind wandered back to my school days at Bonnington Primary School and David Kirkpatrick's Secondary in Leith where all my thoughts and energies had been devoted to playing football. To my joy at signing for Hearts from Tynecastle Boys' Club after I started working as a clerk when I escaped from school. Then, still only sixteen, joining their Edinburgh rivals Hibs after a few frustrating months on the Hearts groundstaff.

I smiled thinking back to my biggest game at Hibs when in one of my first matches, only eighteen years old, I scored the opening goal against the Spanish giants Real Madrid. Just to be on the same pitch as Puskas, Santamaria and Gento was special, but to be on the winning side and get the Man of the Match award was the stuff of dreams.

That Hibs memorable moment was eclipsed two years later when I was picked for my first full Scotland international, in a match at Hampden against the then World Champions Brazil, who were warming up for the World Cup Finals in England the following month.

I recalled with smug satisfaction some of the other big domestic and European matches I experienced at Easter Road in my eight years there, and the excitement I felt when I left for Nottingham Forest in March 1970. Whilst the share of the £80,000 transfer fee I received gave Marion and me financial security we never really settled in Nottingham and relegation had been a bitter blow to everyone at the club.

I wondered what might have happened if Bill Shankly hadn't

rescued me twelve months earlier or if Frank Worthington, Shanks' initial big signing target, had passed his medical. But Frank's misfortune led to my football salvation and I loved every minute of life at Liverpool – even more so with a League Championship medal now in my possession.

Life was very sweet indeed and the future was looking good. I was playing at the best club in England, family life was very happy for Marion and our little daughter Donna Lee and I had some business irons in the fire that I hoped might lead to bigger and better things.

Although I was at the peak of my football-playing career sitting in the dug-out with Shanks that Saturday afternoon had given me insight into the manager's perspective. I realised it was a big, special occasion, but for the first time in my professional career I started to think about life after football. The buzz that afternoon at Anfield whetted my appetite for the prospect of getting my coaching badges and putting my playing experience to good use after I'd hung up my boots.

Still, there was no point in getting too far ahead of myself and anyway there was still a lot of football life left in the old Cormack dog. League Championship success in my first season at Liverpool had made me hungry for more.

I was also hoping that my new lease of life at Liverpool would get me back into the Scottish international picture to enable me to add to the nine caps I had already won.

There was no doubt in my mind that Liverpool's training methods and my year working with Shanks had made me a much better football player, and I desperately wanted to prove that in the dark blue of Scotland.

But first thing's first. My Liverpool team-mates and I still had a two-leg UEFA Cup Final to play to make sure our season finished on a high. The match against the Germans could not come quickly enough, and following that I would have been quite happy to go straight into pre-season training, so keen was I to build on my first season of success at Anfield.

I'd been in football long enough to know that good fortune can quickly turn to bad luck. I had seen it happen to others and I just hoped that the Midas touch I had enjoyed since making my first team debut for Hibs at sixteen would stay with me for the rest of my football career.

2

SUNSHINE ON LEITH

Many years before The Proclaimers wrote their famous song I spent a very happy childhood enjoying the sunshine in Leith.

I'm not saying it never rained – it probably peed down more often than not – it's just that I recall most of my childhood being spent outside in nice weather playing football in the street, my school playgrounds or in nearby Pilrig Park.

Perhaps it is because I was born in the middle of summer, 17 July 1946 to be precise, that I have always had a sunny outlook on life. I am certainly one of life's eternal optimists and my pint tumbler has always been half full.

As I said in the previous chapter, I had a very dramatic entry into the world although I was totally unaware of all the excitement at the time, which is probably just as well. Nevertheless, I think my mum's health scare giving birth to me gave us a special bond that stayed with us until she passed away in 1998.

I was born only a year after the end of the Second World War, and fighting for his country had not been a good experience for my father. Not long after war broke out he joined the British Army's tank regiment. The one positive was that he played for the army's football team, which was full of ex-pros fighting for 'Queen and Country'.

Unfortunately not long after my dad was deployed on active service he was captured by the Germans and ended up in a prisoner of war camp behind enemy lines. But my dad being my dad, he wasn't for spending the rest of the war as a PoW and escaped at the first available opportunity. However, he was quickly recaptured and like Steve McQueen in the film *The Great Escape* was placed in solitary confinement (or 'the cooler' as Steve called it). Contrary to it putting my dad off escaping, this only hardened his resolve to get out and his second attempt was successful. Somehow he managed to get to the island of Cyprus and although it was occupied by German troops he hid out in the Trudos Mountains and local Cypriots gave him food that helped him survive.

His adventures didn't end there, and after my dad returned to London, just seconds after he got out of a taxi, a German bomb exploded which killed the driver sitting at the wheel. You certainly need some luck to survive in wartime.

I have no doubt dad was relieved to get back to his wife and young daughter in Leith. So happy was he to be home that I appeared less than a year later, part of the first wave of post-war 'baby boomers'.

My mum, Barbara (or 'Babie' as she was known to everyone), and my dad, Peter (part of a long line of Peter's in the family that has continued with my son 'wee' Pete) were married on Christmas Eve in 1939. My older sister Stella was born not long after the outbreak of hostilities in 1940 but supporting the Allied war effort meant that my mum and dad had to wait six years before adding to their family. I ended up being the last addition to the Leith Cormack clan. I think the heart shock for my mum when giving birth to me meant that I would not have any younger brothers or sisters.

All my memories of childhood are happy ones in our small but comfortable flat in Bonnington Road. Post-war Leith was a thriving part of Edinburgh with a variety of industries providing work. 'Leithers' are very proud of their own identity and to this day constantly remind outsiders that they are Leithers first and citizens of Scotland's capital city second.

The shipyards provided work for many of the men in the community but there were also thriving paper mills and whisky distilleries where many of the womenfolk also secured gainful employment.

After the war my dad resumed his job with a local painting and decorating business. He used to enjoy working indoors hanging wallpaper, but his speciality was sign writing. He was a dab hand at anything artistic and he used to tell me that he enjoyed the challenge that came with out-of-the ordinary sign-writing jobs. My mum was a trained nursing auxiliary and after the NHS was established in 1948 she worked night duties at the Eastern General Hospital next to Edinburgh Corporations Craigentinny Golf Course.

My parents ensured my sister and I never wanted for anything. Whilst many families in Leith struggled to afford an annual summer holiday or only managed to get as far as Port Seton, a few miles down the East Lothian coast, my mum and dad took us to exotic far-off destinations such as Blackpool or Butlin's at Filey near Scarborough. Sometimes aunts, uncles and cousins would join us on these annual adventures. I especially liked it when my aunt Jessie was there as she loved to play bingo and I would tag along with her as, win or lose, she would always give me some extra holiday spending money.

Being a small town within a city meant that Leith had loads of entertainment venues for the fully-employed citizens to spend their hard-earned cash. There were two cinemas at either end of Great Junction Street, the State and the Palais, and then we had The Eldorado next door to Leith Hospital. 'The Eldo', as it was known to Leithers, was a dancehall five days a week and its close proximity to the hospital came in handy for those patrons who incurred the wrath of the dancehall's doormen or upset the boyfriend of a girl they were chatting up.

But the highlight of the week for me was a Tuesday evening when The Eldo hosted All-In Professional Wrestling bouts. Wrestling was a very popular sport in the 1950s and 1960s, with bouts on the television 'adverts' channel on a Saturday afternoon. I used to love watching the wrestling and even managed to meet Mick McManus, one of my heroes, one year when we were on holiday at Butlin's. The other two wrestlers I remember from The Eldo were Jackie Pallo, who had long, curly blond hair tied with a bow and 'Big Daddy'.

I remember my dad telling me that Big Daddy's real name was Shirley Crabtree. I thought he was making this up until years later I heard one of the commentators on TV repeat what my dad had said. As a tough-guy wrestler, I guess he had no option but to change his name. It was probably the best career move Shirley ever made.

Leith also had its own snooker hall, The State in Duke Street, where in my late teens I would spend many an afternoon and evening. Still, practising my snooker skills kept me away from the distractions of the pubs and the attractions of the opposite sex.

For those wanting to escape Leith's dens of iniquity, public transport was readily available to take them to the 'big city'. Up until the early 1960s Leith also had its own train station for Leithers who wanted to venture even further afield.

Like every other town in Britain at the time, Leith had its own 'Woolies' right in the middle of the busy shopping thoroughfare at the foot of the walk. It was always a treat to get taken to the 'pick 'n' mix' for sweets after a game of football or on my way home from the Sea Cadets where I enjoyed many a happy evening in my youth.

Powderhall, Edinburgh's only greyhound stadium, was also not far from where we lived and in the summer months my pals and I would often head up to St Mark's Park and watch the dogs racing from the hill overlooking the track. Once I had money to burn after turning professional, Powderhall would become a regular haunt on a Thursday and Saturday evening for many of the Hibs players.

When I played with Tynecastle Boys' Club, the manager's son, young Jimmy McLaughlan, got me interested in golf. We used to play every Sunday at his club, Torphin Hill, on the side of the Pentland Hills, and my natural hand-to-eye co-ordination meant that I was lucky enough to learn the basics of golf fairly quickly. Not long after I joined Hibs I managed to get membership of Torphin and shortly thereafter I managed to get my handicap down to single figures. I even managed a hole-in-one just a couple of years after taking the game up. However, I was under no illusion that this was 99.9 per cent luck and 00.1 per cent skill.

I don't recall much about my seven years' education at Bonnington Primary School. The one advantage about living next to my school meant that I didn't have to leave the house until I could hear the school bell. This was especially welcome on cold, winter mornings and I learned to time my run to the playground to perfection. In later years, I employed the same technique to great effect on the football field, timing my late runs into the box to get on the end of a cross and score a goal. A perfect education for a budding attacking midfield player!

The only academic subject, if you could call it that, I ever excelled in and enjoyed was art. I obviously inherited my dad's artistic genes and loved copying images of paintings or photographs. I also enjoyed using colours to create a painting. In later years, I found art a good way of relaxing and, like golf, a great way of escaping the pressures of the football pitch.

The only other subject I looked forward to at school was gym. I had bundles of energy so any sport or exercise was fun to me, and my competitive streak ensured I gave 100 per cent in the sports I played at Bonnington. Whilst I enjoyed everything sport-related, I seemed to excel at ball games. I played tennis at Leith Links in the summer and turned out regularly for the secondary school basketball team.

However, from the first time I kicked a ball, football was my first love. Living next to my primary school enabled me to spend endless hours after lessons enjoying kickabouts and 'take-on' matches with my pals. When there was no one around to dribble past or shoot against I would practice on my own, playing keepy-uppy or kicking and heading the ball against the playground wall.

Once I was old enough I'd spend Saturday afternoons at either Easter Road or Tynecastle, depending on whether Hibs or Hearts were at home that weekend. In those days I didn't have an allegiance to either Edinburgh team, and it was not uncommon for Hearts fans to watch Hibs at Easter Road when the Jambos were playing away, and vice versa.

The player I most admired in my youth was Alec Young, the Hearts centre forward who went on to star for Everton. After I joined Liverpool, many Evertonians used to stop me and recount fondly the times when Alec played for them in the 60s. I'm glad 'The Golden Vision' had long retired from Goodison by the time I was transferred to Anfield in 1972. Two other Hearts players who impressed me were 'The King of Hearts', the legendary centre forward Willie Bauld, and inside forward Johnny Hamilton. Bauld was a member of Hearts 'Terrible Trio' of Conn, Bauld and Wardhaugh and as well as his goalscoring exploits he epitomised the modern professional footballer of that era with his fair hair and handsome good looks.

At Easter Road Gordon Smith was outstanding on the right

wing, and part of the Hibs Famous Five team that helped them win two consecutive Scottish First Division Championships in 1951 and 1952. Gordon was a legend with Hibs fans, but he also went on to win Scottish League Championship medals with Hearts and Dundee and is the only man in Scottish football history to have won three Championship medals with three different clubs. An even greater feat when you consider that none of the three teams were from the Old Firm. The other man I admired at Hibs was centre forward Lawrie Reilly. But more about Lawrie shortly.

When I was ten, my primary school team won the Mackie Shield which was played for by all Leith schools, and the following year we made it a double when we won the Leith Cup. That same year I was picked to play on the right wing for the Leith Primary Schools' Select team at Inverleith Park.

These were the first competitive matches I played and I got a real adrenalin buzz from the moment I started to put my team jersey on in the changing room to the final whistle, especially after we won the two primary school Cup finals.

I was still excited after going to bed at night and remember lying awake for hours imagining that I had been playing for Hearts or Hibs earlier in the day, and replayed over and over again highlights from the match in my head. There is no doubt that the success I enjoyed in these competitive early primary school matches whetted my appetite to become a professional footballer. That personal achievement, combined with watching my heroes playing for Hibs or Hearts, week in and week out, in front of tens of thousands of supporters, gave me a hunger to succeed in football from a very early age.

That desire increased even more when I went to David Kilpatrick's Secondary School. DK's (as it was known to everyone in Leith) was a Junior Secondary, therefore, it was not crammed full of budding Albert Einsteins. I have to be honest and admit that I was a real 'dunderheid' at school. In fact, the teachers told my mum and dad that football was ruining my school work. But I was not interested in academic excellence as my heart was set on becoming a professional footballer. Whilst many of my DK classmates let their fists do their talking, I let my dancing football feet do mine. That's not to say I was a shrinking violet when it came to standing up for myself, but at DK's I gained 'street cred' with my football skills.

I have to admit to feeling ashamed of my report cards, although I felt my parents – my father especially – were secretly just as proud to see me do well at sport. For the three years I attended secondary, DK's had one of the best football teams in the city and in my third year we won the Colonel Clerk Cup, which was played for by all the Edinburgh Secondary Schools.

At that time Hibs' Famous Five centre forward, and one of my football idols, Lawrie Reilly wrote a weekly article about schools teams in the sports section of the *Edinburgh Evening News* that was published every Saturday. Unfortunately his report on my DK team followed a surprising 4–1 defeat at the hands of Tynecastle School. However 'Last Minute Reilly', as Lawrie was known to Hibs and Scotland fans, boosted my growing confidence when he wrote:

David Kilpatrick's inside right, Peter Cormack, is the most gifted player of all. A natural player. I think he could make the senior grade. Had more shots at goal than the other forwards. Lack of physique may be against him but body-building exercises would help. When I joined Hibs I was the same. I was sent to a body-building school for eighteen months and that helped me tremendously.

For a man I had admired from the terracing at Easter Road to draw a comparison to him in the article was praise indeed. Thanks for that, Lawrie! Your words of encouragement were music to my ears and just the added incentive I needed to pursue my dream of becoming a professional footballer.

I recall taking a copy of the article to school the following Monday and after showing it to the headmaster I was given special permission to use the school gym after hours.

For a year I slogged away with weights and medicine balls and whilst the 'weight training' made me physically stronger, I couldn't see any difference in my upper body muscle definition when I stared at myself in the mirror. I was still a skinny wee runt and my dad regularly kidded me on, saying that he saw more meat on the carving knife at our local butchers.

The other thing I vividly recall from that day against Tynecastle School was our school team getting our photo taken with 'Last Minute Reilly'. I didn't notice at the time the photograph was taken, but Lawrie had stood directly behind me and when it was published the following week I took that as a good omen for the future.

I also enjoyed other rave reviews in the local sports paper after scoring in a 3–3 draw with Holy Cross, a team that contained my future Hibs team-mate Jimmy O'Rourke, and I notched a hat-trick in an 8–3 trouncing of fellow Leith team St Anthony's. The victory over 'Tony's' was especially sweet as it ensured the DK boys enjoyed bragging rights over their Leith Catholic pals until the next time we met.

As I said, my sporting success was not just limited to the football field. Without wanting to sound big-headed, sporting excellence seemed to come easy to me at school, which is just as well as anything academic was usually a challenge too far.

Just before I turned thirteen I won four out of the seven boys' events at the DK school sports day and set new records in the 440 yards and the quarter mile. Contrary to Bill Shankly's opinion several years later, I might well have given Brendan Foster a good run for his money if I had chosen distance running instead of professional football.

On the other hand, one of the events I won that sports day was the high-jump with a 'prodigious' leap of three feet eleven inches. Still, maybe before Mr Fosbury invented his famous flop, just under four feet was indeed a giant leap for a young Leith laddie in 1959. What I do remember from that high jump competition is that the landing area was a sand pit that had about as much sand in it as a corporation golf club bunker. Most of my competitors chucked it after their first jump, such was the pain endured after clearing the bar. However, my sporting competitive streak ensured that I was last man standing, but I do think the experience toughened me up and had a positive spin-off in my football career. Diving into headers when the goalie's fists were flying and defenders' boots swinging wasn't half as dangerous or painful in comparison to that DK high jump competition.

In my last year at secondary school I was picked for the Edinburgh Schools Select side for an evening match against Glasgow Schools Under-15 Select. The game took place at Cathkin Park, the home of Third Lanark, which was in the southeast side of Glasgow, close to the national stadium, Hampden. The Edinburgh team also contained Jimmy O'Rourke and that was the first time we teamed up in a competitive match. Neither of us had any idea at the time, but wee Jimmy and I would become team-mates at Easter Road in the not too distant future.

My football career really started to take off when I played for Tynecastle Boys' Club's Under-15 team. Our manager Jimmy

McLaughlan had a great influence on me and when Jimmy said jump I would ask, 'How high?' Jimmy was very professional in his approach to training and would constantly emphasise the importance of getting the preparation right before matches, and he was ably assisted by Joe Foley, his son 'Young Joe' and Johnny Ross. We had a very good group of players at Tynecastle, and I especially remember Ian Grassick, Albert Tait, Ricky Juner, Alan Weir and Ian Blyth who were all excellent players. None of them ended up enjoying the success I had at the game, but at fifteen, with a little bit of luck on their side, I am certain any one of them could have enjoyed successful football careers.

When I look back now over my football career that spanned more than forty years playing, managing and coaching, the year 1962 was definitely the most life-defining. This may seem strange given the first season I had with Liverpool, but if 1962 had turned out differently then the success I enjoyed at Anfield would never have happened.

My first big match that year was a Youth International Trial Match, which took place at Crewe Toll in North Edinburgh. I had an air of confidence going into the trial for two reasons. The first was that I had been picked for the 'A' team and the second was that given the match was near Leith I regarded it as a home game – two very good omens to me. I wasn't aware at the time that I was the youngest player on show but that didn't stop me raising my game and the following week I received a glowing report from 'Craig–Mer' in the *Edinburgh Evening News* sports paper.

Under the headline 'Hearts first in the Queue for Young Tynecastle Star' Mr 'Mer' wrote:

Scouts lined up in orderly and unobtrusive fashion after the Scottish Youth international trial match at Crewe Toll last

Saturday. All had one aim . . . a quiet word in the ear of young Peter Cormack, inside right of Tynecastle Boys' Club Under-Age Juvenile team. Peter was the youngest performer on show, but the general opinion was that he was the star of the game.

Hearts, Hibs, Arbroath and Aston Villa were among some of the Senior clubs represented. All bar one are likely to be disappointed. The exception is Hearts, strong favourites to secure this promising youngster when the time comes for him to step up.

The article continued, 'Willie Hall, secretary of the Scottish Under-Age champions St Bernard's "A", had five of his boys in the trial but he was full of praise for Peter Cormack whose sudden bursts of acceleration when on the ball and his intelligent use of open space reminded him of Denis Law.'

Only a few months earlier I had left DK's and secured a job as a clerk with the Danish Bacon Company, a firm of wholesale grocers in Leith Walk. I was the office junior doing basic clerical jobs such as filing and running errands, which I didn't mind as it got me out of the office. Whilst I enjoyed picking up my weekly pay packet every Friday I was determined that this was going to be a short, temporary stop-gap until I fulfilled my dream of becoming a professional footballer.

Little did I think after that first youth trial match in January my football career was about to hit the 'fast forward' button. A few weeks later a second trial was held back at Cathkin Park against Third Lanark Colts. Our team ran out 2–1 winners and I managed to bag the decisive second goal. Despite my goalscoring performance I was overlooked for the first Youth International match against England. Following defeat by the 'auld enemy' I was selected for the next Youth International against Wales in Bangor on 7 April. Also included in the Scottish team were two players who were to enjoy professional careers in the game. Bobby Watson was a great servant at Motherwell and Denis Setterington played for Rangers and Falkirk. Denis occupied outside right in the youth team and I lined up inside him. Together we formed a good partnership. We drew our first match in North Wales 1–1 and a few weeks later we played Ireland at Cappielow in Greenock.

Before my debut against Wales I received my first ever telegram, not from the Queen but from my team-mates at Tynecastle. I was really touched by their support and have treasured it ever since. It now proudly sits with the many other football mementos I have collected over the course of my career.

Before my Youth International debut I played my first competitive match at Easter Road. On 10 March 1962 Hibs played Everton in a friendly (I think both teams had a free Saturday after getting knocked out of their respective FA Cups a few weeks earlier) and as pre-match entertainment another Youth International Trial Match was arranged between twenty-two possible candidates for the squad. I had been picked to play inside left for the 'B' team, playing in red, and I scored my first ever goal on the famous Easter Road slope as we ran out 2–1 winners. It was probably this performance that secured my place for the Welsh International that was taking place a few weeks later.

In preparation for the match we met at the Scotia Hotel in Great King Street, sadly no longer there, in the centre of Edinburgh, where we were treated to lunch before a bus took us the short drive down to Easter Road. It was a fantastic experience for a young fifteen-year-old just setting out on his football journey.

Although I had previously played at senior grounds they didn't compare to the experience of playing in a stadium where I had watched countless matches and seen great players such as Gordon

Smith, Lawrie Reilly and Bobby Johnstone of Hibs and Willie
Bauld, Alfie Conn and Jimmy Wardhaugh of Hearts.

Because Hibs were playing the English First Division side
following our game there was a decent-sized crowd in the ground
and I got a huge buzz walking onto the park seeing and hearing
the crowd. To make my day complete all the trialists were given
complimentary tickets to watch the Hibs vs Everton match from
the enclosure below the old stand. It was certainly a welcome
change for me, as normally my pals and I used to sneak into
the Hibs ground at a security 'blind spot' we discovered around
the back of the Dunbar End at Easter Road.

You can tell from this report of the game in the *Evening News*
how much of a high I was on during that trial right from the
kick-off:

> In the youth's match curtain-raiser the reds proved the much
> superior team, running out 2–1 winners. They got off to a
> wonderful start when inside left Cormack of Tynecastle Boys'
> Club put them ahead in the opening minutes.

Needless to say, that Saturday at Easter Road I was made up
and it was another big step on my climb up the football ladder.
A week after my scoring debut at Easter Road I turned out for
an Edinburgh Under-Age Juvenile Select against a Celtic Colts
team which took place at Old Meadowbank, the pre-1970
Commonwealth Games Stadium. The *Evening News* report of the
match stated that the game was attended by senior scouts from
Hearts, Hibs, Airdrie, Falkirk, Preston, Wolves and many more
and went on to report that:

> All except Hearts must have envied the inside forward play
> of Peter Cormack of Tynecastle Boys' Club. For one so young
> he stood out against a strong Celtic team. He has promised

to join up at Tynecastle Park when he is seventeen. I believe there is every chance of him being one of Hearts' first youngsters to go on the ground staff.

Things were really moving on apace and the *Evening News* reporter had clearly been given some inside information from Hearts.

On 23 March 1962 I received my first official invitation from Heart of Midlothian Football Club to play in a match they had arranged on Tuesday 27 March at Heriot Watt playing fields on Paties Road, which is now the home of junior side Edinburgh United.

The week following that match I was called in to Tynecastle for an interview with Hearts' legendary manager 'Gentleman' Tommy Walker and he convinced me to become a member of the Hearts groundstaff. As a raw fifteen-year-old I was very nervous sitting face-to-face with a man who had seen and done it all and was respected throughout Scottish football for his success, both as a player with Hearts and Scotland and as a manager with Hearts in the 1950s.

I recall Mr Walker telling me when we sat down in his office that the last Hearts player to be taken on the groundstaff was him – some thirty years earlier. Any reservations I might have had about the move were dispelled when he told me that and I remember thinking at the time that the football omens were looking good for me. No matter how nervous I was then I don't recall it being anything like the nerve-jangling occasion I experienced ten years later when I sat face-to-face with Bill Shankly at Anfield.

The following month I was selected for the Scottish Secondary Juveniles for an evening match against the Scottish Churches at Partick Thistle's ground, Firhill. I was picked to play inside left and Dougie Johnstone was at left back. Dougie, a fellow

Edinburgh lad, would join me in the future at Easter Road for a spell during his professional football travels.

After defeating the Churches I lined up for the Scottish Secondary Juveniles in the final at Falkirk against the Scottish Juveniles, where we ran out winners by five goals to two. I even managed to get on the scoresheet in the final, notching our second goal. The brief press report of the game included the following:

> In the second half the Secondary players made better use of the ball and the outstanding performers were Symington, McLaughlan, Cattenach and Cormack.

Following my two Youth International matches, my focus returned to finish the season on a high at Tynecastle Boys' Club where we swept the boards in the Edinburgh Juveniles.

Over the summer I spent every working day at Tynecastle as the only member of the Hearts groundstaff. Unfortunately for me it really was what it said on the form, and I hated every minute of it. Whilst I wanted to be training and practising for a career as a professional footballer, all I felt I was doing was being used as a glorified 'skivvy'. As far as I was concerned the groundsman, Mattie Chalmers, was a miserable old so-and-so. He had me cutting the grass, sweeping the terracing, cleaning the dressing rooms and whitening the lines. One week I was painting seats in the stand and the next he had me painting the crush barriers. I told him that if I wanted to be an effing painter I could go and work with my dad, but I got no sympathy. I honestly think he was made up having someone around the place that could do all the shitty jobs he had mostly been doing on his own for over forty years. If there was a menial job to be done then it was left for me to do. I had reached the end of my tether and then one day he asked me to park Hearts' state-of-the-art Ransomes Power Unit. This was a miniature tractor that could attach seven trailers, each of them with a special job such as cutting the grass or rolling the pitch. When he asked me to park it in the shed down by one of the corner flags I decided it was payback time. At first I protested that I could not drive, but that cut no ice with my taskmaster so I jumped in the tractor and as I was driving it down the slope leading to the shed, I hopped out and it crashed into a wall. Mattie Chalmers went mad, shouting and swearing, saying that I would be in big trouble for that. But I headed straight for the changing rooms, picked up my gear and made my mind up there and then that I was never going back to Tynecastle.

When I didn't turn up for duty, Tommy Walker came to see me at my house but by this time the nods and winks aimed in my direction by Hibs had me champing at the bit to move to Easter Road. And anyway, Hibs promised that if I signed for them they would buy my mum and dad a new house, and there was no way Hearts could compete with that. They could even have put me in charge of Mattie Chalmers to get my own back but my heart was set on joining the Hibees.

Not only did I escape the Tynecastle groundsman, but within months of joining the groundstaff at Easter Road we moved from our flat in Bonnington Road to the brand new house Hibs had promised, on the west side of Edinburgh. I was delighted that my football abilities managed to give my parents the new house they had always dreamed of.

My next representative outing came in August at the Annual Match between the Edinburgh Secondary Juveniles and Edinburgh Under-Age Juveniles for the James Ford Cup, which was played back at Old Meadowbank. On the Saturday before the Monday night match, my number one fan in the *Evening News*, Craig–Mer, who only a few months earlier predicted my signing for Hearts, wrote this in his column:

Interest will focus on Peter Cormack who has quit Hearts groundstaff and is now to join Hibs. Peter will be at inside right for the Under-Age Select and the Tynecastle Boys' Club skipper will be the centre of attention. This has been a hectic season for this talented young man and honours have come thick and fast. His brilliant displays at inside forward won him his place in Under-Age Select sides, in the Scottish Secondary Juvenile team and the Scottish Youth eleven. Quite a fantastic record for a boy who was only sixteen last month. Playing against older and more experienced players presents no problems to this youngster and he will keep the Secondary defence at full stretch on Monday night.

Craig–Mer certainly seemed to have his finger on the Edinburgh football pulse. In my opinion, I couldn't have signed for Hibs at a better time. The club was in a transition period with older players such as Joe McLelland and Jim Easton coming to the end of their careers and up-and-coming youngsters like Bobby Duncan and Eric Stevenson on the verge of breaking into the first team. Rightly or wrongly I felt my football progress was going to be long and drawn out at Tynecastle, whereas I was convinced that I would have a better chance with Hibs.

But even I was shocked how quickly I would climb that steep learning curve at Easter Road. Within a couple of weeks of joining the Easter Road groundstaff I was playing in the reserve side and made my 'A' team debut against Clyde in an evening match at Easter Road. I was picked for another couple of reserve games, including one at Partick Thistle which included future first team team-mates goalkeeper Willie Wilson and wee Jimmy O'Rourke. In that game I managed to score two goals with my head. In those days, the Saturday sports paper only gave first half reserve match reports and the *News* managed to record: 'Hibs went ahead in twenty-five minutes when Cormack took a neat flick from McCreadie and bulleted a header past Gray in the Thistle goal.'

Then following an injury crisis at the club I was asked to travel with the first team squad for a Saturday league match at Airdrie on Saturday 24 November 1962.

Hibs' season had got off to a bad start and they were languishing near the bottom of the league. On the team bus travelling through to the west on the old A8 road, I sat soaking up the atmosphere, which consisted mainly of the shouts and groans of the players' card school at the back of the coach. I was relaxed, comfortable in the knowledge that I was just going along for the experience. The last thing on my mind, sitting on the team bus, was that I was about to make my first team debut.

After we got off the coach and into the ground the players headed straight for the pitch to stretch their legs and check the condition of the playing surface. I savoured the banter between the established first team regulars and the sprinkling of diehard Diamonds fans that had arrived early at the ground for the sole purpose of winding up their opponents.

When we returned to the sanctuary of the away team changing room, which in those days was housed under the small stand at one of the corners of the ground, I sat quietly as Mr Galbraith read out the team.

In goal Ronnie Simpson, right back John Fraser, left back Joe McLelland, right half Duncan Falconer, centre half Jim Easton, left half Ally McLeod, right wing Jim Scott, inside right Johnny Byrne, centre forward Gerry Baker, inside left Jimmy Stevenson and outside left Peter Cormack.

I never even heard my name being read out as I genuinely was not expecting to be in the starting line-up, and it was only when the other players started congratulating me on getting picked that I realised I was playing.

I read Roy Keane's autobiography many years later, where he described his first team debut under Brian Clough for Nottingham Forest against Liverpool at Anfield. I related that experience to my debut for Hibs at Airdrie in 1962. Unlike Keano, I didn't have a couple of pints the evening before, but I did think, like him, that until that day I was only there to help the trainer put out the playing kit and sample the atmosphere of being with the first team squad.

Getting picked for the starting eleven really was a bolt from the blue, but once I knew I was playing I was totally focussed on giving my all for the team. It may sound daft given how my career was to pan out, but that day, putting on a Hibs jersey for the first time, I had no nerves or butterflies. Maybe it's what sports psychologists now call 'the confidence of youth not having the fear of fear itself' but, in truth, all I could think was that I was getting a game of football and playing 'fitba' is all I ever wanted to do when I was growing up in Leith.

3

BAPTISM OF FIRE

I made my first team debut for Hibs when I was sixteen years, four months and seven days old. Although I was such a tender age, I had considerable confidence in my football ability and all my team-mates gave me tremendous support before, during and after the game.

It was almost a dream debut as I managed to notch our only goal, my first of the ninety-nine I was to go on to score in two hundred and fifty-five competitive appearances in eight years at Easter Road. The down side of my Hibs debut was that we lost the game 2–1, which didn't help manager Walter Galbraith, who had not been long in the top job at Easter Road.

The team and the fans had endured a dreadful start to the 1962/63 League campaign. In the twelve matches played up until my debut we had won four, lost five, drawn three and were sitting near the bottom of the eighteen-team table. Hibs got off to the worst possible start in the league, losing the opening fixture against our Edinburgh rivals Hearts 4–0, and fared no better in the next match at Easter Road going down 5–1 to Rangers. Results picked up after that, I guess they couldn't have got any worse, but a horrendous injury list only added to the manager's already considerable woes.

Still, from a totally selfish standpoint, it was the injuries to the established first team players that gave me my first break at Easter Road and I was determined to make the most of it.

My mum kept many of the newspaper cuttings of my football playing days which have been a handy memory jolt as well as a useful reference source in the compiling of this book. Following my debut at Airdrie, *Edinburgh Evening News* reporter Ian MacNiven wrote in his match report:

Young Peter Cormack won't forget his first outing in First Division football in a hurry. At sixteen years of age Hibs' new forward had an extraordinary experience for ninety minutes at Broomfield on Saturday when yet another defeat by 2–1 sent the Easter Road side tumbling into the league cellar, and with injuries piling up it's hard to see how this present outfit can climb back to a respectable position in the table.

With Gerry Baker and Johnny Byrne early casualties, young Cormack only spent eight minutes in his recognised position at outside left. For the other thirty-seven minutes before the interval he switched to inside left and then spent the second half on the right wing. And in that position at least he had the satisfaction of scoring Hibs' only goal, but with so little support up front it was not surprising that Cormack did not get many opportunities to repeat the feat.

At any rate Cormack now knows that First Division football is no place for weaklings. This was a bruising, hard-hitting ninety minutes with players going down all over the place and the referee seemingly unwilling to take firmer action.

It was inevitable that eventually somebody would suffer for all the fierce tackling.

As it happened centre half, Jim Easton was the unlucky man removed to hospital with a broken ankle.

It is interesting looking back at that match report fifty years on because, as things would turn out, my debut experience reflected my career at Easter Road. My versatility meant I never stayed in one position for very long, and in my first spell at Easter Road I played in every midfield and forward position, and even managed a couple of stints in goal. My goalscoring debut at Broomfield had an additional bonus: I got my first trip on an aeroplane!

On the following Monday the team headed off to Holland to play Utrecht in a second round first-leg tie in the Fairs Cup (the forerunner to the UEFA Cup). The furthest I had travelled up until then had been a holiday to Southport with my family and I was made up to be going abroad in my first season at the club. In the previous round Hibs had beaten Staevnet Copenhagen home and away, but Utrecht were regarded as much tougher opposition. As well as going on my first aeroplane trip I also gave my first interview to a reporter before we left Turnhouse, now Edinburgh, Airport. Speaking to Tom Nicholson of the *Daily Record*, I said, 'I am thrilled but not nervous. I'd been told if I played well on Saturday I'd be going to Holland. Now I'm going and I think it's great.'

Not quite 'I'm over the moon, Brian', but not bad for a young sixteen-year-old Leith laddie about to make his first trip abroad, never mind as part of a professional football team.

On the Saturday I had made my first team debut and two days later I was jetting off for a European tie. It was hard to believe that only a few months earlier I was playing in the Edinburgh Under-16 Juvenile League with Tynecastle Boys' Club. My nightmare experiences as an odd-job man on the Hearts groundstaff a dim and distant memory. What was even better was that my first of what was to be many memorable overseas football trips saw Hibs secure a one–nil victory to take back to Easter Road. Unfortunately, Mr Galbraith went for experience over youth in Holland and I never played in the tie, but it was a tremendous feeling nonetheless. Within months of joining Hibs, my senior football career had hit the ground running.

Despite beating Utrecht home and away our league form didn't improve, and in the four games played before the end of the year we only managed one point, holding Celtic to a 1–1 draw at Easter Road. We lost at home to Partick Thistle and Clyde and suffered defeat at Dunfermline. Around this time, former Hearts inside left Jimmy Wardhaugh, who had taken up journalism after retiring from football, wrote the following newspaper article under the headline 'Young stars may go':

Hibs are perilously placed on the brink of the dark plunge into the chasm of relegation. Market action is badly required. The cost would be negligible compared to what the financial total might be if Hibs do tumble . . . Jimmy O'Rourke, Jimmy Stevenson, Peter Cormack. Conjure a while with those names and try to imagine what they might bring to Hibs on the open market in three years. By then all three will be on the brink of leaving their teens. The trio are sixteen years old at the moment and with another three seasons and the rate of progress they have already made taken into consideration, they could, without much strain on the imagination, each net a cool £30,000 on the transfer market . . . but will these future Scottish caps remain with the club if they take the drop? This brilliant trio are all amateurs and will be free agents at the end of the season. If Hibs go down there are going to be plenty of solid offers to these lads from the spivs and touts that are always on the lookout for the 'quick buck' from clubs. Hibs have built up a sound nursery in the past eighteen months but if they go down and lose these high assets it might take them many years to build from the bottom again.

Given the astronomical sums paid in transfer fees in the twenty-first century, some readers will probably be thinking that £30,000 back then was not really as 'cool' as Jimmy Wardhaugh makes out. But only a few years earlier Hearts had sold Jimmy's team-mate and club captain Dave Mackay to Spurs for a Scottish record of £32,000 and Hibs free-scoring centre forward Joe Baker was sold to Torino in Italy for £75,000 the year before I arrived at Easter Road.

In reality, £30,000 in 1962 was worth several million pounds in today's football transfer market. The one big difference was that, where today the top clubs in Europe are run by mega-millionaires who bankroll players' transfers and wages, back in the early 1960s football chairmen tended to be successful local businessmen who were very careful when it came to spending their hard-earned cash. Up until 1961 the maximum wage a player could earn from football was twenty pounds a week – decent money and a lot more than the average fan took home in his weekly pay packet, but a far cry from the fortunes paid to the top players today. Like every other Hibs fan, I had read the newspaper articles that reported that Joe Baker left Hibs for Torino because the board refused him a wage rise of five pounds a week. Instead of forking out seventeen pounds a week on their star striker it appeared that the Hibs chairman preferred pocketing the £75,000 from his sale to Italy.

Hindsight is a wonderful thing, and looking back to Jimmy Wardhaugh's article all those years later, I can see how right he was about the effect on a football club's pool of young talent if that club slides into relegation. The fear of relegation hung over Easter Road for the whole of 1962/63 and I was never given another run out in the first team that spent the rest of the season trying to stave off the dreaded drop. My time was divided between turning out for the Hibs 'A' team in the Scottish reserve league and being part of the Scottish International Amateur squad. Back then league rules prevented clubs signing young players on professional forms until they reached their seventeenth birthday. However, children could leave secondary school at fifteen and football clubs took promising youngsters on their payroll as groundstaff to enable them to train with the club, and as I knew only too well, after my experience at Tynecastle, do all the menial jobs around the ground.

At least when I was on the groundstaff at Easter Road I had fellow 'skivvies' in Jimmy Stevenson, George Gartshore and Jimmy O'Rourke to share the load, and as well as mucking in together at our chores we used to have a laugh at training. The highlight of every club's training session is the full-scale practice match that usually ends a workout. The groundstaff boys always tried to get in the same side to put our youthful energies to good use by trying to outrun the older players who had used up most of their stamina on the training ground. That was our theory, but we very rarely got the better of the 'aulder heids' in the practice matches.

One day after a hard training session with the first team squad, the groundstaff boys were told by the manager to jog back to the stadium to clean the players' boots for their next match and prepare the communal bath. Jogging back up the road, we started winding each other up, unhappy that we had been excluded from the practice game. By the time we reached Easter Road our anger and frustration had reached boiling point and after running the hot water we decided it would be a good laugh if we threw all the towels in the bath. Not content with just the one rebellious act, I thought I would put my Sea Cadet training to good use and tied together the laces of all the players' shoes.

We decided not to sit around waiting on the players' return, which was probably the only sensible thing we did that day, and headed over to the other side of the stadium. When the first team players returned we were sweeping the terracing opposite the main stand and could hear their abusive shouts from the dressing room. Fortunately none of the players came looking for us, but the trainer was dispatched and we were made to run up and down the steepest part of the terracing for half an hour as punishment. Later we were given a severe dressing-down by the manager and warned that any future reoccurrences would see us thrown out of the club. Needless to say we behaved like angels from there on but were also given some rough treatment in future practice matches by the seasoned pros for our trouble. It was a salutary lesson and one that stayed with me for the rest of my career.

In early February 1963 I was named as a travelling reserve for the Scottish Amateur team who were playing a Junior XI at Airdrie's Broomfield ground. Most of the Scottish team was made up of players from Queen's Park, Scotland's only senior amateur side. Two months later, I won my first Scottish Amateur cap when I was picked to play on the left wing against Wales at the Racecourse Ground in Wrexham.

Playing at centre forward that day was future Scotland manager and current UEFA Technical Director, Andy Roxburgh. The programme notes for the match described Andy as 'a prolific goalscorer who misses few balls in the air, while he keeps the line moving with a vital fluency. He could be Scotland's key forward today if he receives the support he has reason to expect.'

If I didn't know any better I'd swear Andy wrote that pen picture himself. As it transpired I don't recall any of the forwards getting the support we expected that Saturday in Wales and unfortunately Scotland lost the match 3–1. The following month I retained my place in the Scotland Amateur team for an International match against Ireland at the Oval in Belfast. This time I played inside left. Young master Roxburgh wasn't included in the team but wee Tommy McLean, who would go on to win a League Championship medal with Kilmarnock and was an integral part of Rangers' 1972 European Cup Winners' Cup-winning side, played at outside right. We also had 'big' Ally Donaldson in goal and Ally went on to have a very successful professional career with Dundee and Falkirk. Ally was tall, dark and handsome, which you couldn't always say about goalies, and he had the biggest hands I had ever seen.

Sadly, even with Ally's massive hands between the posts we fared no better and Ireland ran out comfortable winners by five goals to two.

The week following the Ireland match I travelled south with the Scottish Amateur squad to play in the English FA Centenary Amateur International Tournament. Also in the squad was Andy Roxburgh and another promising sixteen-year-old – Peter Lorimer from Leeds United. Peter had joined Leeds straight from school and our paths were destined to cross in the years to come.

There were eight countries entered into the tournament divided into two groups with the group winners meeting in the final. Scotland's group included Italy, Switzerland and the Republic of Ireland. The second group contained Germany, Holland, France and England. The tournament was played over ten days in Northumberland and I loved being away with the Scottish team where all we did was eat, sleep and play football.

Two days after the teams assembled in the north-east of England, we played our first match where we beat the Republic 5–2. On the Thursday we were given a day off training and taken on a coach trip to Hadrian's Wall which had been built by the Roman Emperor Hadrian to keep the Scots out of England. As events in the tournament unfolded I bet the English FA wished we had stayed on the opposite side of the wall. The next morning the Scotland squad enjoyed a short training session in preparation for our second game which was taking place the following evening at Darlington against Italy. The Italian amateur footballers turned out to be typical of Italian club sides at the time and were a strong and physical team. However, good old-fashioned Scottish skill and determination won out and we managed to overcome the Italians 3–1.

Sunday was another rest day and the Scottish lads spent the afternoon competing in a putting competition we organised amongst ourselves. If my memory serves me right, I think I managed to win the kitty and annoy the West of Scotland 'golfers' in our squad.

In our final match we fought out a 1–1 draw with Switzerland to top our group on five points. Waiting for us in the final was the West German Amateur team who had maximum points, having scored seven goals and conceded only three in their group games. This must have been the worst-case scenario for the English FA with their oldest and newest rivals battling it out for their Centenary Trophy.

The final was held on the evening of Wednesday 22 May at Roker Park, then the home of Sunderland. We went in at half-time trailing 2–1 but came out guns blazing in the second half and swept the West German amateurs aside scoring four goals without reply. The 5–2 win was a victory for good old-fashioned attacking football and we received great praise in the Scottish press for our performance against the Germans. The press corps north of the border also loved the fact that Scotland's Amateur footballers had won an International tournament held in England to celebrate one hundred years of the English Football Association.

A month earlier Scotland's full International team had beaten England 2–1 at Wembley with 'Slim Jim' Baxter scoring the two Scottish goals. Our tournament winning performance on English soil enabled the more vitriolic elements in the Scottish media to go into overdrive about the Scottish 'double' but my team-mates and I were just delighted with the publicity we got for our efforts in bringing the English Amateur Centenary trophy back to Scotland. Writing these memoirs almost fifty years on I wonder if the Scottish FA still have this trophy in their possession and whether it will be played for again to celebrate the English FA's 200th anniversary in 2063?

The start of 1963 was greeted with a deluge of snow and freezing temperatures that decimated all outdoor sporting events for three weeks and Hibs' first match that year was a Scottish Cup tie at Brechin City at the end of January. Normally the team travelled to away matches by bus, but because many roads were still frozen the Hibs squad travelled to Brechin, in the north-east of Scotland, by train. I was included in the travelling party and I recall the then assistant manager, former Famous Five inside left Eddie Turnbull, handing out a train ticket to each of the players on the concourse at Waverley Station. It was one of the old-style trains that travelled up the East Coast line between London and Aberdeen, which had compartments where eight passengers could huddle together. Woe betides the first person to fart as their life was made hell for the remainder of the journey. Fortunately for me, none of the players in my compartment neither farted nor had a pack of cards, and we amused ourselves on the two hour journey by telling jokes and talking about the forthcoming match. It was clear from the loud shouting and swearing that the compartment next to ours was where the gamblers had gathered and I'm pretty sure, from the racket they were making that some players managed to lose all their loose cash and probably their win bonus in the card game before a ball had been kicked.

Whether it was because it was the Scottish Cup or down to the three-week lay-off or, as is more likely, in an effort to clear their debts before the return journey, all eleven players seemed to put in extra effort and we ran out comfortable 2–0 winners. Whatever it was down to it was a good result nonetheless and made the train journey back to Edinburgh all the more enjoyable. The trip back south was also helped by the 'cairey-oot' many of the players took onto the train with them. Although I did not indulge in the bevvy session the players' booze-fuelled antics kept me entertained all the way back to Edinburgh Waverley.

That was one of the few bright spots in a dismal second half of the season at Easter Road. In the next round of the Scottish Cup we lost 1–0 at home to Dundee and in the quarter-final of the Fairs Cup we went out 6–2 on aggregate to Spanish side Valencia. I was fortunate to be included in the trip for the first-leg tie in Spain and also fortunate to be watching the resultant debacle from the stand. The tie was over after the first leg when the Spaniards ran out 5–0 winners, and it was scant consolation that we beat them in the second leg 2–1 at Easter Road, where I was again a mere spectator. With four league games remaining Hibs were propping up the First Division table with Raith Rovers, and were odds-on favourites to get relegated. Jimmy Wardhaugh's doomsday scenario was staring the club in the face and Easter Road was not a happy place to be around. The omens were not looking good as Hibs faced the short trip to their Edinburgh rivals Hearts who were sitting comfortably in the top half of the table.

Things looked even bleaker after Hearts shot into a two-goal lead, but with their backs to the wall the Hibs team battled back to go 3–2 ahead. Unfortunately, Hearts snatched a late equaliser to deny us the two points we badly needed in our fight to avoid the drop but it was still a point gained, especially after the disastrous start to the match.

However, the fans of both teams trooped out of Tynecastle, convinced it was not going to be enough to save Hibs from relegation.

On the Monday at training I well remember Walter Galbraith telling the first team squad that the players still had control of their own destiny but they would need to take a maximum six points from the final three games to make sure they avoided the dreaded drop into Division Two. To be honest, I don't think there were many players who believed what the manager was telling them and I shared their pessimism. In the thirty-one matches we had played in the league campaign up until that point Hibs had won only five, drawn nine and lost seventeen.

In those days there was not the betting on football that there is today (certainly not legally with the local licensed bookmakers and turf accountants) but if there was, the bookies would have given very good odds for Hibs to win their last three matches. The first of those matches was a tight and nerve-wracking game at home to St Mirren, which the team managed to win 2–1. The penultimate league match was away against fellow strugglers Queen of the South, but Hibs ran out comfortable 4–1 winners and the healthy scoreline did no harm to our goal difference tally.

At last the footballing gods seemed to be smiling on Hibs and as luck would have it the final league match had us playing Raith Rovers who, by this time, were already destined to be spending the following season in Division 2. The final relegation spot was between Hibs and Clyde and although our goal difference was far superior we had to beat Raith to guarantee our survival. And win we did, by a comprehensive 4–0 score-line. That final match took place whilst I was in Northumberland with the Scottish Amateur squad and when the result from Easter Road came through that Saturday tea-time I was the happiest Scotsman in the north-east of England. I was later told that the after-match scenes of euphoria on the Easter Road pitch and in the ground were more reminiscent of a League Championship victory than an escape from relegation by the skin of our teeth.

Whilst part of me was disappointed that I only played in one league match in my first season at the club, I think deep down I was glad that the manager had protected me from getting dragged into the relegation dogfight. As I have said, I had loads of confidence in my football ability, and although I was only sixteen I was already 'streetwise' enough to realise that my light frame and silky skills were no place for the battles the Hibs players had to fight to survive, particularly at the end of the season. I was getting plenty of playing experience in the rough and tumble of the First Division Reserve League and I had the relative luxury of showcasing my footballing skills with my peers in the Scottish Amateur team.

I don't know if I would have signed professional forms for Hibs if the team had been relegated and I certainly have no idea if I would have been offered terms if the club had been starting season 1963/64 in the old Scottish Second Division.

As Jimmy Wardhaugh eloquently said in his 'Young Stars May Go' article:

What future indeed will a youngster feel he has in the Second Division? They have each decided that their living for the next ten years at least is going to be in football. They, like everyone else, must look forward to the future and in this commercialised world players are going where the money lies . . . and no one can blame them.

Fortunately neither Hibs nor I had to wrestle with this dilemma, and on my seventeenth birthday on 17 July 1963 I signed as a professional footballer for Hibernian Football Club. My first season at Easter Road had indeed been a rollercoaster ride; the highs from my dream first-team debut at Airdrie, to going on my first foreign trip for the Fairs Cup tie in Holland and winning the English FA Centenary Tournament with the Scottish Amateurs. The down side was being part of a Hibs squad that for months lived with the relegation sword of Damocles hanging over it. Although it was not a nice or enjoyable experience it was experience that I was sure would stand me in good stead in my future career as a professional footballer. With my contract signed I got down to the serious business of full-time training for the forthcoming 1963/64 season, hoping I would get a chance to stake my claim for a regular place in the Hibs first team.

4

BREAKTHROUGH UNDER BIG JOCK

In the 1963/64 close season Hibs made one of their best-ever signings. Neil Martin had been banging in the goals for unfashionable Queen of the South and Walter Galbraith must have donned a sombrero and poncho to steal him from the Dumfriesshire club for a mere £7,500. 'Neillie' proved to be the perfect replacement for Joe Baker as, like Joe, he was able to score goals for fun, and he proved an instant hit with the players and fans.

Mr Galbraith also brought two experienced inside forwards to Hibs, Pat Quinn from Blackpool and Willie Hamilton from Hearts. Both players had bags of experience and whilst they were good acquisitions to the Hibs squad, I knew only too well that it was going to make my job of getting a regular first team berth in my preferred position that much harder.

When I signed full-time forms on my seventeenth birthday the new manager made it clear to me that I needed to beef up for the challenges of the Scottish First Division. I was five feet eight inches and weighed ten stone. In an attempt to get me to put on more weight my mum dug out an old 'clootie dumpling' recipe and I would eat the fruit pudding every night until I thought it would literally come out of my ears. The trouble was that whilst I was getting more than my fill of dumpling I was burning off the extra calories every day at training, and no matter how much I ate of the Scottish comfort food I never put on an extra ounce. What it did ensure was that it put me off clootie dumpling for the rest of my life.

When stuffing me with clootie dumpling failed to fill me out, it was decided that I should attend boxing training. I know boxercise is quite a trendy keep fit pastime nowadays but back in the 1960s boxing gyms were not graced with overweight executives and women wanting to get themselves fit. Boxing clubs were where teenagers and young men who enjoyed a good scrap went along to toughen themselves up and sharpen their fighting techniques – and I loved the experience. Just because I was signed with Hibs made no difference to the regulars at Sparta Boxing Club, and after several months working out on the heavy punch bags and speedballs I was given a bout against one of the other guys in the club. I never appreciated how draining three three-minute rounds were on your legs until that first fight but I was given the verdict on points.

A few months later I was given my second fight against another local Sparta lad, who went by the name of Ken Buchanan. Although Kenny was a year older than me we were the same height and weight but he had been at Sparta since he was eight years old. Despite his vast experience I think I gave as good as I got in the fight but Kenny was given the verdict on points this time. Shortly after Hibs decided that I had toughened up enough and I stopped going along to Sparta. Seven years later Ken Buchanan was crowned official World Lightweight Champion and only lost the title after his fight with the legendary Roberto Duran was stopped when Duran punched Kenny below the belt at the end of the thirteenth round of their title fight.

With his tartan shorts and immense boxing skills, Scotland and Edinburgh had every reason to be proud of Ken Buchanan because, as well as holding the World title, he is the only living British boxer to be inducted into the Boxing Hall of Fame, and holds the record for a European boxer for topping the bill at Madison Square Garden seven times. His boxing talent took him to the pinnacle of the sport while mine was to come in very handy during some feisty football scraps I encountered over the course of my career.

Walter Galbraith came to Hibs with a reputation as a tough, no-nonsense Scot who had spent most of his playing days and all of his managerial career in England. The signing of Neil, Willie and Pat proved that he could also spot a bargain in the transfer market. During the summer of 1963 Hibs recruited another Edinburgh boy who would go on to be one of the club's best servants. Pat Stanton signed from junior side Bonnyrigg Rose, and after a season playing against ex-pros and long-in-the-tooth hard men (the ones that had teeth, that is) in the East Junior League Pat was more than capable of handling the pace and rigours of the Scottish First Division. Pat was a tough-tackling, creative right half and he added much needed strength and guile to the first team when he was introduced a dozen or so games into the 1963/64 season.

Whilst these four new additions made an immediate impact during the first half of that season, the Hibs defence was still leaking too many goals. The start to the league campaign was almost a mirror image of the previous season. In the opening fixture, again against Hearts, we suffered a 4–2 defeat. If that wasn't bad enough, a week later we were hammered 5–0 away to Rangers and further away defeats followed at Motherwell and Dunfermline. Home form wasn't much better with only three points to show from four games. Despite the new faces it was proving to be a tough challenge for the manager and Walter

Galbraith was beginning to wilt under the strain of the constant criticism he was receiving from the fans and local press.

I eventually got my chance in late October and was drafted in to play at outside right for the home league match against St Johnstone, where we ran out comfortable 4–1 winners. The team had lost three games on the trot and it was a great feeling to be in the side when we broke that terrible run, and on my home debut to boot. John Parke, Northern Ireland's right back, made his debut in that match and he, along with Pat Quinn, received rave reviews for their performances.

The *Evening News'* John Ayres included in his match report:

All round this was a much more impressive Hibs, though there is still a weakness in the half back line. Young Peter Cormack did very well indeed on his return and I am sure he will be given every chance to prove his ability.

That 'every chance' lasted all of two games. I managed to notch our only goal the following week in a 2–1 defeat away to Partick Thistle and the following Saturday we lost 3–2 at Neil Martin's old stomping ground, Queen of the South. That was my last appearance in the first team for four and a half months. My next league outing was in a 1–0 victory over St Mirren at Easter Road where I played right half and the following day the *Scottish Sunday Express* match report said:

But the find of the game was Hibs' seventeen-year-old Peter Cormack who stepped back from inside right to right half. There he tackled like a tiger and his distribution was precise and silky – despite being against St Mirren's Man of the Match.

The following Saturday I kept my place in the team for what

turned out to be manager Walter Galbraith's final match in charge of Hibs away to Aberdeen.

The fifteen weeks I was out of the first team picture were extremely frustrating. I began to think that if I couldn't get a chance when results were bad and with established players' confidence suffering as a consequence then I would never get an opportunity of a decent run in the team. The one huge bonus for me at this difficult time for the club was that I was learning my trade at training week in and week out with Willie Hamilton. For the first six years of his football life Willie played in England where he had gained the reputation as a 'hell raiser'. Many people have likened Willie to George Best, and I was lucky enough to play at Easter Road alongside the two of them. But whilst Bestie was renowned for the birds and the booze, Willie didn't have any time for the ladies, probably because they would have interfered with his gambling and bevvying. I also think Willie would have been the first to admit that he didn't have George's gift of the gab and he definitely wasn't blessed with Bestie's filmstar good looks. But Willie had football ability in spades and I was very privileged to spend my formative years at Hibs learning from this midfield master.

Although results throughout the season had been inconsistent, Walter Galbraith guided the team to mid-table safety and his decision to resign after the defeat at Pittodrie came as a shock to the players and the fans. It seemed less of a shock to club chairman Bill Harrower, who almost immediately announced that Jock Stein would be the new manager.

At the time Mr Galbraith was appointed manager in December 1961 there was much speculation in the newspapers that Jock Stein was going to be Hibs' next boss. But Dunfermline refused to release him from his contract and the Hibs board brought Walter Galbraith to Scotland from Tranmere Rovers. By March

1964 'Big Jock' had firmly established himself as a young, up-and-coming manager following four years in charge at Dunfermline Athletic. In his first couple of weeks at East End Park he saved the club from relegation, and the following season Jock steered the Pars to a Scottish Cup victory over Celtic, the club he had served with distinction as a player.

I saw Mr Stein's appointment as a tremendous opportunity and was certain he would at least give me a fair crack of the whip. My optimism stemmed from previous conversations I had had with Alex Edwards when we played together in the Scottish Amateur team. Alex used to wax lyrical about how great a manager Mr Stein was and how he had given Alex and the rest of the young Dunfermline lads tremendous support and encouragement. Big Jock's mantra seemed to be 'if you are good enough you are old enough', and he as much as said this to me and all the other young lads when he first arrived at Easter Road. I was fortunate enough to play in his first game in charge at home against Airdrie. Despite us winning 2–1 I didn't get a run out in the first team again until four weeks later in a Summer Cup tie against Dunfermline. Jock had an aura about him and all the young players called him Mr Stein but the established pros got away with calling him 'gaffer'. I likened him to a strict but fair headmaster, but guys like Willie Hamilton said he was more like a 'father-in-the-chapel' of the National Union of Mineworkers. At times he was one of the boys but you always knew who was boss and woe betide anyone who got on the wrong side of him.

With Jock Stein's arrival at Easter Road I was determined that the 1964/65 season was going to be 'make or break' for my career at Hibs. It had been more than twenty months since I made my first team debut and that heady afternoon at Broomfield seemed like a lifetime ago. During the previous season I was restless and impatient, playing most of my football in the reserve side. I did manage more games in the first team than the one outing the season before but I was unhappy that when I was picked I was stuck out on one of the wings, only getting snatches of involvement in the game. I was convinced that my best position was inside forward, where I could both create chances and get on the end of attacks in the penalty box.

Although I played only a handful of first team games the previous season, I had a positive feeling going into pre-season training a few weeks before my eighteenth birthday and I put in a lot of hard work in the run-up to the start of the 1964/65 campaign. My number one aim before a ball was kicked was to establish myself as a regular in the Hibs first team. I used to annoy the 'auld heids' in the squad, including Willie Hamilton and Pat Quinn, by putting my stamina to good use in the punishing runs we did on Arthur's Seat. The experienced pros hated pre-season training, they had seen and done it all before and running up and down a hill in the heart of Edinburgh was not their idea of fun. It didn't bother me and the other young bucks like wee Jimmy, Pat and Eric Stevenson. We were determined to establish ourselves in the new manager's plans for the season ahead.

When the hill runs were out of the way we used to laugh at the antics of Willie Hamilton, who would jump over the perimeter wall at Easter Road during warm up laps on the track and then try to convince trainer Tom MacNiven that he had done the same number of laps as the rest of us. Willie probably used up more energy arguing with Tom than he would have done if he had just done the running. Nevertheless, this was all good for team morale and the spirit in the Hibs camp was very good going into the new season.

*

All the players had a big incentive to figure in Mr Stein's early plans as our very first game was the first leg of the first ever Scottish Summer Cup against Aberdeen, which was to be played on 2 August. The final had been carried forward from the end of the previous season because of a typhoid outbreak in the Granite City. My hard work in pre-season paid dividends and I was on the left wing in that opening match. The Dons won the first match 3–2 and we were very confident that we could overcome the one-goal deficit back at Easter Road four days later. After ninety minutes we were 2–1 up with goals from Stan Vincent and Eric Stevenson, and thirty minutes extra-time couldn't break the deadlock. After the toss of a coin won by Aberdeen, the deciding match was scheduled to take place back at Pittodrie on 2 September. Before then we had the group matches in the Scottish League Cup to contend with and our four team group included Airdrie, Third Lanark and Big Jock's previous employers, Dunfermline Athletic. A 2–0 defeat to the Pars on their patch was our only defeat in our six games but we could only manage a 1–1 draw against them back at Easter Road, which meant that they would progress to the next round.

The one consolation for me was that in our final group match against Airdrie at Broomfield I started on the right wing and scored my first senior hat-trick with all the goals coming in the second half.

I found a new 'best friend' journalist in sports reporter John Ayres who recorded my proud moment thus:

> Since coming into the team this season Cormack has played well, first on the left wing and now on the right. The fact that his goals were scored from close range in a position normally filled by a centre forward shows that he was no orthodox winger in the old-fashioned sense.

What John Ayres' comments also reveal is the tactics Jock Stein had us playing at the time. He didn't want anyone holding fixed positions. Both wingers were encouraged to roam across the forward line and switch wings during games. Inside forwards and wing backs would also interchange throughout the ninety minutes and full backs were encouraged to venture forward, which was virtually unheard of in the early sixties.

He exploited this system to the full in later years with Celtic, and the best example I can think of is Celtic left back Tommy Gemmell's equalising goal against Inter in the 1967 European Cup Final. Those familiar with the goal will recall that 'Big Tam' hammered in the shot from the right edge of the penalty box from a cut back by the other Celtic full back, Jim Craig. It was an orthodox position for an inside right or an attacking right half. Not where you would expect to find the left back, and it completely caught out the Inter defenders. In fact, Big Jock's tactical brilliance totally bamboozled the Italians in Lisbon with his team's movement and positional interchanging. Jock Stein thoroughly deserved all the plaudits he received at the time and for many years afterwards, and Celtic nearly won the European Cup for a second time three years later, only losing out in the final to a very good Feyenoord team.

My confidence was sky high after the hat-trick at Broomfield and the replayed Summer Cup Final at Pittodrie on the following Wednesday evening couldn't come quickly enough. Unfortunately it did come two days before the opening of the Forth Road Bridge by the Queen and our bus had to cross the Firth of Forth via the Kincardine Bridge on its journey north. The decider was played at a packed Pittodrie and the following day's papers said that 25,000 fans turned out for the replayed final for the first domestic trophy of the Scottish 1964/65 season. I was back on the right wing and although we went in at half-time drawing 1–1, we had totally outplayed the Dons in the first forty-five minutes, with Neil Martin and me hitting the woodwork and their goalie saving a Pat Stanton penalty.

Mr Stein told us at the interval that if we kept playing the football we had played in the first half we would run out winners and he was proved to be absolutely correct. Twelve minutes from time I won a challenge and slipped the ball through to Jim Scott who ran in on goal and scored. Then five minutes from time I hit a speculative shot which beat the unsighted keeper and crept over the line. I knew after the third goal went in that there was no way back for Aberdeen and at the final whistle Hibs had won their first trophy in twelve years. All the players and the many Hibs fans who had made the long journey to watch the replay were ecstatic and this time the celebrations were merited, as a cup was heading for the trophy cabinet at Easter Road.

Sitting on the bus back to Edinburgh I had a glow of satisfaction for two reasons. Not only did I feel that I had finally established myself in the first team at Easter Road, but I had done so as one of the goalscorers who helped the club lift its first trophy in twelve years.

There was one funny postscript following our victory in the Summer Cup involving Willie Hamilton. Before the replay Jock Stein had informed the first team squad that we were on fifty pounds a man bonus if we lifted the trophy. Several weeks elapsed and each day at training we would take it in turns to bang on at Willie about the missing bonus. In those days the players received their wage packet on a Tuesday and most weeks Willie was skint by the Thursday, after a couple of days at the bookies. One Friday Willie fell for the bait after someone said that the players needed a strong spokesman to take it up with Mr Stein.

'Leave it to me. I'll sort it out with the Gaffer after training,' said Willie.

All the players were bathed and dressed before Willie, and after putting his jacket on he headed up the stairs to Jock Stein's office. As soon as Willie closed the manager's door the rest of us crept up the stairs to try and listen to the conversation. Big Jock probably thought Willie was in to speak to him about his Friday night sleepover but Willie just came right out with it.

'Boss, when are we getting that fifty quid bonus for winning the Summer Cup?'

The next voice we heard was Jock Stein's. 'Hamilton, if you're not down these fucking stairs before I put down this fucking newspaper I'll kick your fucking arse out of Easter Road myself.'

Willie was the quickest man over ten yards in our team, but all the rest of us were down the stairs and back in the dressing room before he had left Big Jock's office. We were all sitting straight-faced when he walked back in and boldly announced, 'That's it all sorted, lads.' We all just burst out laughing but the following week the fifty-pound bonus was in our pay packets. I was on top of the world that night and thought that things could not get any better, but only four weeks later I would experience one of the greatest nights of my football career that still gives me goosebumps almost fifty years on.

Due to our lowly tenth position in the league the previous season Easter Road was a European competition-free zone in 1964/65. But that did not stop Jock Stein from talking the Hibs chairman into inviting the biggest club side in the world at the time, Real Madrid, to play a friendly match at Easter Road. Big Jock was not only ahead of his time when it came to football tactics, he was also a visionary in seeing that the future power base of British club football lay in Europe.

Apparently when Jock first approached the Hibs chairman about playing Real Madrid, Bill Harrower baulked at Real Madrid's asking price of £20,000. But Jock was nothing if not determined, and in the weeks prior to the game he was going around Easter Road telling anyone who would listen about the football and financial benefits for Hibs in staging such a match. And surprise, surprise – guess what? Once again he was absolutely spot-on.

The evening prior to the match hundreds of Hibs fans turned up at the ground just to get the autographs of the Real Madrid players when they appeared for some light training. On the night of the match itself, over 30,000 fans happily paid six shillings (thirty pence), which was double the normal gate money, to watch Hibs take on a Real Madrid team that contained Puskas, Gento and Santamaria, household names to football fans across the world, not just in Scotland.

It will be hard for younger readers to fully appreciate the magnitude of this in the twenty-first century when they can watch European and domestic games live on satellite television virtually twenty-four/seven. But back in the early 1960s there were very few live matches on TV and the armchair football fan had to make do with limited weekend highlights of Scottish football on *Scotsport*, where it was a challenge for the one camera at the game to follow the ball, never mind re-run the best bits of a match.

In fairness, many Scottish football fans in 1964 were familiar with Real Madrid and their top players who had played in, what is still regarded today, the greatest ever European Cup Final. In 1960 the European Cup Final was staged at Hampden Park and over 130,000 fans packed into Scotland's national stadium, whilst many more sat at home watching the match live on their black and white television sets. It was a football classic and Real Madrid defeated the German Bundesliga Champions, Eintracht Frankfurt 7–3. It still holds the record as the highest-scoring European Cup Final, and Real's famous Hungarian forward Puskas scored four goals, with Alfredo di Stefano notching a hat-trick. The game was played just before my fourteenth birthday but the memories of that wonderful football match were still vivid four years later as I psyched myself up for the 'friendly' match at Easter Road.

I was already high as a kite on the back of having established myself in the Hibs first team and in the run-up to the Real match I had to keep pinching myself I was not dreaming that I was about to lock horns against the greatest club players in the world. The date of 7 October 1964 will forever be etched in my mind and was without doubt the greatest game of my career in the green and white of Hibs. Sure it was a 'glamour' friendly match, but for nearly every Hibs player in the squad of thirteen it was going to be one of the biggest nights in their professional career, and we were all determined to do ourselves, the club and our fans proud. And that we did, beating the men in white 2–0 to inflict on them their first ever defeat on Scottish soil. The icing on the cake for me was that I managed to score our first goal after only thirteen minutes' play and I received the Man of the Match award after the game. All the Hibs players also received a gift of a Real Madrid watch from our guests and a commemorative tankard of the occasion from Hibs. Both mementoes still have pride of place in my trophy cabinet at home, and the watch is still in full working order, which is more than can be said of my old footballer's legs these days.

Reporter W. H. Kemp recorded my goal for the history books with the following:

Hibs, to an ear-shattering roar, took the lead with a spectacular goal which Real themselves could not have bettered. Hamilton lobbed the ball out to Martin on the far left. The internationalist sent a fierce low centre to Cormack and the nineteen-year-old [*he got my age wrong but I'll let him off*], swivelling slightly, rocketed the ball into the net from twenty yards.

I have so many fantastic memories from that match. The goal is obviously one I'll treasure for the rest of my life. I scored better and more important goals later in my career at Hibs, Nottingham Forest, Liverpool and Bristol City, but that goal against Real gave me my biggest thrill, coming as it did a few months after my eighteenth birthday. I also don't think Willie Hamilton ever performed better than he did that night. Playing against the biggest club in the world was the stage Willie's talents deserved and he ran the show for ninety minutes, proving that he was indeed a tremendous footballing talent.

The Real Madrid match also highlighted the tactical brilliance of Jock Stein. He had us playing a four-two-four system and the Spaniards were not used to the opposition team being so attack-minded against them. Finally, I don't think I can ever recall the Hibs supporters being as noisy or excited as they were that October night in 1964. Reports in the newspapers of the attendance varied from 30,000 to 35,000, but given the number of people I have met in the intervening years who said that they were at Easter Road that wonderful evening I think there must have been nearer 50,000 people in the stadium. From the deafening noise they made throughout the ninety minutes I think the £20,000 Hibs paid Real was a very good bit of financial business for the club. After the final whistle, the vast majority of the crowd refused to go home and the players had to get out of the team bath to go back on the park and salute the ecstatic fans with a lap of honour. It's these magical moments that players live for, but sadly for most footballers they don't come around often enough.

The publicity I got following the game was great and I was especially pleased for my mum and dad. It made me feel really good that I had done them proud on such a big occasion. On the Thursday morning I went into training feeling ten feet tall, convinced I was ready to take on the football world, but my team-mates and I were brought back down to earth with a thud. After some light training, Mr Stein gathered us together to talk over the previous evening's match. Everyone was still buzzing and Big Jock let us relive the highlights with all the back-slapping and joking that is part and parcel of a happy dressing room after a satisfying performance and result. Once we exhausted the banter and stories he said very quietly and calmly, 'Well, boys, there's no doubt about it, you all did well and I'm proud of the way you played. But remember you are only as good as your last game, and on Saturday we've got a tough league match against Rangers at Ibrox.

'After your Real Madrid exploits they will be desperate to bring you down a peg or two, so no more talk of Real Madrid and get your heads around Saturday's match. The Real game will mean nothing if we don't get a result at Ibrox.'

That was what made Jock Stein the great manager that he was. He was not only a clever football tactician and a first-class man-manager, just as importantly he also knew the right things to say at the right time.

On the Saturday we carried on at Ibrox where we had left off against Real and thumped Rangers 4–2 in front of their own fans. It was Hibs' first victory at Ibrox in twelve years, and I managed to notch two goals from my wandering berth on the right wing. But once again the star of the show was wee Willie Hamilton. As we were coming onto the park at the start of the game Rangers' legendary left half Jim Baxter said to Willie that he would be a far tougher proposition than Ferenc Puskas was on the previous Wednesday. Willie just laughed and told Jim that he'd be better keep his mouth and his legs shut as he would make him eat his words. Wee Willie was true to his word and, if anything, performed better at Ibrox than he did four days earlier against Real. He also won the personal 'nutmeg' competition with 'Slim Jim' hands down and he was the only player I have ever seen who could beat Baxter in his prime at his own game.

To be fair to Jim, he was the first to shake Willie's hand at the end of the match and arranged to treat him to a double Bacardi and Coke afterwards. Willie and Slim Jim were from the same mould. Two football geniuses whose weakness was the demon drink. But with both of them you had to take the full package, personal flaws and all. For ninety minutes on a football park they were masters of their craft and the Scottish game would have been a lot poorer if they had not been given the chance to show the world what they could do.

My newfound fame following the Real Madrid match had an unexpected bonus – I was given a footballer nickname. Nowadays most players' nicknames are fairly bland; 'Gazza' for Paul Gascoigne, 'Crouchie' for Peter Crouch, 'Coisty' for Ally McCoist and 'Dazza' for Darren Fletcher – all much of a muchness. I actually think fans and players were much more imaginative back in the sixties and seventies. Sure there was Bestie, Fergie and Greigie, but at Hibs Pat Stanton was nicknamed 'Niddrie' after the Edinburgh housing estate where he grew up, Billy McNeill was known as 'Ceasar' by the Celtic faithful (although it was Tommy Gemmell who sported the Roman nose), Denis Law was 'The Lawman' and Leeds United had 'Sniffer' Clarke and Norman 'Bites Yer Legs' Hunter. I guess after all the publicity I received on the back of the Real Madrid game it was decided by whoever it is that decides these things that I now merited a nickname and somebody somewhere took it upon themselves to christen me 'Gas Meter' (perhaps not the most creative combination of words rhyming with 'Peter'). Now as football nicknames go, I am the first to admit that mine was perhaps not the most original, and fortunately for me nor was it the most memorable. I am also grateful that I was not burdened with it for the rest of my football career but at the time 'Gas Meter' Cormack was 'over the moon' with his nickname as, if nothing else, it was another sign that I had been accepted by my team-mates and the Hibs fans.

My consistent form and the accompanying complimentary headlines were not restricted to Scotland, and a couple of articles appeared in the press before Christmas saying that Arsenal were keeping a close eye on my progress. One report even stated that their manager, former England captain Billy Wright, turned up at Easter Road to watch me in a match against Partick Thistle. Whilst I was flattered with the speculation, I was in no hurry to leave Hibs. I was delighted that I had become a regular in the first team and Mr Stein's attacking tactics gave me plenty of freedom to wander from my wide berth. We also had a very good squad, and as the old saying goes 'a winning squad is a happy squad', and all the players were enjoying their football. It was a very balanced side with a good mixture of experience and youth, and I was learning every day in training from the likes of Willie Hamilton, Pat Quinn and John Parke.

After our victory at Ibrox we only lost one match in the league before the New Year, ironically against Jock Stein's old team Dunfermline. Three teams were battling it out at the top of the First Division – ourselves, our local rivals Hearts and Kilmarnock. The Old Firm giants Celtic and Rangers were fifth and sixth, and for the first time in several years it looked like a team outside Glasgow could lift the Scottish League Championship.

Going into the New Year we faced two games on consecutive days against Hearts at Tynecastle and at home to Falkirk. Mr

Stein called on his considerable football know-how and put his clout with the chairman to good use by taking all the players to the Scotia Hotel in central Edinburgh for the two nights prior to the games.

I am more than happy to credit Big Jock with this initiative, but in truth it probably had more to do with his wife, Jean. It was common knowledge in the club that Jock had been taking Willie Hamilton back to his house on Queensferry Road, on the west side of Edinburgh, to stay the night before games to make sure Willie was off the drink and in bed at a sensible time. This unusual arrangement had clearly been working a treat given the contribution Willie was making to our superb run of form but I don't think Mrs Stein relished the idea of having Willie as a house guest on Hogmanay and New Year's night.

Therefore all the first team squad had to report to the Scotia at tea time on Hogmanay.

Unfortunately, Big Jock's strategy didn't quite go to plan after the club chairman, Bill Harrower, appeared at the hotel halfway through the evening with a case of champagne for the players to 'have a wee drink to bring in the New Year'. I was in the habit of going to bed at nine p.m. on the eve of matches and most of the other players retired long before midnight. Most of the players, that is, except Willie Hamilton.

To be fair to the wee man, other than when he was under 'house arrest' at Big Jock's, it was probably his pre-match routine to enjoy a few 'shandies' as his way of relaxing on the eve of a game. Anyway, the temptation of the champagne from the chairman was clearly too much for Willie to resist and as the players wandered downstairs for breakfast the next morning we were met on the stairs by Tam MacNiven helping Willie go in the opposite direction to his bed.

Whilst champagne was not normally Willie's drink of choice, he had managed to get through half the case whilst the rest of us slept, no doubt dreaming of scoring the winning goal at Tynecastle the following day. Needless to say, none of the early bedders managed that feat and it was left to the wee man who had been put to bed only a few hours earlier to score the only goal of the game. Willie had another outstanding performance that day and his goal came after a mazy run and shot from a near impossible angle.

The 1–0 victory over Hearts set us up nicely for the visit of Falkirk the following day and we hammered the Bairns 6–0 which included four goals from Neil Martin. Willie Hamilton didn't manage to get on the scoresheet in that match but he had another great game, although I think he had a quieter evening at the hotel on New Year's night.

Our excellent league form followed us into the Scottish Cup where we reached the semi-final after knocking out Clydebank, Partick Thistle and then defeated Rangers 2–1 at Easter Road – the third time we had beaten the Ibrox men that season. But the victory over Rangers was overshadowed when Jock Stein left the club a few days later to take over as manager at Celtic.

Everyone at Easter Road was devastated when it was announced at the end of January that Jock was joining Celtic at the end of the season, or before if a suitable replacement could be found. I was absolutely gutted at the time and quietly hoped that it wouldn't happen if we managed to win the League Championship or Scottish Cup, or even do the double. Big Jock had become a footballing father figure to me and I took the announcement of his intended departure very badly. But immediately following our quarter-final victory over Rangers it was announced that Jock was leaving with immediate effect and that Bob Shankly was joining Hibs from Dundee.

For me it would mean that I would be acquainted with my third manager in as many years at the club and I was apprehensive as I felt that I had managed to gain the confidence and respect of Mr Stein. I also felt that Jock was letting us all down by leaving at such a crucial time in the season. How could he walk out on us when we still had so much to play for? It took me a long time to get over his departure and there is no question in my mind that the timing of his move to Celtic cost us dearly.

Following Jock's announcement, at the end of January the Hibs board managed to persuade Bob Shankly, brother of Liverpool's Bill, to move from Dundee to the manager's hot-seat at Easter Road. Bob was a very experienced manager, having won the League Championship with Dundee in 1962, and he steered them to the semi-final of the European Cup the following season where they were narrowly defeated in the semi-final by AC Milan. I was to spend the bulk of my career at Easter Road playing under Bob, who successfully carried forward the foundations that had been laid down at the club by Jock Stein.

Initially Big Jock's departure had no effect on the team's form. A couple of weeks after Mr Stein left Hibs we beat his new employers Celtic 4–2 at Parkhead with Neillie Martin notching a hat-trick. There are not many seasons when Hibs could boast of beating both Celtic and Rangers in front of their own fans and our confidence was sky high.

Beating both sides of the Old Firm in Glasgow that season also opened my eyes to the sectarian divide in Glasgow. When I scored two goals in the 4–2 defeat of Rangers at Ibrox the previous October I was verbally abused as 'a wee Fenian c***'. That day at Parkhead the Celtic faithful chanted that I was a 'Fucking Orange bastard'. I didn't mind one little bit, and as my team-mates pointed out, the abuse meant that the opposition fans saw me as a threat to their team.

*

The Scottish Cup draw paired us against Dunfermline, which was played at neutral Tynecastle where we had defeated Hearts a few months earlier. But on the day of the semi-final we just didn't perform and went down 2–0. It was the first big disappointment I had faced as a professional footballer, and like every competitive sportsman, I hated losing, and I have never forgotten the pain of that first defeat. Losing the semi-final drastically affected our form in the league run-in where we only managed to win two more games but lost three, including a 4–0 home defeat to Big Jock's Celtic. Just to rub more salt into our very painful wounds, Celtic beat Dunfermline in the final of the Scottish Cup, which was the start of Big Jock's extremely successful thirteen-year reign at Parkhead. Our season petered out lamely after we were knocked out in the semi-final of the Summer Cup by Motherwell.

It had been a real rollercoaster of a year for me personally. At the start of the season my target was to establish myself in the Hibs first team, and that I had achieved. I played in many memorable matches, none more so than the victory over Real Madrid which proved to be the launch pad of my career with Hibs fans and the wider Scottish footballing public. Whilst I was still unhappy at playing out on the wing, Jock Stein's roaming attacking tactics suited my style of play and enabled me to regularly get on the scoresheet, and I was getting invaluable experience training every day with seasoned professionals. The only problem was that all of these positives had significantly raised my expectations and at the season's end I felt deflated that, apart from our Summer Cup success, our poor finish in the final league matches left us four points behind eventual champions Kilmarnock. That and our Scottish Cup semi-final defeat by Dunfermline left a bitter taste in my mouth.

*

Still, after a fifty-two-match season of highs and lows, my work was not yet over. Hibs were going on their first summer tour of North America, playing nine matches in twenty days. Life was looking not too bad for this eighteen-year-old who was heading off to America for the very first time in his life, all expenses paid. At the time there was an advert doing the rounds; 'Join the Army and see the world' it said to get youngsters to sign up to the armed forces. I was seeing a fair bit of the world and at the same time doing something I loved – playing football. But as I was to discover, the tour matches were not as friendly as I thought they were going to be when we headed for Prestwick Airport, and a wee bit of army training might have come in very handy for the scraps we were about to face.

5

GLORIOUS EUROPEAN NIGHTS AND HOT SUMMER TOURS

The second goal in the friendly match against Real Madrid in 1964 was Hibs' 200th goal against foreign opposition. Hibs were in the vanguard of British clubs' participation in European competition. In fact, Easter Road was the first stadium in the UK to have floodlights and in 1955 Hibs were the first British club to play in the European Cup after the Scottish League winners Aberdeen and English champions Chelsea declined the offer from UEFA to participate. Hibs reached the semi-final of that very first European Cup but lost to French champions Reims.

When I arrived, Easter Road still bore the scars of a 1961 Fairs Cup encounter with Barcelona. In my first week at Hibs the groundsman led me down the tunnel to show me the door of the match officials' changing room. It was riddled with stud marks, and whilst for Hibs fans the Fairs Cup win over Barcelona ranks alongside the Real Madrid result, the Barcelona players didn't take the defeat well. My DK schoolmates and I snuck into Easter Road via our usual security blind spot at the Dunbar End for the match and it was my first experience of mob rule on a football pitch. It would not be my last! With the score on the night standing at 2–2, the match was held up for seven minutes whilst the Spanish players harangued the referee and jostled with the Edinburgh 'bobbies' trying to restore order on the pitch after the referee awarded a penalty to Hibs. The conversion of the penalty kick gave Hibs a 7–6 aggregate lead that they managed to hang onto until the end of the ninety minutes. After blowing his whistle for full-time, the referee was chased off the park by incensed Barcelona players who then took their frustrations out on his dressing room door. The door ended up being the Easter Road groundsman's equivalent of Edinburgh Castle, and every visitor to the stadium was given a tourist guide's explanation of the damage inflicted by the Barcelona players. He loved nothing better than regaling visiting match officials and opposition players with tales of the night Hibs knocked one of the biggest teams in Europe out of the Fairs Cup and telling them the story of the resultant attack on the innocent door.

I had caught the European bug after my first trip abroad with the Hibs squad to Holland within days of making my first team debut in 1962. There was something completely different and magical about going abroad to pit your football wits against foreign opposition in their own backyard. Everything about the experience was exhilarating. Perhaps it had something to do with the fact that very few people from Britain travelled over-seas in those days. Today the world is a much smaller place, with no corner of the earth out of reach, but in 1962 even a two-week holiday in the sun to Spain was the stuff of dreams to the vast majority of British people, and the ordinary football supporter never ventured abroad to watch his team.

My first summer tour with Hibs came at the end of the 1964/65 season when the club arranged an eight-game, twenty-day visit to North America. Looking back now, such an exhausting schedule on the back of a tough fifty-two game season would not even be contemplated by clubs, but all the players at Easter Road were excited about an all-expenses-paid trip to play foot-ball in Canada, none moreso than me.

Whilst my eighteen-year-old Leith pals were saving some of their hard-earned wages for a week at Butlins' in Ayr, I was part of the Hibs squad jetting off to Canada from Prestwick Airport. I well remember Willie Hamilton and a few other experienced players getting stuck into their duty frees on the transatlantic flight. Willie had everyone in stitches when one of the air stewardesses asked him if he could drink Canada Dry after they had run out of Coca-Cola for his Bacardi.

'Och I don't know if I could dae that hen, but I'll give it a good try over the next three weeks.'

Needless to say, she never got the joke, but everyone else laughed at Willie's comment. He did indeed get stuck into the bevvy on the trip, but true to previous form the more he drank the better he performed on the park.

The hardest match of the tour came in our first game against Nottingham Forest. Whilst it was our opening game it was Forest's final match of their tour and they had a 100 per cent record going into the game. However, we were the fresher team and ran out 2–1 winners to get our trip off to a good start. Our second game was against a team of British Columbia All-Stars who we beat 9–2. The games were coming thick and fast and Neil Martin and I notched hat-tricks in our third match where we beat Calgary Buffalo Kickers 7–1. We ran up our biggest victory in the fourth match when we overpowered a select team from Concordia 15–1. Their team boasted six continentals, one Scot and four Canadians but we were far too strong for them. I managed to notch a couple and Neil Martin continued his run of goalscoring form by scoring five of the fifteen goals.

Our biggest problem in the next match was not from the opposing eleven players but from swarms of mosquitoes that liked our pale but interesting skin. They descended on us like a plague of, well, mosquitoes, during the national anthems and pestered us for the ninety minutes we were on the park. The mosquitoes only distracted us slightly from beating the Manitoba All-Stars 11–0 and I was delighted to get into the shower at the end of the match to try and cool the bites down. The worst affected was Derek Whiteford who counted twenty-seven individual bites. Willie Hamilton was the least affected and he put this down to the amount of alcohol in his blood stream and suggested to trainer Tom McNiven that this might be the best antidote for future games.

The next 'All-Star' team we faced were Ottawa, but they went the same way as previous opponents, mainly due to a one-man demolition by Willie Hamilton who scored seven goals. Before the match we were shown a beautiful silver tray that would be given to the game's star player and Wille said he wanted to take that home to Scotland for his mum.

Even the ninety degree temperatures didn't put him off and he was outstanding. As well as scoring seven goals he mesmerised the opposition with his ball skills and lethal burst of pace. After being presented with the Man of the Match award Willie couldn't get the prize into his suitcase. Undeterred, he bent the tray in half over his knee to ensure that his beloved mum would get her present from Canada.

Our two toughest matches, both in a football and a physical sense, came against Toronto Italia, which we won 4–0, and a 3–0 defeat of Montreal Italia. The Montreal team didn't take kindly to being outplayed and were determined to leave their stud marks on our legs as a going-away present. At half-time the referee came into our team dressing room and cautioned us for 'undue roughness' which was a joke as we were the ones getting kicked. Following more off-the-ball digs from my marker during the second half, I 'lost the heid' after he punched me in the face and the subsequent free-for-all was reported in the local press as a 'flare up'. An understatement if ever there was one. Finally, mild-mannered Jim Scott of all people was sent off near the final whistle for protesting to the referee about another poor decision. Given the kicking, punching and head-butting that went on it was ironic that Jim got sent off for bad-mouthing the ref.

Still, at the end of the tour we all lived to tell the tale and our statistics were impressive. We had won all eight games, scoring sixty-six goals, conceded only five and beat Montreal Italia by two falls and a submission. More importantly, the trip had been a great bonding exercise for the players. We had been very well looked after by our hosts, staying in the best hotels with plenty of spending money distributed in little brown envelopes by the sponsors. They seemed delighted with the large crowds our games were attracting and we were only too happy to spend their surplus cash. It was a win-win situation that everyone seemed happy with.

Whilst in North America I visited the local tourist attractions and I was particularly impressed with the sound and the fury of Niagara Falls and the spectacular Rockies. It let me see that travel really does broaden the mind. We also saw some top-notch entertainment on the two North American tours I had with Hibs and I was totally overwhelmed when we were treated to live performances by the Everly Brothers, the Drifters, the Four Tops and my favourite of all, Diana Ross and the Supremes. I came home from that first twenty-day trip not only more worldly-wise but also with a stash of LPs and a portable record player. Pretty cool for an eighteen-year-old laddie from Leith only just setting out on his professional football career.

Our fourth-place finish in the league the previous season ensured that we qualified for the 1965/66 Fairs Cup. As luck would have it, we were paired in the first round against Spanish side Valencia who had unceremoniously dumped us out of the competition the last time we qualified in 1962/63. That was in my first season at the club where the Spaniards hammered us 5–0 in the first leg at their Mestalla Stadium, the 2–1 win in the return at Easter Road provided little consolation. However, it was a different Hibs squad that had been assembled in the intervening three years and everyone at Easter Road was looking forward to the first-leg home tie on 8 September.

The Fairs Cup match came early in our season, but we had started well, having won six and lost only one of our first seven matches. We carried that form into the Valencia match and took the lead with a goal from Jim Scott after only five minutes. We battered the Spaniards for the rest of the first half as Valencia packed their defence, allowing us to dictate play. The Hibs players were really fired-up, keen to make amends for the defeat by Valencia a few years earlier, which led to one of the strangest football incidents I have ever encountered. We had just entered the dressing room at half-time when our team captain John Baxter was asked to go to the German referee's changing room. There hadn't been any controversial incidents and we were all puzzled by the summons. A few minutes later John walked in and Bob Shankly asked what the referee wanted. John stood there half laughing and shaking his head in disbelief.

'He said we've to stop shouting at each other.'

Everyone burst out laughing and I said, 'He can get to fuck. He can hardly speak any fucking English and the Spaniards can't understand a word of what we're saying.'

Little did I realise at the time but the half-time incident with the referee was the first of many strange refereeing perform-ances I would encounter in European games at Easter Road in my time at Hibs. The referee's lecture only succeeded in firing us up even more and we tore into Valencia straight from the kick-off but could only manage one more goal from a header by John McNamee, our centre half. I well remember their keeper having one of those inspired performances that happens to every goalie now and again where he made saves with virtually every part of his anatomy to keep the ball out. Still, after the match we were delighted with the result and confident we could score at least one over in Spain, which would require them to put four past us to get into the next round.

Unfortunately the return leg with Valencia did not take place for another five weeks. In the interim we remained unbeaten, winning a further five matches and drawing three before we headed for Spain to defend our two-goal advantage. Before the second-leg we played Celtic in the semi-final of the Scottish League Cup in front of 46,000 fans at Ibrox. A double from Neil Martin had us leading 2–1 going into the dying minutes but Celtic's flying left winger Bobby Lennox equalised in the final minute to force a replay. It was really frustrating getting so tantalisingly close to a Cup Final and I recall wondering at the time if we had blown our best chance of beating Celtic in Glasgow.

Valencia were doing well in La Liga that season and 65,000 noisy Spaniards packed into the Mestalla for the return match. It was a tremendous atmosphere but despite playing really well and creating chances throughout the ninety minutes we didn't manage to score. Valencia scored a typical continental curling free-kick early in the first half but we managed to keep the score to 1–0 at half-time. I recall manager Bob Shankly telling us at the interval to carry on the way we had been playing and a goal would come. He was right but unfortunately it was Valencia who scored it fifteen minutes from full-time from the penalty spot. Ironically the penalty came from a quick Valencia counter attack at a time when we were dominating the game and looking the likelier team to score.

Two–nil for Valencia was the final result and at that time there was no extra-time or penalties to decide the outcome. Therefore, the referee called the two captains together to toss a coin to determine the venue for the third and deciding game. As luck would have it we lost the toss and had to return to Valencia at the beginning of November. I don't remember very much about that match other than it lashed down for the full ninety minutes and we were humped 3–0. I do recall the Spanish players being magnanimous in victory and complimenting us on the tough three matches we had given them, but to me that was of no consolation. We had lost the tie and were out of the Fairs Cup and that season's European adventure had ended in the first round. The experience only made me more determined to ensure that we qualified for Europe the following season and get another crack at foreign opposition.

I have no doubt that that season's Fairs Cup disappointment ended up taking a heavy toll on my form and that of the Hibs team. There certainly wasn't an immediate European hangover, as on the Saturday following our return from Spain we hammered Hamilton Accies 11–1 at Easter Road. Unfortunately most of the media focus of the game was on a wee boy's dog that ran onto the park and held the game up for five minutes whilst the players tried to retrieve the confused mutt for the distraught owner. We were 10–0 up at the time and some Hibs players wondered if it was a desperate attempt on the part of a Hamilton fan to get the match abandoned, but it turned out the dog and its young owner were both local Hibs fans who probably sneaked into the game at my now not-so-secretive security blind spot.

As well as that being the highest victory of my eight years at Easter Road, the Hamilton match was also the day the covered enclosure was opened behind the goals at the bottom of the Easter Road slope. Over the coming months and years, the enclosure would be known as 'The Cowshed' to Hibs supporters and it was from there I received both adulation and abuse in equal measure. In those days, supporters would change ends at half-time and Hibs fans especially liked to gather in The Cowshed when we were shooting down the Easter Road slope. The Hibs players always preferred to be playing down the slope in the second half and if our captain won the toss he always chose to kick uphill in the first half. There were many games where we were behind at half-time but often turned the match around going down the slope in the second half. Shooting into the goal in front of our fans in the The Cowshed was another part of that 'lucky' tradition.

Whether it was down to the disappointment of Celtic's equalising last-minute semi-final goal or getting knocked out of Europe, the rest of season 1965/66 was a huge anti-climax. Our league form was unpredictable and no matter how many goals the forwards managed to score, the defence seemed to concede one more. A typical example was when we managed to put four past Dundee United at Tannadice but they went one better, scoring five. Whilst I managed to get on the score sheet that day I didn't put all the blame for our defeat on the shoulders of our defenders. After getting back to 3–3 from being 3–1 down, United's fourth goal was miles offside and their winning goal came from a twice-taken penalty. That result more than any other put paid to our chances of qualifying for the following season's Fairs Cup and our miserable league campaign was complete. It was a bitter blow to the players and our supporters when Hearts knocked us out of the Scottish Cup in the fourth round in early February, winning 2–1 at Tynecastle. A season that had started so promisingly ended in bitter disappointment and there would be no exciting European journeys to look forward to the following year.

It was hard to take, but at the end of the season I was still only nineteen and these setbacks were only strengthening my resolve to make it to the top of the football tree. A couple of weeks after the season ended, I was called into the Scotland squad by new manager John Prentice and given my first full cap against the World Champions Brazil. Once again football had shown me how quickly your luck and your emotions can change.

The 1966/67 season saw Colin Stein break into the Hibs first team. Colin had been signed as a defender from junior side Armadale Thistle but was quickly transformed into a strong, bustling centre forward who knew where the goals were. I had established myself at inside left and Allan McGraw, who Bob Shankly had got from Morton, added a bit of experience and composure to the midfield. Whilst we lost out to Rangers in a tough League Cup group at the start of the season our good form helped us to the quarter-final of the Scottish Cup against an Aberdeen side led by former Hibs Famous Five member Eddie Turnbull. Eric Stevenson gave us the lead which we looked likely to hang onto but we were denied with a late equaliser. Aberdeen totally outplayed and outfought us in the replay ten days later at Pittodrie where we were well beaten 3–0. That result was another setback to the team's confidence and our form for the remainder of the season was poor, winning only three more league games. Fortunately we had done enough up until then to finish the league in fourth place, one point ahead of Dundee, which guaranteed us another crack at Fairs Cup glory the following season, and what a rollercoaster ride that would prove to be.

*

Following the success of our North American Summer Tour adventure in 1965, Hibs were invited back two years later, along with fellow Scottish teams Aberdeen and Dundee United, as well as Wolves, Sunderland and Stoke from the English First Division. The tournament organisers had learnt from the previous event and it was a more ambitious, bolder and brasher event lasting all of six weeks, involving twelve teams from some of the top leagues in the world.

One particular match stood out for all the wrong reasons. On Saturday 17 June we faced Italian Serie 'A' team Cagliari in Toronto, and as things would turn out it made our previous final match two years earlier seem like handbags at five paces. Italian teams have always been known for their uncompromising, tough approach, but the Cagliari team took that to new levels.

Right from kick-off the Italians intimidated us by their rough-house tactics and unfortunately, in my case, they succeeded in provoking a reaction. At corners and free-kicks they made sure they included a handful of flesh when they grabbed your jersey and they would constantly niggle, kick and trip you off the ball whenever they thought the referee wasn't looking.

After I put us 1–0 ahead, one of the Italians was sent off for sticking the head on Jim Scott, but I evened up the sides before half-time after I foolishly retaliated after being kicked and punched once too often. Before I was sent off I warned our trainer Tam MacNiven that if the ref didn't start to take action about the Italian team's fouling I would not be responsible for my actions. Less than ten minutes later I put my Sparta Boxing Club training to good use and hooked an Italian defender after another late tackle. Unfortunately the referee did not take into account the mitigating circumstances and I made an early trip to the dressing room.

Things went from bad to worse in the second half and a mass brawl erupted after the referee awarded us a second goal ten minutes from the end to put us 2–1 ahead. The Cagliari players went mad, chasing and pushing the referee and were joined by hundreds of Italian fans who invaded the park.

Thankfully I watched this from the safety of the main stand but some of my team-mates were not so lucky and had to run a gauntlet of angry Italian fans and players to escape to the sanctuary of the dressing room. The referee was forced to abandon the match and we were credited with a 2–1 victory. It had been a nerve-wracking experience for everyone at Hibs and none of us relished the prospect of the remaining three group games against Sunderland, Brazilian side Bangu and Shamrock Rovers. However, the organisers apologised to us for the behaviour of Cagliari, who were warned that they would be sent home in disgrace if they repeated their unruly tactics in any other matches. The Hibs players were happy to see the tournament through as we were receiving red carpet treatment everywhere we went in North America. The Yanks in particular were exceptionally friendly and their 'brown envelopes' were bigger and better than everyone else's. It made the remaining three weeks extremely bearable and none of us were in a hurry to give up the five-star treatment we were receiving from our extravagant hosts. With money to burn and plenty of distractions away from football at the horse racing tracks and casinos, nobody in the Hibs party wanted to cut short the trip.

We returned to Scotland during the second week of July and the eleven-game tour meant that the normal slog of pre-season training was avoided as we were already match fit four weeks before the start of the 1967/68 season. In fact, our exertions in North America probably cost us qualification from our League Cup section where we lost at home to Dundee and away at Motherwell. Either that or several of us were suffering from delayed jet lag. We made up for this with our fans when we went to Tynecastle on the first day of the league season and beat our Edinburgh rivals 4–1. I managed to score our second goal with a diving header but our star man was Pat Quinn who broke a twenty-three month scoring drought in style by notching a hat-trick. Pat was signed four years earlier by Walter Galbraith at the same time Willie Hamilton arrived at Easter Road but, whilst Willie had moved on a couple of years earlier Pat had established himself in the side as our midfield general.

Pat's previous claim to fame before he came to Easter Road was scoring for Scotland against England at Wembley, which is pretty much near the top of every Scottish schoolboy's dreams. Unfortunately it was in the match in 1961 that England won 9–3, and six years on Pat was still being constantly reminded of this by his Hibs team-mates when we thought he was getting too big for his size six boots. Pat's favourite story of the Wembley debacle was when the players trudged into the dressing room after the drubbing. According to Pat, the first person in the communal bath was the Scotland goalkeeper Frank Haffey who had been at fault for several of England's goals. Frank apparently fancied himself as a bit of a singer and proceeded to sing his heart out without a care in the world. This was the final straw for several of the Scotland players and they let rip with a stream of expletives, but Frank carried on singing regardless. Needless to say, Frank never won another cap for Scotland but Pat always joked that this had more to do with his singing abilities than his performance between the sticks.

Eleven days after our opening-day victory at Tynecastle we ran out onto the Easter Road pitch for a first round first-leg Fairs Cup tie against Portuguese side FC Porto. During the close season Bob Shankly had signed Scottish winger Alex Scott from Everton. Alex had previously moved to Goodison from Rangers and had considerable experience in top-flight football. Alex gave our team a new dimension with his direct running and tricky wing play, and he ran the Portuguese defenders ragged for the sixty minutes he was on the park that September night. Scottie set up countless chances for us and we ended up winning 3–0. I bagged two of the goals, one a header from a Pat Quinn free-kick and the second after getting put through on goal from a defence-splitting pass by Alex Scott. It could easily have been double that score, and we were so much on top for the ninety minutes that we travelled to Portugal full of confidence for the return leg three weeks later.

However, it was a totally different Porto team we met on their home patch who were ably assisted by a 'homer' Spanish referee and they gave us the fright of our lives. I didn't help our cause any by getting sent off for an innocuous push on a Porto defender who was practising his hacking techniques on the backs of my legs. After the Portuguese scored two early goals, Joe Davis steadied our nerves by coolly slotting home a penalty which had the Porto players and fans going crazy, and their third goal came too late to cause us any further embarrassment. The experience in Portugal should have been a salutary lesson for us but things looked bleak after the first-leg tie away to Napoli in the second round. We travelled to Italy in late November following a tough league match at Aberdeen where we had lost 1–0 and I was suspended for the first-leg tie after my sending-off against Porto. This time the team went one worse than the FC Porto game, losing 4–1 to a skilful, strong, fast and physical Italian team. It was agonising watching from the stand and after the final whistle I told my dejected team-mates that Colin Stein's away goal gave us hope of overturning the deficit in the home leg in Edinburgh. Sometimes managers and coaches say these things to try and get a positive reaction from their players. In this instance, I totally believed the Italians had weaknesses that we could exploit at Easter Road.

The one person that did not apply to was their young goal-keeper Dino Zoff. Six months after we faced him Dino would make his Italian international debut in the quarter-final of the European Nations Cup and go on to pick up a winners' medal in that tournament. Zoff became a fixture between the posts for the Italian national team winning one hundred and twelve international caps over the next fifteen years and he ended his career captaining Italy to World Cup glory in Spain in 1982. But on 29 November 1967 Dino Zoff couldn't stop Hibs over-turning the 4–1 first-leg deficit in another glorious European night at Easter Road. Don't just take my word for it, one Scottish national newspaper the following day boldly declared; 'This was Hibs' night for miracles', with the report of the game beginning:

> Salute this glorious Hibs team . . . and change that famous saying about Naples to 'See Edinburgh and die'. For last night Hibs wrote the greatest chapter into their long and glorious history.

If I'm not mistaken I think the actual saying is 'See Capri and die' but let's not quibble about a little journalistic licence. Tom Nicholson's article neatly summed up the feelings of the Hibs supporters who witnessed one of the greatest ever comebacks in Fairs Cup history. For Hibs fans this was up there with the Barcelona and Real Madrid results and one of the best nights of my entire football career.

From the first minute we tore into the Italians with a hunger and desire that they clearly were not expecting and ironically, whilst we had the same Spanish referee that sent me off against Porto, this time he was not as sympathetic to the home team as he had been in Portugal. But neither Dino Zoff nor the referee, Señor Rigo, could stop us that evening and, to be honest, I don't think there was a team anywhere in Europe that could have withstood the onslaught we unleashed. The first mistake the Italians made was choosing to kick downhill in the first half after winning the toss. That meant for the second forty-five minutes we would be shooting into our favourite end with The Cowshed packed to the rafters with screaming Hibs fans.

Our goal rout started after only five minutes from the last player anyone in the stadium, never mind the Napoli team, expected would score. Bobby Duncan had established himself as our regular right back a few seasons earlier but the one thing Bobby was not renowned for was scoring goals. In fact, I don't think Bobby had managed to score in any of his previous first team appearances but he more than made up for that against Napoli. The Italians had done their homework before the game and when Bobby picked up a loose ball just inside our half they were quite happy to let him amble forward unchallenged. Twenty-five yards from goal Bobby let fly and the ball rocketed into the top right-hand corner of Zoff's net. It was one of those goals that if you happen to score it in training you curse, wishing you had saved it for a game. But Bobby didn't even score goals like that in training. In fact, the players used to joke that he wouldn't score in the local brothel with a ten bob note on the end of his knob. Still, Bobby's rocket that night against Naples had Easter Road jumping and the Italian players quaking in their boots.

A few minutes later I was hauled down in the box and the referee awarded an indirect free-kick – Hibs fans hurled a stream of abuse at Señor Rigo for this blatant injustice but it only increased the players resolve to beat both the Italians and the dodgy continental ref. Despite battering the Italian defence for the rest of the first half it looked like we were only going to have one goal to show for all our efforts. Then right on half-time Colin Stein made a forceful run to the bye line and when Zoff fumbled his low cross-cum-shot Pat Quinn was on hand to fire the loose ball into the Italian net. The Hibs fans erupted, sensing the impossible comeback was now on. Two–nil up with forty-five minutes to come shooting down the hill – we came out for the second half needing one goal and banged in three just to make sure. From the whistle to start the second half the Italians didn't know what hit them and the three goals were no more than our build-up play deserved. In fact, it could have been a lot more. I scored the all-important third goal when I outjumped the Italian defence from an Alex Scott corner kick and headed the ball past the soon-to-be Italian international goal-keeper. Two minutes later Pat Stanton headed in our fourth goal and the Hibs fans went crazy, singing, 'Easy, easy' – and they were right, it was. Colin Stein completed the rout ten minutes from time after he picked up a loose clearance and slipped the ball past a totally dejected Zoff.

The headline accompanying Tom Nicholson's match report said it all: 'Impossible five-goal fight back shatters Italians' and we marched proudly on to the next round of the Fairs Cup to face Don Revie's Leeds United. After our heroics against Napoli, we feared no one and everyone at Easter Road relished the chance to add Leeds' scalp to that of FC Porto and Napoli.

The first leg of the Fairs Cup tie against Leeds at Elland Road was only five days before Christmas. The Leeds team was full of British internationalists and included three Scotsmen: Billy Bremner, Eddie Gray and my ex-Scotland Amateur team-mate Peter Lorimer. As is the norm with these England versus Scotland club encounters, the media on both sides of the border billed the match as a 'Battle of Britain'. It was the first time I experienced playing against a top English league team in a competitive match and I was determined to rise to the occasion.

Nowadays players from both sides shake hands when they line up before a game but the first contact I had with a Leeds player was when Norman Hunter put me up in the air with one of his infamous 'Bites Yer Legs' tackles. It wasn't the last time Norman and I would tangle that evening and we would go on to see a lot more of each other in years to come.

And I wasn't the only Hibs player singled out for special attention by the uncompromising Elland Road side either, and Colin Stein was carried off on a stretcher before half-time after two ground-shaking tackles by Billy Bremner. Despite losing a goal in the first five minutes we were holding our own, with Leeds getting more desperate as the minutes ticked away, realising that after our previous exploits 1–0 was not a convincing lead to take to Scotland. They threw everything at us in the last ten minutes and just before the final whistle our keeper, Willie Wilson, made a miraculous point-blank save from the Leeds centre forward Mick Jones. At the end of the ninety minutes the Hibs players were the happier team trooping off the Elland Road pitch, and despite losing to Eddie Gray's scrambled goal we strongly fancied our chances in the return match at Easter Road which was held on the second Wednesday in January.

I was particularly happy the day after the first-leg match after reading the post-match quotes. The Leeds manager Don Revie made no secret that he would have preferred a bigger winning margin. 'I would have liked two goals of a lead but Hibs put up a splendid display,' he said. The press report also included a comment by the Coventry City manager, Noel Cantwell. 'I thought this was a tremendous performance all-round by Hibs and for me Cormack was supreme. That boy would be a terrific asset to any English club.' I was flattered by the praise but determined to keep my feet on the ground for the return match at Easter Road on 10 January 1968. The Saturday prior to the return leg we beat Dundee United 3–0 at Easter Road and the team's confidence was sky high for taking on the Mighty Leeds.

Colin Stein had recovered from his injury in the first leg and shot us into an early lead to level the tie on aggregate. This really lifted the 40,000 Hibs fans who crammed into Easter Road and we battered Leeds for the rest of the first half. However, poor finishing, desperate defending and bad luck kept the tie delicately balanced as the game entered the last fifteen minutes. On more than one occasion my Hibs team-mates and I had reason to question the impartiality of Welsh referee Clive Thomas. He was on first-name terms with all the Leeds players, which wasn't surprising given that he made his living from English football, but in our view he allowed them to get away with several crude tackles that disrupted our rhythm.

The 1967/68 season had seen the introduction of a four-step rule for goalkeepers and after collecting a cross, Willie Wilson was penalised by Mr Thomas for taking more than four steps. All the Hibs players surrounded the referee, arguing that the rule had not been breached but the referee was adamant and awarded Leeds an indirect free-kick near the penalty spot. We lined ourselves up, expecting Billy Bremner to touch it to Peter Lorimer for one of his rockets, but Billy fooled us by chipping the ball onto big Jack Charlton's head at the back post for him to equalise.

Leeds held out to win the tie on aggregate and we were distraught in the dressing room after the match, none more so than Willie Wilson. It was Willie who had kept the score at 1–0 in the first leg with his fantastic late save and it was an injustice that he was penalised for the foul that led to the Leeds equaliser. It was another example of the highs and lows of life as a professional footballer, even more so on the unpredictable European stage.

The Leeds result also had a damaging effect on the rest of that season. Up until getting knocked out of the Fairs Cup we were battling with Celtic and Rangers at the top of the league. Four weeks after our European exit we went out of the Scottish Cup at Airdrie and subsequently lost against both Celtic and Rangers at Easter Road in the league. Still, our forty-five point third-place finish ensured that we would be back in the following season's Fairs Cup, and after our exploits in 1967/68 all the players were looking forward to another crack at Europe.

Following the indiscipline problems of Cagliari and their ex-pat fans, a proposed summer tour of America fell through and at the last minute the club arranged a pre-season trip to Africa. The tour could not have been more different from the trips to North America, and whilst Nigeria and Ghana didn't offer the glam and razzamatazz of Canada and the United States, it was nevertheless a once in a lifetime experience. Whereas everything in North America was in plentiful supply, with us receiving every luxury imaginable, our summer trip to Nigeria and Ghana really opened my eyes to genuine hardship and poverty. It was a humbling experience for everyone at Hibs and whilst we were well looked after by our hosts, it was the spirit and friendliness of the local people that I most remember from that African trip.

What really struck me was despite the basic living conditions the people were happy and cheerful – always smiling, happy with their lot. In Lagos there was one young Nigerian boy who followed us wherever we went. He introduced himself to a group of players at the hotel and asked if he could get a job helping us. He was a lovely lad and some of us would give him our complimentary Coca-Cola, biscuits and sweets that had been given to us by our hosts. On the day we left Lagos to travel to Ghana for the next leg of the trip, I handed him some of my training gear and his eyes swelled up with tears. It truly was a humbling experience and let me see how lucky I had been in the upbringing I had with my mum and dad in Leith.

In fairness to the African teams we came up against, their level of football skill was a lot higher than the local teams we played on the first North American tour in 1965. The conditions also suited the African players, particularly the first match where we played against a Nigerian Olympic IX with the temperature over 100 degrees Fahrenheit. All the Hibs players struggled in the heat and humidity and several team-mates suffered from heat exhaustion after the match. We managed to secure a 1–1 draw and I scored our goal with a header. After that first match we played Northern Lions in Kaduna three days later, winning 1–0 courtesy of another 'trademark' Cormack header. We played one more match in Nigeria against Western Rovers and secured another 1–0 win thanks to a goal from Colin Stein.

The first of our two Ghanaian matches was against a Ghana Select side that ran out 1–0 winners. Bob Shankly ingratiated himself with the local organisers, players and fans with his fulsome praise of the Ghana team's performance, and this ensured that we received royal treatment for the remainder of the trip. Though we had a hairy bus journey to the stadium for our final match in Kumasi against North Ghana XI. A tropical storm hit the area as we headed for the ground and the roads quickly resembled fast-flowing muddy rivers. When we eventually reached the stadium the pitch was flooded but dozens of fans cleared the water, so keen were they to see the 'whities' from Scotland. The muddy conditions were much more akin to what we were accustomed to and we ran out comfortable 2–0 winners.

Of all the trips I went on as a footballer, the 1968 Hibs summer tour to Africa was the most memorable because it felt like we were missionaries spreading the football gospel to people whose one pleasure in life was playing and watching the beautiful game.

The first-round draw of the 1968/69 Fairs Cup paired Hibs with Olympia Ljubljana from Yugoslavia. The first leg of the tie was in Yugoslavia and, like our final African tour match, the conditions were much to our liking with rain lashing down for the ninety minutes. We ran out comfortable 3–0 winners and a 2–1 victory in the second leg at Easter Road saw us comfortably through to the second round where we were drawn against East German side Lokomotiv Leipzig. This time the first leg was at home where Hibs paraded a new centre forward who was making his home debut. A couple of weeks beforehand Colin Stein was transferred to Rangers for £100,000, at the time a record fee between two Scottish clubs. Colin proceeded to score three hat-tricks in his first three Rangers matches, including one against us in a 6–1 doing at Ibrox. The Hibs fans were unhappy with the board of directors at Colin's transfer to one of our rivals, and in an effort to placate them Joe McBride was signed from Celtic. Colin's departure was quickly forgotten when Joe scored a hat-trick in our 3–1 defeat of the East Germans. The following Saturday he went one better, banging in four goals in a 5–0 hammering of Morton. The return leg with Leipzig would be a test of our travelling stamina as well as our football strength.

Because Leipzig was behind the Iron Curtain, there were no direct flights from Scotland, so we he had to fly to Amsterdam and then endure a five-hour bus journey into East Germany. The arduous travel arrangements didn't stop us winning the away leg 1–0 with a Colin Grant goal that gave us a comfortable 4–1 aggregate victory.

The only memory I have of my first trip behind the Iron Curtain was of the spartan furnishings and lack of heating in our East German hotel. No wonder all the locals seemed miserable and their mood was in total contrast to the smiling Africans we had met a few months earlier.

The Fairs Cup quarter-final draw paired us with a West German side this time. The famous Hamburg FC who boasted the West German centre forward Uwe Seeler, who had played against England at Wembley in the 1966 World Cup Final. The first-leg tie was played in freezing German fog the week prior to Christmas and like our first-leg tie the previous year in Leeds, we lost 1–0 to an early goal but we were confident that we could overcome the Germans back at Easter Road.

The Hibs fans again turned out in their droves, eagerly anticipating us putting Hamburg to the sword. There was controversy before the kick-off when the Hamburg goalkeeper appeared in a green top but the Swedish referee turned away our protest for him to change. This only increased our resolve and we tore into Hamburg in the same fashion that we had set about Napoli the previous season. Joe McBride scored two goals and we had a further three disallowed. Two were given as offside – one when the linesman mistook the Hamburg goalie for a Hibs forward and the other when Joe smashed in a shot which came back out after hitting the stanchion holding up the nets. Then Hamburg stole a goal when Seeler slipped his marker and the away goal took the West Germans into the semi-final. At the end of the game all the Hibs players were devastated that for the second year in succession we had been robbed of progressing in Europe through no fault of our own.

It was another bitter pill to swallow and our poor league form resulted in us finishing twelfth in the league and well out of places for the following season's Fairs Cup. The Hamburg game was the last European match I would play for Hibs, but the glorious European nights I enjoyed at Easter Road were going to stand me in good stead in the future where I would more than make up for the disappointments and injustices I had endured.

6

THE LONG FAREWELL

Football has seen many changes from when I played in the 1960s and 70s and without doubt the biggest change for players has been the Bosman ruling governing contracts and transfers. I have no doubt that if Bosman had been in existence when I started my playing career at Hibs I would not have ended up spending almost eight years at Easter Road first time around. I am 100 per cent certain that if football agents had existed in my playing days then I would have been auctioned off a lot earlier in my career.

After I established myself in the first team under Big Jock every now and again an article would appear in the newspapers linking me to one club or another. Initially such speculation was extremely flattering and boosted my confidence on the park and my self-esteem off it. But as time wore on it became a distraction and started to have a negative effect on my performances on the football pitch.

In the 1950s, 60s and 70s, Scottish football was a regular conveyor belt of good quality players for the richer English teams. Nearly every top English side had two or three Scots in their best eleven, with some Scots regarded as the most talented and skilful players in the English league. In fact, Anglo-Scots could have easily made up an English select side, and any world XI in the 1960s would have been delighted to include Denis Law and Pat Crerand from Manchester United, Ian St John and Ron Yeats from Liverpool,

Dave Mackay, John White and Alan Gilzean from Spurs and Billy Bremner and Eddie Gray from Leeds United. For ambitious Scottish league players outwith the Old Firm of Celtic and Rangers, a transfer to the English First Division was regarded as natural progression once you had served your apprenticeship with the Scottish club and I wasn't any different in that respect from any other player. So when talk of transfer interest first appeared in the press in December 1964 linking me to a move down south I was very flattered, but at eighteen I knew I still had a lot to learn. The Arsenal manager Bertie Mee probably thought that as well and nothing came of the initial speculation. Two years later, after my Scotland debut against Brazil, I was linked to a move to Blackpool who had just sold Alan Ball to Everton for £110,000. The Blackpool manager, Ron Suart, was quoted in the Scottish press as regarding me as an ideal replacement for the little England World Cup-winner but that remained as idle tittle-tattle and to my knowledge no approaches to Hibs were ever made by Blackpool.

In the second half of the previous season I started to get some stick from a section of Hibs fans. I knew I hadn't been playing up to my own high standards, but I thought the criticisms from my own supporters were unjustified. It reached the stage that the *Evening News* ran a story telling the Hibs fans to get off my back. Initially I didn't want to dignify the critics in the press, but when the paper said they were running the story I told the reporter, 'I'm used to it now and it doesn't bother me.'

Manager Bob Shankly was more direct and he told the journalist, 'I just don't understand this anti-Cormack feeling. Some of the crowd even start hounding him before the kick-off.' The article ended with the reporter stating that 'we should warn Hibs supporters that such treatment has caused other good players to ask for transfers – and get them'.

In some ways I think drawing attention to the issue actually helped improve the situation. By bringing the criticism out into the open it confronted the critics head on and the reporter's comment about it possibly chasing me away from Easter Road was a wakeup call for the boo-boys. When the Blackpool interest appeared shortly thereafter, my view about a move away from Easter Road had changed from two years earlier and I was interested in the speculation but nothing came of it. I suppose that's where an agent, acting as a go-between for clubs and players, can be advantageous.

On top of the press transfer speculation, I was upset with having to play centre forward at the start of the 1966/67 season and was constantly in the manager's office at this time pleading my case. I had a good relationship with Bob Shankly who I both liked and respected. To be fair to him, his hands were continually tied at Easter Road. For example, when Neil Martin was sold to Sunderland in 1965 for £50,000 the manager was not given any transfer money to buy a replacement.

Bob accepted that he didn't see me as a long-term replacement for Neil at centre forward, but because it was in my nature to give 100 per cent wherever I played the team won seven out of ten games with me leading the line and I bagged five goals. The manager and I would agree every time we discussed it that inside forward was my best position but he kept reminding me that he had to try and make the best hand with the cards that he had been dealt by the Hibs board. I was getting totally frustrated at the punishment that was being dealt out to me week-in and week-out by big, hard centre-halves who loved nothing better than clobbering centre forwards from behind when the ball arrived at their feet with their backs to goal. Unfortunately, the tackle from behind was still an integral part of the Scottish game with waist-high tackles the norm. I knew I faced serious injury if I continued playing

centre forward and thankfully big, bustling Colin Stein's trans-
formation in the Hibs reserves from a defender to a rampaging
goalscoring centre forward meant that I could revert to my
midfield berth, and I thrived in that role, creating chances for
the forwards and getting on the end of crosses with late runs
into the penalty box.

The next press speculation about a big money move down south
appeared in the *Daily Express* in October 1967. '£100,000 bid for
Cormack' was the paper's back-page headline, but to say it was
strange is an understatement. The article stated that just before
he resigned as Chelsea manager Tommy Docherty made an offer
to buy me for £100,000 but Bob Shankly had given him short
shrift and stated, 'Cormack is not for sale under any circumstances no matter what the fee.' The Doc had transformed the
Stamford Bridge side and the previous season they lost to Spurs
in the FA Cup Final at Wembley. But Tommy was a very volatile
character and had fallen foul of the English FA who subsequently
suspended him for twenty-eight days. Whilst I was naturally
flattered that Tommy had enquired about my services I'm not
sure, looking back now, as to whether it was a genuine bid or
just another one of his media stunts to keep his name in the
papers. In any event, the Hibs manager made the club's position crystal clear in the matter of my transfer which ensured
there wasn't any other transfer speculation for the remainder of
season 1967/68.

The highlight of the 1968/69 season was getting to my first, and
as things would turn out only, major domestic Cup Final during
my time at Easter Road. After losing our opening Scottish League
Cup group match 1–0 to St Johnstone, where I was carried off
in the first half with torn ankle ligaments, the team won four of
the next five matches to qualify for a two-leg quarter-final against

East Fife which we won 6–2 on aggregate to set up a semi-final against Dundee. The semi-final was played at neutral Tynecastle, which had been the scene of our Scottish Cup semi-final defeat by Dunfermline three and a half years earlier. With the tie delicately balanced at 1–1 we went down to ten men when Allan McGraw limped off injured with fifteen minutes left. However, Allan came back on with his knee heavily bandaged but could only manage to hobble around the park scarcely even nuisance value to the Dundee defence.

We won a corner in the last minute and the ball ended up at Big Al's feet on the six-yard line, he swung his bandaged leg and the ball flew past my ex-Scotland Amateur team-mate Ally Donaldson and into the Dundee net. Our joy was unbridled and we celebrated with the fans when the final whistle went straight after Dundee kicked off to restart the match. I'm convinced Allan scored the last-minute winner to get carried off the park shoulder high by his team-mates – he certainly couldn't have walked off given the swelling on his knee and in years to come he would receive a lot of publicity about the plight of injury-ravaged ex-professional footballers as he ended up requiring the support of two crutches to get around. But Allan's last-minute goal more than made up for the Dunfermline Scottish Cup defeat and Celtic's last-minute semi-final equaliser at Ibrox in October 1965.

Celtic waited for us in the final, but the match was delayed for six months after a fire destroyed part of the stand at Hampden. That delay, probably more than anything else, scuppered our chances of winning the League Cup. Not long after our semi-final victory, Colin Stein left Easter Road for Ibrox, and whilst Joe McBride proved himself more than capable of filling Colin's boots he could not play in the final as he had previously played for Celtic in the earlier rounds of the competition.

*

I really enjoyed the build-up to the Cup Final. On the Monday prior to the game the Hibs squad headed down to North Berwick and were based at the Marine Hotel on the outskirts of the town. We enjoyed a couple rounds of golf on the North Berwick West Course and training was very relaxed throughout the week.

Sadly the preparation for the game was the highlight of our week. Unfortunately for me and my team-mates, the manager's solution to the void created by Joe being cup-tied was to play me at centre forward. Celtic's centre half and captain, Billy McNeill, must have had one of his easiest matches at Hampden as I was no match for him when crosses came my way, and there were very few occasions in the ninety minutes when the ball landed at my feet. In truth Celtic totally outclassed us that April Saturday, running out comfortable 6–2 winners. I was in my seventh year at Hibs and that Hampden hammering more than anything else convinced me that it was time for me to seek pastures new. The League Cup Final was also our last chance of gaining entry to the following season's Fairs Cup and at the end of the season we sat twelfth in the league, well out of contention for the European places.

Transfer gossip linking me to two English clubs appeared in the press shortly before the start of the 1969/70 season. Newcastle United had just won the Fairs Cup and had previously signed centre half John McNamee and Jim Scott from Hibs. Both were successful fixtures in their first team and the Newcastle manager, Joe Harvey started the speculation when he said at a press conference that he had an 'arrangement' with Hibs whereby they would contact him as soon as I became available.

At the end of the previous season I had put in a transfer request and I returned from my last 'boys' holiday to Majorca with some Hibs team-mate pals to newspaper headlines about a £100,000 transfer 'mystery'. Whilst Joe Harvey was proclaiming that 'Peter Cormack is our number one target. We are prepared to spend a six figure fee for his transfer', Hibs manager Bob Shankly was pouring cold water on the story saying, 'Newcastle United have never been in touch with me about Cormack. And in any case the position about Cormack's future is unchanged; we would not consider parting with him until we had signed a suitable replacement.' When the reporter, Alister Nicol, spoke to me about the speculation I gave him my honest opinion. 'Naturally I'd be delighted to get a move to English First Division football, but for the present my only aim is to get fully fit.' Before Joe Harvey's utterances, the Scottish press said that Leeds United were about to put in a six-figure bid to Hibs for me. Their manager, Don Revie, had apparently identified me as a transfer target after the two Fairs Cup games I played against his team, but despite the newspapers saying that Leeds were about to make a firm move for my services they ended up signing Allan 'Sniffer' Clarke from Leicester City for £165,000.

Despite my transfer request and rumours of an imminent move appearing in the press every now and again, not all the Hibs supporters gave me a hard time. The vast majority of the fans were very friendly and supportive when I met them at club functions or out and about in Edinburgh.

Around this time I also gained the distinction of being the first player in Scottish football to have his own female fan club, and when the press heard about this it naturally became public knowledge – much to the amusement of my team-mates. Out of all the newspaper headlines I made during my playing career, 'Female fans honour "Peter the Great"' is not the most memorable. But at its height the 'Peter Cormack Female Fan Club' boasted around 100 members in America, Canada, Holland and of course Scotland – well, Edinburgh at least. The club president was Mary Weston who used to regularly contact me to find out what I had been doing in order to help the monthly magazine editor Ann Ramage compile her articles. Membership fees were all of a shilling (five pence) and at Christmas my female fans presented me with a silver mug, which I am sure would have been deemed as very apt by the male boo-boys at Easter Road. The final honour was when the female fan club created a green tie, complete with my photograph on it, which they sold to raise funds for the club. If anyone is still the proud owner of a 'Peter the Great' tie I'd love to hear from them.

For some reason membership of the fan club took a nosedive when I announced my engagement to Marion, and I often wondered over the years what happened to Mary, Ann and Kathy Duncan, who was the fan club's treasurer. They certainly didn't get rich quick on the proceeds of the fan club, but I genuinely welcomed their support, particularly when some of their male Hibs supporter colleagues were not as appreciative of my 'silky skills' as the female fans.

I missed the start of what would prove to be my last season at Easter Road due to injury and in my fifth match of the season I scored both goals in a 2–0 home win against St Mirren. Sadly this was Bob Shankly's final match in charge at Hibs and he resigned following the disappointing start the team had made after missing out on qualification from the group stages of the League Cup. I was sorry to see Bob leave as he was a good manager and tactically he came into his own in European matches. He had taken his previous club Dundee to the semi-final of the European Cup and was extremely unlucky with Hibs, losing out at the quarter-final stage in successive years of the Fairs Cup. I am convinced that if we had beaten either Leeds or Hamburg we could have gone all the way in Europe, but sadly that little rub of the green deserted us on both occasions. I also think Bob had reached the end of his tether with the Hibs board and he felt that he was fighting a losing battle trying to keep his best players at the club.

I had made my position clear that I wanted away, but Bob was insisting that Hibs found a replacement before they would consider selling me. Whilst I understood his position I felt it wasn't helping my cause, but Bob assured me that I would be the next person to leave Hibs once the circumstances were right for the club. I respected Bob's straightforwardness and he always kept me informed when clubs expressed an interest in me with Hibs, but I was refusing to sign a new contract, so keen was I for a move. Post-Bosman clubs now move heaven and earth to sell a prized asset before their contract expires in order to recoup a transfer fee. Prior to that, players were still classed as belonging to a club even when they were out of contract.

Bob Shankly was replaced by Willie McFarlane, and I was the first player in the queue for a meeting with the new manager within days of him taking the hot-seat at Easter Road. Willie had played right back for the great Hibs Famous Five team and cut his managerial teeth with Stirling Albion. Despite Willie being a fellow Leither, I was intent to impress on him my desire for a move. After our first meeting in his office he re-affirmed the commitment given by his predecessor that I would be first to leave once the right offer came along. But that wasn't the case. During the festive period, Peter Marinello was transferred to Arsenal and a few weeks after Willie arrived I played for Scotland against West Germany in a World Cup qualifying tie in Hamburg. Following the match I was offered an improved one-year contract from Hibs which I was happy to sign on the condition that I could leave at the end of the season.

I did not start the New Year and the new decade well when I managed to get myself sent off in the Edinburgh Derby at a packed Easter Road. Over 36,000 fans saw me make an early exit halfway through the second half after I had a boot at Hearts left back, Peter Oliver. 'Ollie' was a very good and quick full back and had been giving me a hard time but after one hefty challenge too many I had a wild swipe at him and earned myself an early bath. To make matters worse, I gave referee Gordon a mouthful of abuse before I headed up the tunnel.

My transfer frustration and sending off against Hearts might have been the worst possible football start to the New Year, but a few weeks later Marion and I became engaged and organised a party for friends in the number five Masonic Lodge in Leith's Queen Charlotte Street. Initially Marion and I decided to limit the guest list to close friends and their partners but a flu epidemic not only laid low many of the guests, it also stopped the band we booked from making it. Marion eventually telephoned our respective parents to get them off the subs' bench and join the celebrations. The 'auld yins' certainly livened up the proceedings and made sure the party went with a swing.

Peter Marinello's transfer to Arsenal for £100,000 not only shocked the Hibs fans, there was nobody more surprised than Peter at the swiftness of his move to London. Whilst I was delighted for 'Nello', who had proved himself to be a quick and skilful right winger in the short time since he had burst into the Hibs team as a teenager, I was really angry that the Hibs manager and board had gone back on their commitment to me.

I told the press, 'I'm a bit fed up as no one stood in (Peter) Marinello's way. I'll stay until the end of the season and honour my contract but then I'm going to England if it can be arranged.'

I was not the only Hibs player unhappy at the club's decision to sell Peter Marinello over the festive period. Club captain Pat Stanton and I were taking it in turn to discuss our futures with

Chairman Bill Harrower and eventually Pat agreed new terms with Hibs a couple of months into the New Year.

The week before Marion and my engagement party, Peter made his debut for Arsenal against Manchester United at Old Trafford and scored the only goal of the game. The English media immediately christened him as the 'new George Best', but unfortunately things never worked out for Peter at Arsenal and his debut was the highlight of his career.

Whilst Nello got his dream English move I was livid with Hibs, and manager Wille McFarlane in particular, who had said that I would be the next person out of Easter Road.

My anger and frustration was only compounded when reports appeared in the Scottish press that Arsenal's biggest rivals, Spurs, were about to table a £125,000 offer to Hibs for my services. At the end of January Spurs manager Bill Nicholson watched me play for Hibs at Firhill in a 3–1 defeat and afterwards he told the *Scotsman's* John Rafferty, 'I must now assess what I have seen and give consideration to an offer, to the size of one and to the form of one.' It was clear that 'Bill Nick' had not made up his mind if he was going to make a bid to take me to Spurs and I fretted for days afterwards. In truth, I did not have a great game against Thistle and did not help the team's cause by missing a penalty kick with the score at 2–0 for Partick. If I had converted the spot-kick we may have been able to kickstart a comeback, but it was not to be.

Shortly thereafter I was given a fourteen-day suspension and seventy-five pound fine by the SFA Disciplinary Committee for my sending off on New Year's Day, which meant missing two league matches. Given I had received two previous suspensions of seven and fourteen days for cumulative bookings, the punishment for my sending-off was relatively tame. Bill Nicholson returned to watch me in my first match following the suspension against Rangers at the end of February, but again I did not do myself justice, although we battled our way to a 2–2 draw. The Spurs manager's only comment after the game was that he would be back, but unlike Arnie he never was.

Three days after the Rangers game I was sent off again, against St Mirren at Love Street, this time for having a kick at Iain Munro. Having appeared before the SFA just a few weeks earlier I knew they would not be so lenient next time around and I was at the lowest point of my career at Easter Road. I was annoyed with myself for letting my quick temper get the better of me but the upshot of my indiscipline was that I got my long sought-after transfer and Hibs received a far smaller cheque in the process.

After my second sending-off I was summoned to the manager's office expecting to receive a severe carpeting from Willie McFarlane. But all Willie said was that the chairman had decided that in view of the likely lengthy suspension I was facing the club had decided to cut their losses and would accept the first offer they received for me. They had already notified clubs in England that I was available and hoped that a bid would arrive before the English League's mid-March transfer deadline. A few weeks earlier I had spoken to Bob Shankly who was scouting for Nottingham Forest, and as soon as I got home I telephoned Bob to tell him of my conversation with Willie and he told me to leave the rest to him.

I played my final match for Hibs against St Johnstone at Easter Road on 21 March 1970 and scored in the 4–1 win. On the following Monday I met the Nottingham Forest manager, ex-pat Scot Matt Gillies, at Easter Road and the deal was done very quickly.

Forest ended up forking out £80,000 for my services and Hibs chairman Willie Harrower's churlish comments in the press left a bad taste in my mouth. 'We tried very hard to encourage Cormack to stay. It was the unanimous decision of the board to try and keep him, but the player wanted away. In view of his pending appearance before the referee committee, we felt that it was prudent to transfer him before the end of the season.'

Clearly Mr Harrower was preparing the ground for an onslaught of criticism from Hibs fans, but manager Willie McFarlane was more circumspect. He was reported as leaving Easter Road 'grim-faced' and his only comment was, 'I have nothing to say – I have had nothing to do with this. Any comment must come from the chairman. He handled this deal.' I was just delighted that after years of press speculation, and in particular the previous couple of months surrounding a possible transfer to Spurs, I had at last secured my 'dream move' to English football. As well as looking forward to the professional challenge of playing at a higher level, I was also relieved that my football future had been resolved before my wedding to Marion the following July. My mum and dad were also about to emigrate to join my sister Stella in Australia and they were relieved that my transfer had gone through. After my sending-off against St Mirren, my mum had told the press that she wanted me to give up football but I quickly disabused her of that idea.

I had no regrets about leaving Hibs as I had given eight good years to the club. There were far more highs than lows. I had played in two hundred and fifty-five competitive games, scoring ninety-nine goals. My goalscoring record was even better in tour matches and friendlies, notching twenty-one goals in twenty-seven matches. Without doubt the highlight for me was playing in the 2–0 friendly against Real Madrid when I was only eighteen and scoring the first goal in that match. But I had also enjoyed many memorable Fairs Cup encounters at Easter Road, none more so than the 5–0 demolition of Napoli at the end of November in 1967.

My biggest disappointment in a Hibs jersey was the Scottish League Cup Final at Hampden in April 1969, both for the result and the fact that I didn't get the opportunity to play in my best position that day. During my time at Easter Road I played in every forward position, both right and left half, and even had a 100 per cent success rate the two occasions I deputised in goal.

Despite the occasional love/hate relationship I had with some Hibs fans, I know that the vast majority recognised the contribution I made to the club in the time I was there and no one could dispute that I always gave my all when wearing the green and white. It was unfortunate my departure came about in the way that it did, but Hibs decided to cut their losses before I faced the beaks at the SFA. When my second ordering-off offence was considered by the SFA's Disciplinary Committee they imposed a twelve-week ban. At the end of season 1969/70 my wish had been granted and the following season I would be earning my crust in the English First Division. But first things first – I had a wedding date in July with Miss Marion Robertson and before then we would have to go house-hunting in Nottingham. My life was to change in more ways than one.

7

FIGHTING FOR SURVIVAL AT FOREST

Over the years many football fans have asked me if I thought I made a mistake moving to Nottingham Forest in 1970. My answer has always been the same – no. I never hesitated in signing for Forest after I sat down with the manager Mattie Gillies and my old mentor at Hibs, Bob Shankly, and I have never regretted moving to the City Ground in March 1970 – and given the way my playing career panned out thereafter, how could I? Football supporters always love to speculate on everything and anything to do with the beautiful game, and players are no different. I'd be lying if I said I'd never wondered if my playing and managerial career might have worked out differently. I've probably thought about countless possible scenarios millions of times over the years but I have always come to the same conclusion regarding my playing days – I couldn't have wished for a better career after I joined the Hibs groundstaff in 1962.

As I said before, up until the Bosman ruling, football clubs had total control over players until clubs agreed a transfer fee. The facts in my case were that, despite much media speculation and enquiries by some big English clubs, Hibs had shown no desire to sell me on. In fact, both managers, Bob Shankly and Willie McFarlane, were on record that I was going nowhere until the club signed a replacement for me. That just doesn't happen since Bosman, as players become free agents at the end of their contract and can sign for whoever they choose but then the club doesn't receive a penny in transfer fee. My only regret is that I took my frustrations onto the pitch, which resulted in two sendings-off in quick succession. It is easy, all those years later, in a period of calm reflection for me, to feel embarrassed and apologise for that happening, but in truth the intransigence of the Hibs board had pushed me to the limit.

After I moved down south I enjoyed an unblemished disciplinary record, well, almost, but for one exception at Liverpool and an aberration, ironically, when playing for Bristol City against Hibs in the Anglo-Scottish Cup – which I'll get to later.

Nottingham Forest had not been strangers to me whilst I was at Hibs. My first encounter with Forest came in the opening game Hibs played in their North American tour in 1965, which Hibs won 2–1. Forest visited Easter Road for a pre-season friendly in August the following year, with Hibs again coming out on top, winning that encounter 3–2. For one of the oldest clubs in the world, Nottingham Forest did not have a great record of winning trophies. Despite being formed in 1865, Forest have only won the FA Cup twice, in 1898 and 1959, and up until they won promotion to Division 1 in 1957 they had spent all of the twentieth century in England's lower leagues. Forest held their own in the First Division during the 1960s and the nearest they came to success was when they got to the semi-final of the FA Cup in 1967 losing 2–1 at Hillsborough to eventual winners Spurs.

Matt Gillies became manager in 1969 after ten years in charge at Leicester City. Although I had never met Mattie before, I knew of him as he had transformed Leicester's fortunes and went on to win the League Cup in 1965. He was regarded as a shrewd judge of football talent and had a very successful record of wheeling and dealing in the transfer market when he was at Filbert Street.

It helped me that although Matt had spent most of his football career in England he hailed from West Calder, fifteen miles from Edinburgh, and I immediately took to him when we first met with Bob Shankly.

Bob also sang Mattie's praises and said to me that he regarded him as good a manager as his brother Bill and Matt Busby at Manchester United. It was high praise indeed, but unlike Shanks and Jock Stein, Mattie was not one for donning a tracksuit and mucking in at training. No, he left that to the Forest coach Bob McKinlay. Bob was an Anglo-Scot who had previously played centre half for Forest and, as I was to discover, was a bit of a sergeant-major on the training ground.

The first thing Mattie said to me on my first day at Forest was that he wanted me to play as an attacking inside forward, and that was music to my ears. I dare say, Bob Shankly probably marked his card about the number of times I had 'nipped his heid' about being played out of position at Hibs. Mattie was a good salesman and spoke highly of the 'excellent squad of professionals he had gathered at Forest, none better than Ian Storey-Moore'. I knew some of the players and Storey-Moore was often bracketed alongside Georgie Best in the football talent stakes.

Within a couple of hours Matt had me convinced that Forest were on the verge of winning the First Division Championship and competing with the big guns in Europe. Unfortunately he couldn't have been further from the truth, but his prophecy was to prove right within a decade, although only after Brian Clough and Peter Taylor took the helm at the City Ground.

Once I signed on the dotted line, Matt and Bob whisked Marion and me off to Nottingham and after a guided tour of the stadium we spent the night at a city centre hotel. Our next mission was to find ourselves a house before our forthcoming wedding in July. The club were very helpful in our house-hunting adventure. At the time most of the Forest players lived in the Ruddington area of Nottingham, but when Marion and I set out looking there weren't any properties in that neck of the woods that caught our eye. We eventually found a really nice house in Padleigh's Lane on the other side of the River Trent. The property was only a few of years old and the couple selling were already considering an offer of £6,200. We managed to gazump the other bidders by £100 by getting the sellers to leave all the light fittings. As things would turn out, the area would have a few more Scottish residents in the not-too-distant-future.

Things were indeed moving apace. In a matter of weeks I had a new club, my first house and on 4 July 1970, Marion and I were married at St Bernard's Church in Edinburgh. We had a great wedding reception at The Ravelston Dykes Hotel with our families and all our friends and then we enjoyed a short honeymoon in Cala Rajada.

Once the wedding nuptials had been taken care of it was back to Nottingham for pre-season training in preparation for my first full season in the 'toughest league in the world'. Nowadays, the English media and Sky TV hype the English Premiership as the best football league in the world. I don't want to get into a debate about the merits of that viewpoint, but there is no doubt in my mind that during my lifetime the top division in England has always been the most competitive league in the world and I'm not just talking about some of the uncompromising defenders it has spawned.

Although I had been given a twelve-week suspension by the SFA, it didn't apply to leagues outside Scotland, and I was looking forward to making my debut at the City Ground against Newcastle on 28 March. Unfortunately Newcastle's manager Joe Harvey had other ideas.

Joe was maybe still upset that he had not signed me from Hibs at the start of that season, and because I signed for Nottingham Forest two weeks after the English League's transfer deadline, teams could object to the opposition fielding a new signing in vital league games. Newcastle were challenging for a top six place which would have got them into the Fairs Cup and they black-balled my home debut for Forest. Marion and I watched the game from the centre stand where Forest battled their way to a 2–2 draw.

With a week's training under my belt, I made my debut for Forest at West Brom on Saturday 4 April 1970, but it was a debut to forget as we were on the end of a 4–0 drubbing. I didn't cover myself in glory, and in truth my lack of match fitness showed. As a consequence, Mattie Gillies decided to rest me for Forest's final league match against Coventry City three days later at the City Ground. Watching the 4–1 home defeat from the centre stand made me realise that I was in for a challenge when the new season got under way in August. Fortunately the team had finished in fifteenth place, well clear of the dreaded relegation zone.

Whilst I took time to settle to the pace of the English First Division in that first match, I was pleased to have got the game under my belt before my first pre-season training, especially as it came immediately following our wedding. Whilst the first pre-season at Forest was no tougher physically than what I had experienced at Hibs, the difference was that most days we had to report back to the training ground in the afternoons where we would do ball work and practice set pieces. At first I found this routine quite tiring – either that or I was still getting accustomed to the rigours of married life! It was this focus on fitness, skill and the work with individual players on their role in the football team that for me made the difference between Scottish and English teams.

In that first full season's summer training at Forest Matt Gillies was working with us on a four-three-three system. The good thing for me was that I was given an attacking inside left role and my job was to principally support our two front men, fellow Scotsman Alex Ingram and Ian Storey-Moore.

I had played against Alex when he was with Ayr United and knew him to be a tough, uncompromising centre forward in the Mick Jones, Jeff Astle and Joe Royle mould. My main job was to feed off all the scraps that Alex could throw my way and get on the end of the regular supply of crosses that Ian Storey-Moore fired into the penalty box. Ian was a couple of years older than me and had been a regular in the Forest team since 1962. There was no question he was the star man of the side and I was certain playing alongside him wouldn't do my own game any harm. Ian's England international career was hampered because he wasn't in one of the more glamorous sides, and I am certain he would have enjoyed more than the one measly cap if he had played for one of England's big teams. The other stalwarts in the Forest team at this time were the captain and right back Peter Hindley, goal-keeper Jim Barron, centre half Liam O'Kane and tough-tackling midfielder Bob Chapman. Other players on the fringes of the first team included centre forward Duncan McKenzie and fellow Scotsman John Robertson. Off the park Robbo looked nothing like an athlete, never mind a professional footballer, but at training he could make the ball talk with his left peg. However, it would take several years and the arrival of Brian Clough for Robbo to blossom in the first team.

I saw firsthand at training that Duncan McKenzie was a class act and he was not short of confidence in his footballing abilities or in the talking stakes. He was constantly telling anyone who was prepared to listen how good a player he was but despite having been at Forest for several seasons he had failed to hold down a regular place in the first team and the season before I arrived was sent on loan to Mansfield Town.

Duncan would eventually move to Leeds United in 1974 joining up with Brian Clough during his brief forty-four days in charge at Elland Road. Despite the big price tag on his head and considerable animosity from many players and fans at Elland Road, he managed to score twenty-seven goals in his sixty-six appearances and received a European Cup runners-up medal after Leeds lost to Bayern Munich in 1975. Duncan even managed legendary status at Everton despite only being there for two years, helped considerably by a Man of the Match performance against Liverpool in the 1977 FA Cup semi-final. But Duncan's biggest claim to fame at Forest was that he could jump over a Mini and throw a golf ball from one end of the pitch to the other. Unfortunately I never saw him perform these unusual feats so I had to take his word for it.

After several weeks of twice-a-day training I was raring to go in the pre-season trip to Sweden which gave all the team the chance to get match fit and put our set-piece drills into practice. I also realised it was an opportunity for me to prove to my team-mates what I could bring to the table and it let me see what they had to offer. I think it is fair to say a mutual respect and understanding developed very quickly in the couple of weeks we were away. I was immediately struck at the power and pace of the Forest outfield players and how relatively comfortable they all were on the ball. This was not always the case at Hibs but where players in Scotland had a weakness in one or more department of their game they more than made up for it by concentrating on playing to their strengths. Fortunately I was able to make a good impression on the tour for the manager and my new team-mates by bagging three goals.

I have no doubt that the enforced lay-off following my transfer the previous March not only helped ensure that I was fully rested before the start of my first season in English football, it also gave me a fresh hunger and desire to succeed at my new club.

We had one more friendly match to play after the Swedish tour and my home debut at the City Ground was against a team I had a score to settle with – the German club side Hamburg. I still nursed a grievance at the manner that they knocked Hibs out of the Fairs Cup the previous year and I managed to grab the only goal of the game with a header, which gave me a lot of satisfaction. Unfortunately my dream home debut was spoiled when I missed a penalty, following which I vowed never to volunteer for any future spot-kicks. It was a promise I was destined not to keep. The headed goal against Hamburg was my fourth header of the pre-season, and this run continued in Forest's second league game at home to West Brom when I nodded us 3–1 ahead with less than ten minutes to go. It seemed we were heading for our second league win after opening the season with a comfortable 2–0 victory at home to Coventry. But after Bob Chapman went off injured we lost our way and the Baggies scored two late goals to scrape a 3–3 draw. Still it was a damn sight better than the 4–1 drubbing I experienced a couple of months earlier on my Forest debut.

West Brom's late comeback let me see how hard teams in England battled for the full ninety minutes. The saying 'every point is a prisoner' definitely applied in England's top flight. Despite dropping a point, Forest's fans seemed to be happy with their new Scottish signing and after suffering for a brief spell from the boo boys at Hibs I was determined to keep the Nottingham Forest supporters on my side.

The rest of the league campaign was almost a mirror reflection of the match against West Brom where good performances were interspersed with some bad luck and disappointing results. Our league highs included a 4–1 home defeat of Wolves at the end of August and an early season 3–1 over Blackpool at the City Ground where I managed to score the third goal. I also enjoyed scoring at home when we entertained Manchester United, but unfortunately my goal was scant consolation in a 2–1 defeat.

My best league performance of the season came in March when we beat Everton 3–2 at the City Ground. Commenting on my scoring two of our goals a local press report the following day stated:

> Peter Cormack, slim-line package of pure soccer skill, three times lifted himself above the skulduggery going on around him to win a game Everton won't be sorry to lose . . . It was Cormack's head which directed a precision centre from Lyons past Everton's teenage keeper Dai Davies. It was Cormack who rapped in the shot that Davies could only parry to Moore. And it was Cormack who went into a near-post gap that Davies, Wright and Labone must swear that wasn't there, to snatch the third with an eye-of-the-needle header.

In my first season at Forest our fans had the satisfaction of seeing our best form at the City Ground as we only managed five wins from the twenty-one away league matches. We made up for our earlier season draw when we beat West Brom 1–0 at the Hawthorns.

That victory on 9 January was our first away win of the season but we had to wait another two months for our next victory on the road. That came against Tottenham and it gave me added satisfaction to score the only goal of the game in front of the White Hart Lane faithful. My goal in the 1–0 win let Bill Nicholson and the Spurs fans see what they were missing in not signing me from Hibs when they had the chance. We then won three of our last five away games, the first when Forest beat our local rival Derby County 2–1 at the end of March. We had Ian Storey-Moore to thank for a superb display that culminated in him scoring the winning goal.

Our two final away wins both came in April. First of all we beat Manchester City 3–1 at Maine Road and then I grabbed our first goal in a 3–1 defeat of Blackpool.

Arsenal finished the season as League Champions, one point ahead of Leeds, and became only the second team in English football history to win the coveted double after they beat Liverpool 2–1 in the FA Cup Final after extra-time at Wembley. Nottingham Forest secured thirty-six points and ended well clear of the two relegated teams, Burnley on twenty-seven points and Blackpool, who finished bottom on twenty-three points. Blackpool was the only team we managed to do the double over in the league and at the end of my first season in the English First Division Nottingham Forest ended up in sixteenth place; a respectable enough position but not one that the manager, players or fans were happy with.

Unfortunately our Cup form mirrored that of our league performances. In the second round of the League Cup we managed to overcome Huddersfield Town 2–0 in a replay at the City Ground after drawing 0–0 on their patch. I endeared myself to the Forest faithful when I grabbed the second and decisive goal in the Cup tie with another trademark Cormack header after I got on the end of a great Ian Storey-Moore cross. That second round win set us up for a third round tie away to Second Division Birmingham but they deservedly beat us 2–1. Forest enjoyed a better run in the FA Cup that season, finally falling to Spurs in the fifth round at White Hart Lane and ironically the 2–1 scoreline was a repeat of the semi-final result from four years earlier. Before then Forest endured an epic third round struggle against Luton Town. We drew the first match at the City Ground 1–1 but the replay turned out to be one of the most exciting games I was involved in during my eighteen-year playing career. In the first half I opened the scoring but Malcolm MacDonald, later of 'SuperMac' fame, equalised a couple of minutes later. The score stayed at 1–1 until the seventy-fifth minute when I crossed for our substitute Graham Collier to put us ahead. A minute later we went 3–1 up when I laid on an opening for Barry Lyons to score. But in a matter of moments Luton levelled the tie with a penalty kick and a goalmouth scramble equaliser, both scored by that man MacDonald. With the game heading for extra-time our left winger for the night, Ronnie Rees, struck a dramatic winner when he chipped their goalkeeper.

It was indeed a memorable Cup tie and I have to admit to feeling a wee bit sorry for Malcolm MacDonald after he ended on the losing side despite scoring a hat-trick. Our subsequent two FA Cup ties that season were dull by comparison. In the fourth round we scrapped a 1–0 win against Leyton Orient before finally losing out to Spurs.

My first season at Forest coincided with the introduction of the Anglo-Scottish Cup, which would subsequently run for ten seasons. The trophy was played for by English and Scottish clubs which failed to qualify for any of the three European competitions. Known for the first couple of years as the Texaco Cup, Forest were drawn against Airdrie in the first round in the inaugural year of the competition. The first leg at the City Ground ended 2–2 and that scoreline was repeated after extra-time in the second leg at Broomfield at the end of September.

I think it is fair to say that Scottish teams and their supporters were more up for this Scotland versus England club competition than English clubs and their fans. More than 13,000 noisy and excitable Airdrie fans were out in force for the second-leg match and they reserved most of their abuse for the Scottish players in the Forest side.

This put the Forest Anglo-Scots, Alex Ingram, Dave Hilley and me, in the firing line but Dave's and my response to the stick was to score a goal apiece. Unfortunately Alex's response was to miss an open goal from a few yards out 'to continue his goalless night-mare' as the *Nottingham Post* reporter put it in the following day's match report.

The local Airdrie hero was their bustling centre forward Drew Busby, who scored the Lanarkshire side's four goals over the two legs. Drew would go on to carve out a successful career for himself as a rumbustous centre forward with Hearts.

Early in the first half I scored with a header but Busby took the game to a penalty shoot-out, and we made a little bit of history as the first football match in Scotland to be decided by penalty kicks. As the *Nottingham Post* reported, 'Airdrie won the penalties 5–2 in the super-charged atmosphere of Broomfield Park'. Only left back John Winfield and I managed to convert our spot-kicks, whereas Airdrie scored all five of theirs, and needless to say the local fans were ecstatic at their team taking the scalp of an English First Division side. After winning the penalty shoot-out the little Broomfield stand at the corner of the ground, where the dressing rooms were located, was shaking late into the night and my English team-mates were just grateful to get back on the team coach and on the road to Nottingham safe and sound after the nerve-wracking experience.

When I reflected on my first season at Nottingham Forest after our final league match away at Leeds on 1 May, I was relatively satisfied. I knew that I had performed consistently after quickly establishing myself in the Forest first team and I had struck up a good understanding with Ian Storey-Moore, who ended another season as the club's top goalscorer. Although I finished a distant second, grabbing eight goals in the league and a handful in Cup competitions, I took a lot of satisfaction from the fact that nearly all my goals had been headers. I only missed one league match due to injury and played thirty-six at inside forward and five as our main striker. There was no doubt the centre forward berth was the one that gave manager Matt Gillies the biggest headache, and in the forty-two league games eight different players wore the number nine jersey. I got two of my eight league goals whilst wearing the number nine on my back but I made it clear to the manager that I was not happy having big, uncompromising centre halfs clobbering me all over the park. Whereas in Scotland I could sometimes avoid the worst of the hacking with my speed and agility, in England the markers were quicker and stronger than their Scottish counterparts.

Unfortunately things didn't work out at Forest for Alex Ingram and in his twelve league appearances that season Alex failed to score. The glaring miss at Airdrie was probably the final nail in Alex's coffin and shortly afterwards he was transferred back to Ayr.

The enigmatic Duncan McKenzie led the line on three occasions but Duncan was even less happy than me at the treatment that the number fives dished out to guys who wanted to get the ball at their feet and play silky soccer. Our centre forward dilemma was finally eased when Forest signed my old Hibs pal Neil Martin from Coventry City halfway through the season. Coventry had signed Neillie from Sunderland for £90,000 a few years earlier and his goals helped them avoid relegation, and so Mattie Gillies also turned to Neil to solve our goalscoring problem. Whilst Neil only managed one goal in his twelve appearances he laid on chances for the rest of us and it was no accident that our best performances and results towards the end of the season came after Neil arrived.

Neil and his wife Mima's arrival in Nottingham was also an added bonus for Marion and me, especially after they bought a house nearby. The move away from family and friends in Edinburgh had been a challenge for Marion, especially when I was playing and travelling to and from away games, so having a friendly face nearby was great for her. Neil and Mima had been in England for almost six years so were more accustomed to the periods apart but they also welcomed the chance to renew our acquaintances and we have remained the best of friends ever since. Their arrival coincided with Marion discovering she was pregnant with our first child and it was comforting for her to have Mima closeby during her pregnancy and on call after Donna Lee was born on 2 December.

My performances in that first season in English football also earned me a recall to the Scotland setup and I played in two of the Home Internationals that May including my first appearance against the 'auld enemy' at Wembley.

So whilst I could look back on my first season at Forest as a personal success I also realised that the following season was going to be a tough challenge. I had quickly learned that there are no hiding places in the English First Division and whilst I was confident I was up to the challenge I had niggling doubts about some of my team-mates. It wasn't that they weren't capable of holding their own in the rough and tumble of top-flight English football, they had already proved that. My doubts were about the average age of the team. Most of the players had been at the City Ground for a number of years and their best days were probably behind them. I couldn't see many of the young players in the reserves making a breakthrough and went into the close season wondering if the manager would be able to strengthen the squad with some new signings.

One new face at the City Ground would prove to be a future hit as a player and football manager but Martin O'Neill's arrival from Distillery made no immediate impact on our fortunes in his first season in English football. Like his future coaching partner John Robertson, it would take the arrival of Brian Clough at the City Ground to transform his career and Nottingham Forest's fortunes.

Near the end of my first season at Forest the *Derby Evening Telegraph* ran a feature headed 'Cormack Talent Blossoms'. In the article I told the reporter, Bob Bryant:

I'm a better player today than I was when I left Scotland. Football here is taken more professionally than back home. I've never trained so hard in my life and I think I have bene-fitted from things like tactical talks and personal training in individual skills.

Obviously I'm a marked man now. But you tell me what striker isn't in these days of tight massed defences.

I've had my share of knocks this season but you forget all about the bruises when you score goals . . . But to score goals you've got to keep out of the way of defenders who are always breathing down your neck. I just try to keep on the move all the time which foxes defences.

Not only had a move to the English First Division improved me as a footballer, I had also come a long way from that first inter-view at Edinburgh Airport as a raw sixteen-year-old teenager who could only mutter a few clichéd words when asked how it felt to be travelling abroad.

At the end of the season my big mate Neil Martin told me that when he moved to England his second season at Sunderland was a lot tougher than his first 'because people's expectations were a lot higher, plus managers and defenders had had a chance to size you up and work out your strengths and weaknesses'. With no significant additions to the squad, and whilst I had no doubts about my own ability to build on my first season at the City Ground, I had my doubts about the Forests board's ambitions and I also feared that the strength in depth of our squad would make the 1971/72 season a battle for survival. Sadly I was not to be proven wrong.

In my two seasons at Nottingham Forest I never ever got used to running onto the park with the loudspeakers blaring the theme tune from the *Robin Hood* television programme of that time. I had to constantly remind Matt Gillies and my team-mates that I met, wooed and became engaged to 'my Maid Marion' long before I signed for Nottingham Forest. Opposition fans and players used to rip the piss out of us something rotten as we were leaving the changing rooms, and whilst the tale of 'Robin Hood riding through the glen with his merry men' echoed around the City Ground before each home match we were sliding down the table and heading for the Second Division. I wasn't the least bit surprised when Brian Clough eventually binned the Robin Hood theme tune after he became manager at the City Ground.

For the new season Matt Gillies and coach Bob McKinlay decided to pair Neil Martin and me as the Forest striking partnership. Despite the success I had in the attacking midfield berth the previous season, they were convinced that Neillie and I were the answer to the team's lack of goals. I didn't agree with them and made my views crystal clear but come the start of the league campaign Neil wore the number nine jersey as our target man and my job was to be up there for his lay-offs and knock downs.

We could not have had a harder opening match away to Liverpool and they put us to the sword, winning 3–1. This game marked the Liverpool debut of Kevin Keegan and as well as running our defenders ragged for ninety minutes he opened the scoring early in the first half. I had never heard of or seen Keegan before his debut but we would go on to become team-mates and the best of friends after I moved to Liverpool. Unfortunately for Forest players and fans, *Match of the Day* chose our opening match at Anfield as their main feature and I had to endure the edited highlights of our comprehensive defeat later that Saturday evening.

All my misgivings and apprehensions were there for everyone to see as Liverpool destroyed us in front of the Kop and the BBC cameras.

We fared no better in our next match losing 2–1 away to Leicester City but fortunately things improved when we overcame West Ham 1–0 in our first home game on the second Saturday of the season. The start of the season turned out to be a real struggle and we never developed any cohesion or consistency. I managed to score our only goal with a header in a 1–1 draw away at Coventry and it was Neillie's turn to be unhappy with the boss after he was taken off against his old team after sixty-five minutes.

A few weeks later an old knee ligament injury from my Hibs days returned with a vengeance, which kept me out of the side for seven weeks. It was torture sitting in the stand every week watching the team struggle, unable to help as they became rooted to the foot of the First Division. We only picked up three points in the seven league games I missed, which included a 6–0 hammering at Spurs, a 3–2 defeat at the City Ground by Liverpool and another home defeat to fellow relegation strugglers Huddersfield Town. I had always found it frustrating watching from the sidelines and it was doubly difficult as my Forest team-mates' confidence was taking a battering with that dreadful run of results. Lady Luck was also not on our side.

At the end of October we entertained our local rivals Derby County at the City Ground and with the score at 0–0 the normally clinical Ian Storey-Moore missed a penalty kick. The confidence just drained from the team after that and Derby ran out comfortable 2–0 winners. That defeat left us five points adrift at the foot of the table. Duncan McKenzie replaced me in the team when I was out injured and initially he grabbed his chance with both hands (or should that be feet?), but after a couple of sparkling performances Duncan's magic faded fast. He was still in the starting eleven at centre forward when I made my comeback at the end of November away to Newcastle United on a snow-covered St James' Park.

The previous Saturday we had trounced West Bromwich Albion 4–1 at the City Ground in what was Martin O'Neill's debut. But just when it was beginning to look like we had turned the corner Newcastle beat us 2–1 to keep us firmly lodged at the bottom of the table. I was pleased with my comeback given the length of time I had been absent and hit our only goal, a shot after taking a knock down from Neil who had only just come off the bench to replace a struggling Duncan. My goal was eclipsed by two from Newcastle's new £175,000 recruit Malcolm MacDonald and SuperMac, as the Geordies quickly christened him, grabbed the winning goal ten minutes from the end to leave us in serious relegation trouble. In our next six matches we only managed four points from a possible twelve after losing away at Manchester United and Sheffield United and at home to Leeds. The Man United result was 'sair to bare' as both Martin O'Neill and I managed to score at Old Trafford, but we still lost 3–2 through two goals by Brian Kidd and one from Denis Law. We then scrambled two points by drawing with Arsenal at the City Ground and Manchester City at Maine Road and our only victory in that period was a 1–0 win at home to Everton.

Whilst December had been a poor one on the pitch, team morale in the dressing room improved with the arrival of left back Tommy Gemmell from Celtic. Big Tam was a legend with Celtic fans after scoring their first goal in the 1967 European Cup Final, and he was a legend with me after he chased Helmut Haller and kicked him up the arse in a West Germany versus Scotland World Cup Qualifier I played in during my final season at Hibs. I would constantly remind Tam of his infamous indiscretion following which he had to run a gauntlet of beer bottles thrown by West German fans, but he never regretted the incident and always said,

'That dirty German bastard deserved all he got.' Tam had been a regular in the Celtic team for a long time and had scored their only goal in the 1970 European Cup Final, which they lost 2–1 to the Dutch champions Feyenoord. Big Tam was also not short of confidence and kept everyone amused with his Glesga patter, and although very few of the English lads understood what he was saying half the time they just joined in when Neillie and I laughed at Big Tam's antics and jokes. One of Forest's young new recruits was given the job of cleaning his boots and Tam christened him Pelé. Viv Anderson would go on to be the first black player to play for England but he was made up with his new Forest nick-name after Tam arrived. Tommy was even more opinionated than Duncan McKenzie, which is saying something, and when they disagreed, which was pretty much all the time, Tam would tell him to 'eff off, ya big English poof'.

Big Tam was not impressed with the Forest training regime, particularly the hard running session on a Thursday after our Wednesday day off. He collared Bob McKinlay after a few weeks of gruelling Thursday sessions and told him that players were tiring at the end of matches because the tough workout was too close to match day. The coach responded by saying that he knew most players went for a drink on a Wednesday and the tough session was necessary to sweat out the booze. Tam said, 'Well, why don't you give us a Monday off and murder us on the Tuesday?'

I looked away and smiled, as I knew what Bob's answer was going to be.

'We can't do that, Tam – the manager always plays golf on a Wednesday.'

It was the only time I ever saw Big Tam speechless. A few minutes later he said, 'I cannae fuckin' believe that. We're breathing oot oor arses on a Saturday cause Mattie plays fuckin' golf every Wednesday.'

I shrugged my shoulders and said, 'I know, Tam, I sometimes play with Mattie. He's not a bad golfer.'

It was Big Tam's turn to shrug his shoulders and he wandered off shaking his head muttering, 'Big Jock wouldnae organise training at Celtic around golf. Wait until I tell him, he'll no' fuckin' believe me.'

Tommy Gemmell's best footballing days may have been behind him but his signing that December certainly lifted the spirits in the Forest dressing room. However, whilst our morale may have improved, our performances on the park didn't get any better. We continued to struggle in the league and in the third round of the FA Cup we lost 3–1 away to Second Division Millwall. That was our second Cup defeat in London that season as Chelsea had knocked us out of the League Cup in a second-round replay after a 1–1 draw at the City Ground.

Our league fate was pretty much sealed after Derby hammered us 4–0 at the Baseball Ground on 19 February. Brian Clough's side were beginning to be talked about as title contenders, and whilst Derby would go on to lift the First Division Championship, with Leeds losing out by a single point for the second year running, Forest never got out of the relegation zone.

Two weeks after our defeat at the Baseball Ground, Ian Storey-Moore was paraded by Brian Clough and his assistant Peter Taylor before a Derby County league match as County's new signing, but two days later Ian signed for Manchester United for £200,000. The selling of Forest's talisman two months before the end of the season sent out the message to Forest's fans and players that the board had resigned themselves to the team going down to the Second Division. From my perspective, this was a disaster on their part and whilst it might not have made any difference at the end of the day as the results subsequently proved, we might have been able to turn things around. The City Ground was not a happy place those last few weeks although we threatened to pull off the impossible after beating Chelsea 2–1, courtesy of two Tommy Gemmell specials, and Coventry 4–1. But any faint hope was short-lived after we lost 6–1 at Leeds and 3–0 to Arsenal at Highbury.

The Leeds match saw me don the goalkeeper's gloves for my one and only appearance between the sticks in English football. Going into the match Leeds had won eight games on the trot, scoring twenty-five goals in the process and 40,000 fans packed into Elland Road on a wet and windy March night, looking for them to add to that total against the team at the bottom of the league.

After going behind in fifteen minutes we equalised just before half-time when a shot from Alan Buckley hit me on the shoulder then ricocheted off goalkeeper Gary Sprake into the Leeds net. At the half-time whistle Sprake chased after the referee, claiming I had knocked it in with my arm but 1–1 it stood at the interval. Leeds came out with their tails up for the second half and after fifty-two minutes our goalkeeper Jim Barron split his lip, diving bravely at the feet of Allan Clarke. Jim had to go off to have stitches put in the wound and I had no hesitation putting on the keeper's green jersey. I may have managed two clean sheets deputising in goal at Hibs but that 100 per cent record meant nothing to ruthless Leeds who were chasing a championship title.

In four minutes I managed to concede two goals thus not only shattering my clean sheet record but managing to kick-start Leeds into a goal scoring spree. I had no sooner slipped on Jim's gloves when Peter Lorimer thumped a corner into the six-yard box that I fumbled and Eddie Gray gleefully poked home. Two minutes later, a fast-flowing Leeds attack down the left wing ended with Allan Clarke stroking the ball past me. I was delighted to see Jim Barron waving to come back on after I had picked the ball out of the net for a second time and decided there and then that if a goalkeeper ever got injured in future I would not be as keen to deputise. We steadied the ship after that and Leeds led 4–1 going into injury time, but somehow we managed to concede another two goals before the ref blew his final whistle. In fairness to Mattie Gillies and my Forest team-mates, they didn't blame me for the two goals lost when Jim was getting treatment, which is more than can be said for the *Yorkshire Post* whose headline the following day read: 'Brave keeper's injury opened the flood gates'.

After losing to Arsenal we beat Newcastle at home 1–0 and then on the Easter Monday we defeated Stoke City 2–0 at the City Ground but it was a case of too little too late, and in our final league match of the season against Everton at Goodison only 21,500 spectators turned out for typical drab, end-of-season 1–1 draw. I managed to score the Forest goal in what turned out to be my final appearance for Nottingham Forest. That point ensured we didn't finish bottom of the table but we only ended higher than Huddersfield Town because of a better goal aggregate. We had taken almost half our points total for the season from the six teams above us in the league but it was our failure to pick up points against the top fifteen that proved to be our downfall. Our respective twenty-five points was four less than the twentieth team in the division, Crystal Palace, and no matter how I analysed the statistics it didn't change the fact that the following season Nottingham Forest would be playing in the English Second Division after fifteen continuous seasons in England's top flight.

After Ian Storey-Moore was sold to Man United I sat down with Matt Gillies to find out where my own future lay. I had made my opinion clear to the manager and the chairman before Ian left that I thought it was crazy to sell our best player when there was still two months of the season left. I think the Forest board panicked into selling Ian to United after Cloughie had paraded him in front of the Derby fans. Most Forest fans were relieved that at least Ian hadn't been sold to their nearest rival but the timing of his departure did nothing for team morale in the dressing room, especially as we still had almost a dozen league matches left to play.

When I met with Mattie he told me that the board would be looking to offload several of the first team squad as they knew that gates would drop dramatically and as a consequence revenue would fall considerably, with the club playing in the Second Division. When I asked him if that included me he said, 'Peter, you are our best player at the club and they hope to make a profit on the £80,000 they paid Hibs.' I was dreading the final game at Goodison, as in the run-up to it I was sure that after the match I would be depressed at the thought of playing the following season in Second Division.

I knew that the Forest board's lack of ambition meant that they would not be going on a summer spending spree – in fact, the opposite would be the case. They would be tightening their belts, not loosening them to splash the cash on new players to try and get back in the top flight at the first time of asking. It seemed that the Nottingham Forest board's biggest concern was the forthcoming football league, AGM, where they were about to propose the revolutionary idea (well, at least it was in 1972) of playing football matches on a Sunday. The Forest board had made it known that every player in the squad was up for sale, and if I was still at the City Ground come the beginning of August it meant that none of the First Division managers thought that I could do a job for them. Fortunately I had our little baby Donna Lee to take my mind of my football woes and then as soon as the season ended the transfer rumour mill started up and the wheeling and dealing began in earnest for the new season.

The FA Cup winners Leeds United signed Trevor Cherry from

near neighbours Huddersfield Town, England's World Cup hat-trick hero Geoff Hurst signed for Stoke City for £80,000, Steve Kindom moved from Burnley to Wolves for £100,000, Ian Ure left Manchester United on a free transfer to St Mirren, and Bobby Hope moved across England's second largest city when he signed for Birmingham from West Brom for £60,000.

Whilst all that was going on, George Best failed to turn up in Troon to meet the Northern Ireland squad for a Scotland versus Northern Ireland Home International. George was later tracked down in Marbella and subsequently announced that he was going to retire from football, saying that he was a physical and mental wreck and had been drinking too much in the previous four months. For several weeks during the close season the occasional story appeared in the press that Bill Nicholson was going to take me to Spurs. But despite the paper talk I heard nothing from Bill or Forest. I then read about Liverpool's interest in Huddersfield Town's Frank Worthington.

Frank was a proven goalscorer, and Liverpool manager Bill Shankly talked in glowing terms about how Frank would be the ideal foil for Kevin Keegan and John Toshack in the Liverpool forward line. After his debut against us on the first day of the season, Kevin had gone on to establish himself as a goalscoring revelation in his first season at Anfield.

Then the press reported that Frank had failed a medical at Anfield due to high blood pressure. The papers said that after the medical Frank was told to go on holiday and report back at Anfield for a second test after his break. Unfortunately for Frank, two weeks of late-night partying in Magaluf didn't help his high blood pressure and the readings in the second medical were higher than the first time around.

A few days later as I was sitting having breakfast with Marion and Donna Lee, I received a telephone call from Mattie Gillies. He told me to report to his office and not go to the training ground with the rest of the players. When I went into his office Mattie told me that a club were interested in signing me. I was certain that at last Bill Nicholson had made his move and I was on my way to Tottenham Hotspur.

'No, it's no' Spurs that have contacted us, it's Shanks,' he told me.

At first I thought he meant Bob Shankly and I asked him who Bob was scouting for.

'It's no' fucking Bob, you daft bastard,' he blurted out. 'It's his brother, Bill. He wants you to go straight to Liverpool for a medical.'

I was in a daze and jumped in a taxi to catch the next train to Liverpool. The taxi trip and the train journey to Liverpool were a total blank, and the first thing I remember is meeting Rueben Bennett at the Anfield players' entrance.

'Welcome to Liverpool, Peter. We better not keep the boss waiting, he's looking forward to meeting you.'

And with these few words I was ushered into the great man's office to meet a football legend who would transform my football career in England and shape my philosophy on how football should be played. It was without doubt the most important day of my football career and a day that changed my life for the better.

8

THIS IS ANFIELD

When I turned up for my first day's training at Liverpool's Melwood training ground I was excited and nervous. In my two years at Forest I had played twice at Anfield, and although we had been comprehensively beaten 3–0 and 3–1, both occasions burned in my memory because of the atmosphere created by the Liverpool fans. Anfield was without doubt the best stadium in England to play football in the 1960s and 70s and that was all down to Bill Shankly. When Shanks set about transforming Liverpool Football Club after his appointment as manager in 1959 he did so with the stated aim of making Anfield a fortress for visiting teams. Everything he did, from his training methods, changing the colour of the team strip to all red and erecting the 'This is Anfield' sign above the tunnel as the players walked onto the park, had a purpose in Shanks' greater scheme of things. In transforming Liverpool Football Club Bill Shankly revolutionised football thinking and the way clubs, managers and players went about their business. He had a simple philosophy to football training and how the game should be played. When constantly pestered by the media for his secret to success his response was usually, 'Football is a simple game. It's coaches that make it complicated.'

Where Nottingham Forest were a step further up the ladder than Hibs in training and organisation, Liverpool were on the very top rung in everything they did at the football club. Whereas training at Forest may have been organised around the manager's golf day, at Liverpool players were banned from going anywhere near the golf course during the football season. The emphasis at Liverpool was on the 'professional', and players were expected to train properly, eat a healthy, balanced diet and make sure they rested between training and matches. During one memorable training session at Nottingham Forest, coach Bob McKinlay set up the first team to take on invisible opponents. Honestly, there were no opposing players, not even cardboard cut-outs – it was surreal. I think it was meant to be a confidence booster, and whilst we managed to bang in a few goals against the invisible men it probably had the opposite effect than was intended and our bad patch in the league continued.

As soon as I walked into Melwood on my first day at training I knew I had arrived. I was comfortable in the environment and immediately welcomed into the Liverpool football family. One of the first things my new team-mates did was give me a nickname. They weren't keen on 'Gas Meter', which was also a huge relief to me, and settled for my middle name, Barr. In later seasons I think some of the new recruits thought that it was spelt with one 'r' and my nickname had something to do with an indiscretion involving alcohol.

Unbeknown to me when I signed in Bill Shankly's office, the £110,000 fee equalled Liverpool's highest transfer paid two years earlier to Cardiff City for John Toshack. Because of this and the fact that I was Liverpool's only close season signing, the local media were out in force when I arrived for my first day at training. I was warmly welcomed by team captain Tommy Smith who shouted over Brian Hall, Steve Heighway and Peter Thompson for the handshakes in front of the cameras.

After the paparazzi headed off, Peter Thompson pulled me aside and asked me what kind of car I was driving and its colour.

I was taken aback at 'Thommo's' question and asked him why he was asking. 'It's just that when I signed for Liverpool in 1963 I was driving a cracking blue MG sports car. But when Shanks saw the colour of the car he told me to get rid of it. You play for Liverpool, not Everton. You can drive any type of car in any colour except blue, was the boss's ultimatum.' I burst out laughing at Thommo's piece of advice but heeded the warning. Fortunately Marion and I had a white car with a red stripe along the side which I was sure would please Shanks no end.

At least Thommo's welcome was friendlier than Tommy Smith's. As soon as the media left Smithy started winding me up about the way I ran. When I was at Forest I was warned about Tommy before we played Liverpool. Ian Storey-Moore hated playing against him and told me that Smithy's greeting usually consisted of him threatening to 'break his fucking back' if he went past him. Ian's response to this was to stay as far away as possible from Tommy. Come to think of it, I don't think I tangled very often with Smithy in the games I had played against Liverpool with Forest.

On my first day at Liverpool Tommy said, 'See the way you run, Peter lad, you know on the tips of your toes – you look like a fucking poof.'

I just laughed at his comment and said, 'Well, Smithy, you're safe on two counts. The first is that I'm not gay and second, if I was, you're the last person I would fancy.' Tommy and the other lads laughed at my reply but I don't think Smithy was 100 per cent convinced of my answer and an hour or so later he welcomed me to my first Melwood practice match with one of his trademark crunching tackles.

As I slowly got to my feet Tommy smiled at me and said, 'Welcome to Liverpool.' For the rest of the training match I gave as good as I got and in the changing rooms afterwards Tommy came over to me ruffled my hair and said, 'You'll do for me, lad.'

I knew there and then that I had won his respect and we were the best of mates for the rest of my career at Anfield.

After a few weeks' hard graft in pre-season I could see that Bill Shankly had a squad of players of the highest order. I didn't realise at the time but the combined transfer fees for the fifteen players that played in all of the sixty-six competitive matches that season was £455,000. As transfer dealings go, pound-for-pound we were probably the most successful club side in the history of English football. Not only would that squad go on to win the First Division Championship twice, lift two UEFA Cups and the FA Cup, it was also the backbone of Liverpool's first European Cup success in 1977. There was a great balance to the squad. Experienced guys like Tommy Smith, Ian Callaghan, Peter Thomson and Chris Lawler lived and breathed Liverpool Football Club and had seen and done it all before, with Shanks winning two League Championships and the FA Cup in the mid-1960s. I was one of the 'new kids on the Kop block', along with Kevin Keegan, John Toshack, Steve Heighway and Brian Hall. I might have had ten years' first team experience under my belt but I quickly realised that with a big price tag on my head I had a lot to prove to my new team-mates and the most knowledgeable football supporters in England on the famous Kop at Anfield.

Shanks might have made me feel ten feet tall when he told the press that he thought my signing was the 'final part of his jigsaw' but he was also putting me under pressure to hit the ground running when the time came for me to slip on the famous red Liverpool shirt. The 1972/73 season and making my home debut against Manchester City couldn't come quickly enough and I was flying in training and loving my new life at Anfield.

*

The previous season Derby County had won the League Championship with fifty-eight points and three teams finished only one point behind – Leeds, Liverpool and Manchester City. In the pre-season build-up Shanks made it clear to us that his priority for the season was winning the league and every day at training he would never tire of telling the players that. Shanks reminded me of Jock Stein in so many ways. Both were from Scottish mining communities and playing football had been their escape from working down the pits. Shanks and Big Jock were also tracksuit managers and loved nothing more than working with the players on the training ground. I especially enjoyed training at Liverpool, as everything was organised around ball work and short, sharp fitness sessions, but the highlight of every session was the organised game at the end. That's where the boss's competitive streak came into its own and a session would not finish until his team were in the lead.

It was hilarious but you daren't laugh at him or your life would not be worth living. It was even worse if you were refereeing a game and gave a decision against his team. Retribution was swift and usually involved an extra punishing training workout. I only ever made the mistake of giving a decision against Shanks' team once when I refereed a match whilst recovering from injury. As the rest of the squad made for the changing rooms after I blew the final whistle, Shanks made me do several laps of the park and then some stomach work with a medicine ball as my punishment for 'a shocking refereeing performance' as he put it. When I eventually got into the dressing room half an hour after the rest of the players they were already bathed and dressed. To say I was not in the best of moods is an understatement. Smithy came up to me, put a consoling arm around my shoulders and said, 'That'll teach you, lad. If you ever ref another game just make sure Shanks' team wins.' The rest of the players burst out laughing and I vowed never to referee another match after that. But Shanks' football pride was great for team spirit at the club.

That first season at Anfield, Shanks spent several hours discussing with me what he thought my best position would be in the team before we went on a short summer tour. Initially he wanted me playing up front to support Keegan and Toshack, but I wanted a deeper role. The dilemma had not been resolved before I played my first match for the Reds in a friendly against Bochum. Nobody was any the wiser after the match either as my old knee ligament injury returned with a vengeance and I was stretchered off during the match – my dream Liverpool debut turning into a nightmare. Following my injury, Shanks never spoke to me for weeks and I wondered what was going on. Eventually I decided to have a quiet word with Ian Callaghan who was the most experienced player in our squad. 'Don't take it personally, Barr,' he said, and then assured me that Shanks did that to every player who was injured. 'Believe me, Barr, it doesn't matter who it is, if you are on the treatment table you are no use to him so he just ignores you. It's all part of Shanks' make-up. He thinks that if he doesn't speak to you you'll get fit sooner.'

After my heart-to-heart with Cally I felt much better and was determined to get back playing as quickly as possible. The injury to my knee ruled me out for the start of the league campaign and I missed the first six matches where the team took nine points, their only defeat away at Leicester City. Included in the run of four wins were victories over the two Manchester clubs, Chelsea and West Ham. Whilst I was out, fellow Scot Brian Hall, who was one of Shanks' young recruits from university, played at inside right and as well as playing superbly, 'Little Bamber' scored our first goal in the opening match of the season against Manchester City. Because Brian and Steve Heighway were university graduates the Scousers on the Kop had christened them 'Little

Bamber' and 'Big Bamber' after Bamber Gascoigne, the quiz-master of the TV programme *University Challenge*.

After the Leicester defeat I made my debut against the reigning champions Derby County at the Baseball Ground on 2 September, exactly a month after my knee injury. I always liked playing against Derby on their home patch and revelled in the atmosphere generated by the close proximity of the fans to the pitch. The Baseball Ground had a tendency to turn into a mud heap in the second half of the season and I was glad that we were getting it in relatively pristine condition three weeks into the season. The Derby manager Brian Clough had done a fantastic job with the quality squad of players he had assembled to win the league the previous season and he spent most of that summer telling the football world that his team would go on to win the European Cup. I liked Cloughie and whilst his brashness sometimes got up other people's noses, I had the utmost respect for what he had achieved at Derby.

After my two years at their nearest rivals Forest I had seen and heard a lot from 'big mouth' or 'motor mouth', as some of the football media unfairly labelled him, but I was determined to put his gas at a peep in my Liverpool debut. Unfortunately Cloughie and his players ruined those plans and my first league appearance for Liverpool saw us lose 2–1. I felt I had done alright in the ninety minutes but by my own standards I knew I could do a lot better. I played another ninety minutes in a League Cup tie the following Tuesday at Carlisle where we scrambled a 1–1 draw. Fortunately I retained the number eight shirt for my home debut the following Saturday against Wolves.

By the time of the match against Wolves there was some talk in the media of Liverpool facing an early-season crisis. The draw at Carlisle following back-to-back league defeats even had some football journalists writing off our season and Shanks, the football psychologist that he was, used this to his advantage.

Before we went onto the park he cut out one of the offending articles and held it up in the middle of the dressing room. 'You know what I think of this piece of crap, lads?' and he crumpled the newspaper cutting into a ball and kicked it into a corner of the changing room.'That's the easy part, boys. Now you go out there and show those so-called football journalists just how good you are and let these Liverpool fans see that they've got a team to be proud of.'

After Shanks' team talk, all eleven players were bursting to get onto the Anfield pitch and we flew at Wolves right from the kick-off. Emlyn Hughes gave us an early lead and I was full of running, patrolling the right side of midfield. The two previous games had been stepping stones to getting match fit and as well as covering loads of ground my touch on the ball was back to its razor-sharp best.

Despite controlling play for most of the first half we went in at the break with only Emlyn's goal to show for our superiority. Then, as so often happens in football, the team that had been totally outplayed in the first half came out with their tails up and Wolves scored an equaliser at the start of the second half. In years to come I would be good pals with Steve Kindon and it was ironic he scored his first goal for Wolves after his transfer from Burnley in the same match as I scored on my Anfield debut. After Stevie scored the equaliser I could feel the tension amongst our fans on the terraces but Shanks was coolness personified and told us to keep playing the way we were and not to panic.

We began to take control of the game and Kevin Keegan chased down a long ball near the Wolves corner flag on the right. In truth, the pass wasn't even seventy/thirty against Kevin, but his speed and strength won him the ball and he quickly fired over a long cross which carried to the left-hand side of the penalty box where Stevie Heighway rose and headed it towards the edge of the Wolves six yard line. When Kevin won the ball I instinctively started running towards the Wolves goal and when Stevie's header landed on the six yard line I threw myself head first to bullet the ball past the onrushing Phil Parkes in the Wolves goal.

The Liverpool fans may have been ecstatic and relieved to see us take the lead again but there was no happier person on the planet at that moment than me. I picked myself up and ran towards the Kop and was quickly grabbed by Emlyn Hughes. Later that night I watched the TV highlights of the game on *Match of the Day* and I was struck by the fans' reaction in the Kop when I scored my goal in front of them. When my header went in and I instinctively ran towards them I hadn't noticed the Kopites swaying forward like one gigantic tidal wave. Watching the Liverpool fans' reaction on TV gave me goosebumps and let me see what Shanks had said about just how much their football team meant to them.

After putting us back in the lead I was really buzzing and not long afterwards I won a penalty kick after my ex-Scotland teammate Jim McCalliog bundled me over just inside the box. As far as I was concerned it was a stonewall penalty but Jim wasn't happy and managed to get himself sent off for bad-mouthing the linesman. Tommy Smith clinically dispatched the spot-kick at the second time of asking and a few minutes later Kevin Keegan put the result beyond doubt with a near post header.

Looking back on it now, my debut goal was not only the turning point in that match, it was quite possibly the turning point of Liverpool's season and defined my career at Anfield. As well as putting us 2–1 ahead, I won a penalty kick and even managed to get myself booked for a clumsy challenge on, guess who, yes Steve Kindon, such was my devotion to the cause. Although Wolves pulled a consolation goal back near the end, that 4–2 victory set us on our way to a thirteen-game unbeaten run in the league at Anfield. The Wolves match also preceded our first UEFA Cup tie of the season at home to Frankfurt which we won 2–0. It was the start of a history-making campaign that would culminate in Liverpool winning its first of many European trophies. But winning the UEFA Cup was not in the minds of the players that September. Bill Shankly had said before the start of the season that the club's priority would be winning the league, and beating Wolverhampton Wanderers had put us back on track after the setbacks at Leicester and Derby.

In our next league match at Anfield we hit top form demolishing Sheffield United 5–0. It was a superb team performance and I thought we might go on to hit a record score after I notched our fourth goal in the fifty-first minute, but no one in red was complaining that day after we hit five goals without reply. That victory also put us back on top of the First Division.

After my discussions with Shanks earlier in the season about where I would best fit in the side I had quickly established myself on the right side of midfield, linking seamlessly with the defenders and Kevin and Tosh up front. I felt comfortable in the role I had created for myself and the manager was singing my praises to my team-mates, the fans and the football media.

Things were great for me on the park and life was sweet for Marion, Donna Lee and I away from the football club. After my first week at Liverpool I received a pleasant surprise with my first pay packet. The contract I had signed was for one hundred pounds a week plus an appearance fee, along with a fifty pound win bonus and a further bonus for winning trophies. The basic weekly wage was more than double what I had been getting at Forest and made me one of the highest earners at Anfield. After speaking to some of the other players and meeting their wives, Marion and I bought a detached villa for £13,500 at Ainsdale, near Southport. It is a beautiful part of England with large sand dunes, beautiful beaches and some of the best golf courses in Britain, including Royal Birkdale, home to many Open Championships over the years.

I quickly settled into a nice routine where if I wasn't training in the afternoons I would be home by two o'clock to enjoy a cup of tea with Marion and then take baby Donna Lee for a good long walk. The only socialising we would do was on a Saturday evening when Marion and I would go out for a quiet meal if we had been playing at home. After a few months The Bold Arms in Southport became a regular haunt for us because it was handy, the food was very nice and we never got any hassle. Occasionally we would go out with some of the Liverpool players and their wives or girlfriends for an Italian or Chinese meal, but mostly Marion and I enjoyed our quiet Saturday evenings at The Bold.

I had established a regular routine over the years that I never changed in the eighteen years I played. The night before a game I would be in bed by nine o'clock and my pre-football meal was usually eggs on toast. The only variation I allowed was deciding whether I had the eggs scrambled, poached or boiled. That good living habit had stood me in good stead at Hibs and Nottingham Forest and I made sure I followed it religiously at Anfield. I have never met a footballer who didn't have at least one superstition and that pre-match sleeping and eating routine was mine. I have no doubt that the settled family life, training every day with the best players in England, plenty of rest and a balanced healthy diet was helping my performances on the park for Liverpool and resulted in me playing the best football of my career in that first season at Anfield.

There was one additional perk that Marion and I enjoyed. Every Friday a local Liverpool fan would appear at Anfield and distribute parcels to the players packed with butcher's meat in exchange for complimentary match tickets. Either he came from a big family of Liverpool fans or was the most popular supporter down at his local, but none of us ever asked any questions, so grateful were we for the quality supply of butcher meat – liver, bacon, sausages, pork chops and T-Bone steaks – to die for. Every week – rain, hail or snow – the butcher meat parcel provider appeared at the players' entrance and all the married guys took advantage of it. No wonder we were the fastest, fittest and strongest team in the league.

My biggest playing highlight that year came on Saturday 7 October 1972, ironically exactly eight years after my greatest moment at Hibs when I scored against Real Madrid at Easter Road. Derbies are always great games to play in and I had always enjoyed the Hibs versus Hearts matches in my eight years at Easter Road. It therefore goes without saying that I was looking forward to playing in my first Merseyside Derby at Anfield against an Everton team that included Howard Kendall, Roger Kenyon, Colin Harvey and Joe Royle. Although Everton had finished a distant fifteenth the previous season, manager Harry Catterick was an experienced and shrewd operator and no one at Liverpool was under any illusion that we were in for a gruelling ninety minutes. The Everton players and fans were certainly up for the match after Shanks received two Manager of the Month awards fifteen minutes before the kick-off. For some obscure reason one award had been held over from the previous season and the other was the August award after Liverpool's great start to the league campaign.

In many ways the game was typical of local derbies the world over where a cautious start, with more brawn than brain, was followed by good attacking, free-flowing football from both sides once the early nerves disappeared. The second half was end-to-end play and in seventy minutes only a brilliant save by Ray Clemence prevented Joe Royle giving Everton the lead. This came after a sustained period of Everton pressure but seven minutes later I scored the most memorable goal in my four years at Liverpool to settle the outcome of the match. I watched play develop down the left and when the ball reached Steve Heighway I gambled on 'Big Bamber' getting in a cross. Stevie didn't let me down and he fired a fast, long cross that eluded the Everton defenders. I came flying in at the back post and threw myself forward catching the cross flush on my forehead. I knew as soon as I made contact that it was a goal and the ball flew into the corner of the Everton net.

Unfortunately the goal was scored at the Anfield Road end of the ground and I had to wait until I watched the *Match of the Day* highlights to see the 26,000 Liverpool fans packed into the Kop going absolutely nuts at my goal. After I jumped to my feet to acclaim my goal big Larry Lloyd held me up in front of the ecstatic fans saying, 'Barr, you'll be a fucking Liverpool hero for life to these fans.' Fortunately we managed to hold on to win my first Merseyside Derby, and more importantly the victory put us two points clear of our challengers at the top of the English First Division Championship.

The first half of the season was not all plain sailing though. Whilst our home form was superb our form away was not as consistent. We lost two big matches, at Elland Road and Old Trafford, and one thing seemed certain – the destination of the championship was going to go to the wire. I had quickly settled into the team and was receiving rave reviews most Saturdays, working hard to live up to Shanks' label of being 'the final piece in his jigsaw' when an old Achilles heel returned with a vengeance – and I'm not talking about a previous injury.

The Tuesday after the Everton game we played West Brom at Anfield in a League Cup tie, which we eventually won 2–1. It had been a bruising encounter with no quarter given by either side and we only scraped through with a winning goal from Kevin Keegan in the last minute of extra-time. The Baggies players and fans were not best pleased and thought they should have taken more from the game.

Eight weeks later we travelled to the Hawthorns for a league match where I managed to get myself sent off for retaliation. It was my first indiscipline in more than two years and whilst we didn't lose the match Shanks totally blanked me after the game and I spent two sleepless nights over the weekend knowing I would have to face him in his office on the Monday morning. I kept running the incident over and over again in my head wishing I had kept my temper in check. Also uppermost in my thoughts was Shanks' reaction to injured players who he treated like lepers. 'If that's what he does when you're injured, what the hell will he be like for an unnecessary sending-off,' I said to Marion repeatedly that weekend.

On the Monday morning I sheepishly crept into his office when the call came to face the music, fully expecting to be hauled over the coals for my moment of madness. Shanks was one of the few people I have met whose facial expression hardly changed in day-to-day settings. He would have made a great poker player, although he never gambled. When I looked at him across his desk I had no idea from the look on his face what he was about to say.

'Peter son, you let a lot of people down on Saturday. You let yourself down, your family, your Liverpool team-mates but most of all you let down the people that pay your wages – the supporters of Liverpool Football Club.'

I sat staring at my feet, expecting no less than a heavy fine and a warning that any repeat behaviour would find me looking for a new club.

As Shanks continued I was not expecting him to say what he said next: 'You know, Peter son, you have exceeded even my expectations in your first couple months here and those Liverpool fans worship you. They work hard all week and what keeps them going is their Saturday afternoon watching Liverpool Football Club. Always remember that what you do on that park will determine if their next week at work will be a good week or a bad week.'

I was beginning to shift uncomfortably in the chair, feeling humble and embarrassed.

'Now I don't want to see you sitting in that chair again. The next time you want to kick somebody up the backside, do it to Tommy Smith at training and after that you'll never kick anyone again.' I smiled at the comment and thought to myself, 'I'm not that fucking stupid,' but Shanks continued, 'I've had a word with Bob Paisley and Doc Reid and they have made a detailed list of all the injuries and the bruises that these dirty West Bromwich players inflicted on you on Saturday. I have already sent a telegram to the FA's disciplinary committee requesting a personal hearing and that Bob and our club doctor accompany you when you appear before them. Liverpool Football Club will support you 100 per cent and do everything we can to stop them suspending you.'

I was gobsmacked and didn't know what to say and mumbled, 'Thanks, boss.' It seemed pathetically inadequate given what Shanks had said to me but it was all I could think of.

'You are far too important to the team to be watching from the sidelines. Let this be a salutary lesson, son. These West Brom players knew that by stopping Cormack they stopped Liverpool playing and that's why you were targeted on Saturday. Away and see Bob Paisley and Doc Reid and get your story right for that hearing.'

After walking in feeling miserable and thinking my career at Anfield was hanging by a thread I walked out feeling ten feet tall. I also swore to myself that would be the first and last time

Shanks would have to go out on a limb for me. When I subsequently appeared at the FA I received a severe reprimand, thanks to the collective efforts of the club.

Over the important Christmas holiday period we took a maximum eight points from four matches and in the last game of the calendar year I scored our only goal in a 1–0 victory at Crystal Palace. It was a great end to the year and my first six months at Liverpool.

Unfortunately my good fortune did not last long into the New Year. After knocking Burnley out of the FA Cup in a replay at Anfield we were drawn at home to Manchester City and despite 56,000 fans cramming into Anfield on the first Saturday in February we could only manage a 0–0 draw. Four days later City beat us 2–0 in the replay at Maine Road and I suffered a recurrence of the knee injury which had kept me sidelined for four weeks at the start of the season.

The team had mixed fortunes in the six games played in my absence. We lost our unbeaten home record the following Saturday with a 2–0 defeat by Arsenal which included a superb breakaway goal by John Radford when he ran from the halfway line. In the second Merseyside Derby at Goodison three weeks later Emlyn Hughes was outstanding and scored both goals in the last ten minutes to give us a 2–0 win. Nobody celebrated a goal better than 'Crazy Horse' and he eclipsed my derby winner five months earlier by grabbing a double in front of the end where the Liverpool fans were packed into Goodison.

I returned to the first team on 17 March where we needed a win at Stoke City to remain at the top of the league. Fortunately we came away with both points when Brian Hall scored a late winner after coming off the bench. We then won three of our next six league matches but lost away at Birmingham and Newcastle and drew at home to Tottenham. Spurs goalie Pat Jennings was their hero that day after saving a penalty kick from Kevin Keegan in the first half and a second penalty from Tommy Smith five minutes from full-time. In between he made several outstanding saves with one stop in particular from me in the 'how did he manage to get to that?' category.

We went into our second-last league match against Leeds on Easter Monday knowing that if we won it was going to make life extremely difficult for our nearest challengers Arsenal to overtake us. The Leeds match was also my fiftieth game for Liverpool in my first season at Anfield and I was raring to go. Leeds' title challenge had faltered several weeks earlier but they were still our biggest rivals and I had played in the match earlier in the season at Elland Road which we lost 2–1. Leeds were also looking forward to meeting Sunderland in the FA Cup Final twelve days later and all their players were playing for a spot in the starting line-up at Wembley. In many ways it helped us that the Leeds match came only two days after we had narrowly lost at Newcastle.

The shortened build-up didn't afford a lot of time for pre-match nerves, and on the Sunday all of the players reported to Anfield to get injuries from the Saturday checked out and enjoy a relaxing massage to soothe away the previous day's aches and pains.

On the Monday night Liverpool fans crammed into Anfield full of hope and expectation and the gates were closed half an hour before kick-off. The game might have meant nothing to Leeds in terms of league points but their professionalism and pride ensured that they were up for the game. If the boot had been on the other foot we would have relished the opportunity of denting their League Championship ambitions. Leeds United and Liverpool enjoyed a tremendous rivalry at this time and several of their players were making their competitive intentions abundantly clear. With fifteen minutes gone Norman Hunter reacquainted himself with my left ankle and initially I thought I might have to leave the field. But after some treatment I continued and managed to run off the stiffness.

I had first encountered Norman playing for Hibs in the Fairs Cup a few years earlier and 'Bites Yer Legs', as Norman was known, would always introduce himself with a crunching tackle.

It was an evenly-matched game and we went in level at half-time. Shanks was the calmest person in the dressing room at the interval and he told us to keep our discipline at the back, be patient and a goal would eventually come. Fortunately he didn't have long to wait. Two minutes into the second half I opened the scoring and that settled us and got the fans right behind us. It may not have been the best goal I scored out of the twenty-six I got for Liverpool in my four years at Anfield but it was the most satisfying as it set us on our way to clinching the League Championship. In saying that, there was a lot of sharp inter-passing before I latched onto the ball in the penalty box and fired a half volley beyond David Harvey in the Leeds goal.

I immediately headed for the fans behind Harvey's goal to celebrate and was quickly joined by ecstatic team-mates. There was no way back for Leeds after that and Kevin Keegan put the icing on our Championship cake with a second goal five minutes from the end of the match.

After the final whistle we were told that Arsenal had only managed to draw their match which made it virtually mathe-matically impossible for them to win the league. We celebrated with the fans after the Arsenal result came through and I have never enjoyed a celebratory bottle of beer as much in my life. However, that was as good as the festivities got that evening.

Whilst League Championship success was guaranteed we were playing the semi-final second leg of the UEFA Cup against Spurs at White Hart Lane two nights later. I might have managed to

Childhood holidays were a great chance to practice my football skills!

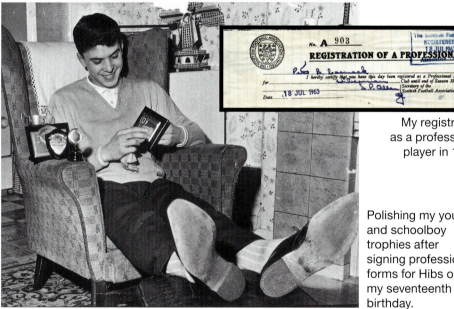

My registration as a professional player in 1963.

Polishing my youth and schoolboy trophies after signing professional forms for Hibs on my seventeenth birthday.

Mattie Chalmers driving the tractor around Tynecastle several years before I crashed it into the perimeter wall and walking out on Hearts.

My greatest game at Hibs. Opening the scoring against Real Madrid on 7 October 1964.

Admiring my Man of the Match award and Real Madrid watch with Hibs manager Jock Stein.

'Cormack the Cat' – my first of two clean-sheet stints in goal was against St Mirren after Willie Wilson got injured.

The Peter Cormack Fan Club President, Mary Weston, tries out one of the 'Peter the Great' ties. Does anyone still have one of these?

PETER CORMACK FAN CLUB

THIS TIE IS A WINNER

IT'S THE LATEST LINE in club ties for the Peter Cormack fan club. Hibs' 20-year-old forward is the only player with an official fan club, and now a tie is going on sale with his picture on it. Even George Best does not have that!

Admiring the tie are, left to right: Mary Weston, club president; Kathy Duncan, treasurer; and Ann Ramage, who is the editor of the club's monthly magazine.

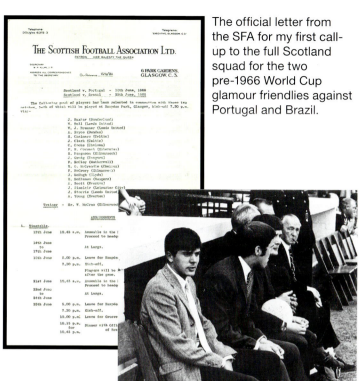

The official letter from the SFA for my first call-up to the full Scotland squad for the two pre-1966 World Cup glamour friendlies against Portugal and Brazil.

Returning from Hibs' 1965 North American Tour where I bought my first portable hi-fi.

Torn ankle ligaments kept me sidelined for four weeks at the start of my final season at Hibs.

I get a close-up view of Stevie Chalmers opening the scoring against Brazil on my Scotland debut in June 1966.

My biggest match in 1970 was getting married to Marion at St Bernards Church in Edinburgh.

Posing for the cameras after signing for Nottingham Forest in March 1970.

My dream first season at Anfield. Here Chris Lawler and I show off the First Division Championship trophy to the best football fans in England on the Kop.

I enjoy a celebratory bottle of beer whilst Ronnie Moran straps my injured ankle after we clinched the title by beating Leeds 2–0 at Anfield.

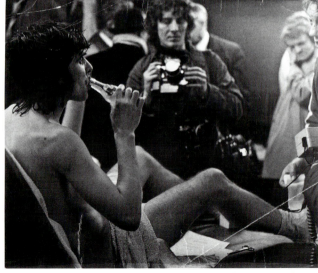

My best mate at Liverpool Kevin Keegan and I celebrate on the Wembley pitch after we destroyed ~~Liverpool~~ to lift the FA Cup in 1974.

Newcastle?

Four weeks after his shock resignation, Shanks led out his Liverpool for the last time alongside 'Cloughie' in the charity shield at Wembley.

I put one in the net for Liverpool as Tottenham Hotspur's goalkeeper can only lie on the ground and watch.

I was at the front of the queue
of players and fans that
welcomed George Best back
to Easter Road after I returned
to Hibs in February 1980.

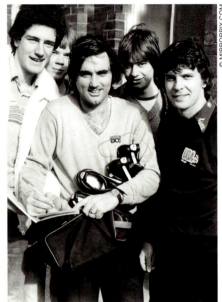

Celebrating with the Bristol
City players after our Anglo
Scottish Cup success against
Alex Ferguson's St Mirren.

My only Scotland appearance against the 'auld enemy' at Wembley in
1971 ended in a 3–1 defeat. Here the legendary Gordon Banks plucks
across out of the air as I am about to pounce.

I'm showing the Anorthosis players the exercise routine I want them to do with my Cypriot coach Demi.

I loved my four seasons coaching some very good players at Hibs in the late 1980's.

I line up with the Botswana squad before the independence centenary game against Malawi in September 1986.

Sitting proudly with the Partick Thistle squad at the start of my first full season in charge at Firhill in 1981.

Marion, Donna Lee, wee Pete and I frequently enjoyed our trips to the local Southport sand dunes during my time at Liverpool.

One of several 'Cormack Creations' I designed when I turned my artistic skills to clothes designing. I just can't believe the polka boots never took off.

My second season at Anfield was transformed when I took possession of the number five shirt after shaving off the 'tache.

Kevin Keegan and I enjoyed a healthy rivalry in the fashion stakes and here we acknowledge the Liverpool fans on one of our many European adventures.

stay on the park after Norman's crunching tackle but my ankle ballooned after the match ruling me out of the game against Spurs. For once Shanks broke his own 'cold shoulder' policy and spoke to me before the team left Anfield for the semi-final in London.

'Peter son, you just make sure you get yourself fit for the final. We will need our best eleven on the park. Now that we've won the league I want Liverpool to be the first English club to do the double of League Championship and European silverware in the same season.'

I wasn't aware that hadn't been done previously and in the lead up to the final Shanks kept using it as a tool to motivate the players. In truth, the team was already motivated as Bill Shankly had moulded a squad of players who had a collective professional pride and who would help each other out, off and on the park.

Not only were they great individual footballers, but each and every one of that squad worked their socks off in training and during a game. Somehow Liverpool were able to bottle that recipe, and it would be the formula for dominating English and European football for the next twenty years.

Over the years many people have asked me what was the secret to Liverpool's success during the 1960s, 70s and 80s. It's quite simple, really, and can be answered in two words – Bill Shankly. I regret that only four of my eighteen playing years were at Anfield. These four years were the most successful period of my football career and they were also the happiest. That wasn't just down to the two League Championships, two UEFA Cups and the FA Cup winner's medal I won playing for Liverpool. Shanks created a legacy with his simplicity of approach to everything at Liverpool that made it very difficult for his successors to fail. Three of Shanks' backroom staff from the Boot Room at

Anfield went on to manage the club and they were successful because they followed his tried and tested strategy.

The team I was fortunate to grace in 1972 also had a great balance of youth and experience and we developed a tremendous counter-attacking strategy that time and time again would catch teams cold. It became second nature for all the outfield players to go looking for a quick throw from Ray Clemence as soon as he caught the ball to set up a counter attack. That was when teams were at their most vulnerable and we exploited it to the full over and over again. The beauty of Shanks' football philosophy was its simplicity. Every Liverpool player was comfortable on the ball and our 'passing and movement' strategy became second nature to us. Honed on the training ground at Melwood we then carried that into matches with Shanks' mantra ringing in our ears, 'If the opposing players don't have the ball they can't hurt you.'

Often in media interviews Shanks would modestly say, 'There is no secret to success in football. You just have to work hard and eliminate the mistakes. The team that makes the least mistakes will win the football match.'

But everyone at Anfield knew the real reason for the club's success was Bill Shankly's burning ambition to make Liverpool Football Club the best team in the world. Others can argue whether he succeeded in that or not, I just know that he was without doubt the best football manger I ever played under and my life and football career would have been a lot poorer for not knowing him.

9

UP FOR THE FA CUP

The 1973/74 season saw two firsts for me. The first of the firsts came when I played in the FA Cup Final and as things would turn out, it would be my only Cup Final appearance in England. The game against Newcastle saw me back at Wembley three years after I had played at the famous Twin Towers in a Home International match for Scotland. My one and only appearance against England had not been enjoyable or memorable and afterwards I vowed that the next time I stepped on the hallowed Wembley turf it would be a much happier experience. The second first saw me take over the number five jersey at Liverpool. No, Bill Shankly had not taken leave of his senses thinking that I was the ideal replacement for our centre half Larry Lloyd after he got himself injured! I may have been used in various positions during my career but one role I never fancied was centre half.

Many football fans over the years have come up to me and offered their opinion as to why, for the remainder of my career in the Liverpool first team, I wore the number five jersey. Some have suggested that it was my lucky number – sorry, wrong. Many wondered if maybe on one of the first occasions I wore five on my back we thumped the opposition and I played a blinder. So with footballers being the superstitious creatures that they are, maybe I decided to stick with it. I was going to say – nope, wrong again, but then I checked our results after I first wore the number five shirt against Coventry at Anfield on 5

February 1974. We did win that match 2–1 thanks to goals from Alec Lindsay and Kevin Keegan, and we then went on an eleven-match unbeaten run but that was not the reason I continued wearing number five on my back. The most common view expressed by curious fans over the years is that Shanks being Shanks, he started trying to confuse our opposition by switching the numbers we all wore on our shirts. Now, whilst I'm sure he might well have worked that flanker in some big matches it was not the reason. Anyway, Kevin Keegan wore the number seven shirt for the duration of his career at Anfield and if we wanted to disguise anyone it would have been Kevin, but the best disguise we could have given him was a haircut.

Ok I'll put you out of your misery – the reason I ended up with the number five shirt is really very simple: nobody else wanted to wear it. With Larry Lloyd out of the team injured, Phil Thompson had established himself in the centre of the back four and Emlyn Hughes was moved back from midfield and the two of them struck up a great central defensive partnership. So much so that when Larry did get himself fit he couldn't get back into the side and was eventually transferred to Coventry for £240,000 at the start of the next season. But whilst Thommo and Crazy Horse became fixtures in the heart of the Liverpool defence, neither of them wanted to wear the centre half's shirt. It got to the stage that Shanks was becoming demented with their stubbornness. One day at training Phil and Emlyn were arguing for the umpteenth time about the number five when Shanks erupted, 'Jesus Christ, if you two don't sort it out I'll drop both of you and put Larry and Smithy back in the team.'

I hadn't given it any thought before then and without thinking blurted out, 'Boss, if it means I'll get a game I'll wear the fucking number five jersey.'

A couple of days before I had been clicking my heels on the subs bench against Norwich City but went on and scored our only goal in a 1–0 victory. I don't know if I would have been in the starting eleven for the next game against Coventry but by solving the number five dilemma I was back in the first team and remained there for the rest of the season. Given that we went on to win the FA Cup perhaps the number five shirt was my and the team's lucky mascot that season.

After winning the First Division Championship the previous season I went into the new campaign full of confidence that we could repeat the feat. As well as hoping to win back-to-back league titles I had high expectations that we could go all the way in the European Cup. Whilst I was certain that Liverpool now had the players who could go on to bigger and better things in my second season at Anfield the guys who had seen it and done it all before cautioned me against getting too carried away. I can remember Tommy Smith saying to me one day at pre-season training, 'It can be a bit like a hangover, Peter lad.' I wasn't sure what Smithy meant and he went on to explain that in his view, given the number of games we had played in winning the league and UEFA Cup double and the emotional peaks and troughs involved, there was every chance that we might suffer a reaction at the start of the season. Shanks was also saying publicly that there would be a psychological impact for the players from the previous season's exertions but, to be honest, I thought they were both wrong. As things would turn out, however, they were absolutely spot-on.

One surprise Shanks sprung on us all in pre-season training, and particularly on Smithy, was that he made Emlyn Hughes captain. To be fair to Tommy, he never said anything in the dressing room against the decision and never once let his feelings show but it must have been a kick in the teeth. Bad enough losing the team captaincy, but Emlyn and Smithy never got on and that must have made it doubly painful for him, but like the great professional he was, he accepted the Boss's decision and just got on with it. I wasn't a great fan of Emlyn's either, and whilst I respected him as an exceptional footballer his people skills left a lot to be desired. I wasn't the only player at Liverpool that wasn't a member of the Emlyn Hughes fan club and neither were the fans at opposing team grounds. The regular chant away from home was 'Emlyn Hughes, you're a wanker, you're a wanker', and whilst Crazy Horse enjoyed the attention I think most of the Liverpool players smiled when they heard this and hummed along to the chant.

For what it was worth, I told Smithy that he was still the club captain as far as I was concerned, even though it was Emlyn who tossed the coin on match days.

The league season started well enough and I was wearing the number eight shirt in our opening match at home to Stoke City. We got off to a flyer when Steve Heighway opened the scoring in the sixth minute but we huffed and puffed for the rest of the game and it ended 1–0. In our next league match we lost by the same scoreline at Coventry and that inconsistency dogged us for the first half of the season. Whilst we struggled to find our form our biggest rivals Leeds United had no such problem and went on a twenty-nine game unbeaten run in the league.

During this time Shanks' reaction to Don Revie's side's blistering start and our indifferent form was to remind everyone that 'the league is a marathon not a sprint, and it's the team that lasts longest over the course of the season that wins the championship race'. I always laughed when he rolled out his 'marathon' comment as it reminded me of his Brendan Foster remark that he made on the first day I met him when I signed for Liverpool.

I never failed to be impressed by Shanks' positive outlook. Where others would sow doubt and dwell on the negative he always outflanked the doom-mongers and more often than not outfoxed the opposition managers.

My own form mirrored that of the team and as a consequence I was rested for the two European first-leg ties against Jeunesse d'Esch, the Luxembourg part-timers. In truth, I didn't mind missing out on both matches as the team struggled to overcome them, eventually going through 3–1 on aggregate. I didn't break my scoring duck that season until the week after the second leg match against Jeunesse when I scored our first goal in a 2–2 draw against West Ham at Upton Park in the League Cup. Unfortunately we lost the next two league matches, both 1–0, away at Southampton and league leaders Leeds. The defeat at Elland Road dropped us to seventh in the league table, eight points behind Leeds. Despite those two setbacks I retained my place in the team for our second round first leg European Cup tie away to Red Star Belgrade. Although we lost 2–1, I was sure Chris Lawler's away goal would be enough to ensure our place in the next round. Before the return leg we beat Sheffield United in the league and West Ham in the League Cup replay, and then I was on the subs' bench for a league trip to Highbury, where two goals in the last fifteen minutes from our new captain, Emlyn, and John Toshack gave us a good 2–0 victory over Arsenal.

I assumed Shanks had decided to rest me for the Arsenal game for the return match with Red Star the following Wednesday. Well I had to assume that, as it was the boss's policy never to discuss with a player why he left them out. If I had any criticism of Shanks it would be for not communicating with players that he was dropping from the side. Like his attitude to players that were injured, it was as if you were invisible when you were not picked for the team. As far as Shanks was concerned his priority was to put the best team on the park for Liverpool and it was definitely not his job to try and pacify or mollycoddle players that he had not picked. I saw this firsthand when Larry Lloyd was dropped from the team after Phil Thompson and Emlyn Hughes established such a good partnership in the centre of defence. After several frustrating months in the reserves, one morning at training Larry had a go at the boss for leaving him out. Shanks was initially taken aback, probably at the shock of someone having the audacity to question him.

'Look, if you want to get in the team I'm not stopping you. You are!' Shanks curtly responded, and a few months later Larry was transferred to Coventry City. I know Larry was unhappy to leave Liverpool after five very successful years, but as things would turn out his subsequent transfer to my old club Nottingham Forest would see him go on to even bigger and better things and he ended his career with League Championship and European Cup winner's medals.

In contrast to Larry's predicament, whilst I was dropped to the bench for the Arsenal match Tommy Smith wasn't even stripped after travelling to London with the squad. I knew this was a bitter pill for Smithy but he never put his personal feelings before the interests of Liverpool Football Club. After the match all the media interest surrounded Smithy's absence but his reaction to the omission was to say nothing publicly and redouble his efforts to get back into the team. Knowing Smithy as I do, I have no doubt words would have been exchanged in the privacy of the manager's office but that was where it was left between Shanks and him.

Neither Tommy nor I were back in the starting line-up four days later for the return European Cup tie against Red Star Belgrade. We watched from the bench as Red Star totally outplayed Liverpool to win the match 2–1 and go through 4–2 on aggregate.

The Yugoslavian side might have been regarded by many as one of Europe's lesser lights but they were a very good side that played fast, attractive and attacking football. Going out in the second round of the European Cup was a bitter disappointment to everyone at Anfield but I think Bob Paisley and Joe Fagan learned a great deal from that game that would stand them in good stead in future European ventures. The following Saturday I returned to the team in the number eight shirt for a home match against Wolves, which we won 1–0 courtesy of a first-half Steve Heighway strike.

That victory set us on an unbeaten five-month run at Anfield and we only lost one match in the league before Christmas, away at Burnley. I celebrated my return to the team by regularly getting on the scoresheet. I scored one of our four goals in a 4–2 win over Bobby Robson's Ipswich Town the week after the Wolves match. I then scored our only goal in a 1–0 league victory over West Ham at Anfield on 1 December and followed that up a few weeks later scoring in a 1–1 draw with Norwich City at Carrow Road. During December we beat our Merseyside rivals Everton 1–0 at Goodison and the Saturday before Christmas defeated Manchester United 2–0 at Anfield with goals from Kevin Keegan and Steve Heighway. Whilst George Best was in the Man United starting line-up he was a shadow of the player he had been and seemed all out of sorts and disinterested in what was happening on the park. It didn't come as a surprise to me when a few weeks later he announced he was packing football in after flying off to Marbella in Spain. I could see Bestie's mind was not on the game and he was virtually anonymous for the entire ninety minutes. For the second year running, in the final game of the year, I notched our only goal in a 1–0 away win over Chelsea at Stamford Bridge. That goal was an interesting role reversal as I scored with a header from a John Toshack cross. Usually it was Tosh

157

who got on the end of crosses in the opposition's box. Our good run of form coincided with Tommy Smith's return to the team. Unfortunately Chris Lawler was having cartilage problems that required surgery and Smithy was drafted in at right back. Tommy was determined to prove a point and he ended up making the right back position his own for the remainder of his career at Anfield.

Following the defeat to Burnley on Boxing Day we trailed league leaders Leeds by nine points but whilst we went on a twelve-game unbeaten run, Leeds started to falter. Their twenty-nine-game unbeaten run ended at Stoke City at the end of February but at the time they were still eight points ahead of us.

On 16 March we beat Leeds 1–0 in a pulsating top-of-the-table clash at Anfield to reduce the gap to four points. We had Steve Heighway to thank for a match-winning goal with less than ten minutes left on the clock. Whilst we were playing out a goalless FA Cup semi-final against Leicester City on 30 March Leeds were losing at West Ham in the league which left us four points behind them with three games in hand.

I was convinced Leeds had blown it, and although we faced nine games in April to Leeds's six, I was sure that the momentum had now swung in Liverpool's favour. Our first hurdle was Queens Park Rangers at Anfield and we overcame them 2–1 but the following week we lost our first match in five months away to Sheffield United at Bramall Lane. We then drew our next two matches, both 1–1, at Manchester City and Ipswich but returned to top form handing out a 4–0 thrashing to Manchester City at Anfield. But our League Championship fate was sealed in the next two home games when we could only draw 0–0 with Everton and lost 1–0 to Arsenal. The Arsenal result was doubly disappointing, for as well confirming Leeds United as First Division

Champions it was also our only defeat in the league at Anfield that season. Our form during the second half of the season had pushed Leeds all the way but to use Bill Shankly's marathon analogy, Leeds had enough stamina to carry them through to the finishing line in the Championship race. We were down but not downhearted as our second half of the season run had taken us to the FA Cup Final. Finishing the season with a Cup Final appearance at Wembley had been one of my burning ambitions after moving to England four years earlier and I was determined to end my second season at Liverpool on another high.

Walking out at Wembley for an FA Cup Final may have been a first for me and several other team-mates but it was not the first time Bill Shankly proudly led out a Liverpool team for English football's end of season climax. Shanks' Liverpool had been to Wembley twice before, winning the FA Cup against Leeds in 1965 and losing after extra-time against Arsenal in 1971. The year 1965 was the first time Liverpool had won the FA Cup in their ninety-plus-year history. I didn't know much about the '65 final but that was more than made up by Tommy Smith and Ian Callaghan who loved to talk through their memories of the match to while away long boring coach journeys. From what both of them said it had been a great occasion and although it was some nine years and hundreds of games ago they could both recollect even the smallest detail of the day. The Liverpool versus Arsenal final occurred in my first season in English football and I watched the match at home on television with Marion. It had not been the most memorable of ninety minutes but the game burst into life at the start of extra-time when Stevie Heighway scored from the bye line, beating Arsenal and Scotland goalie Bob Wilson on his near post. Unfortunately for Liverpool, Arsenal equalised a short time later through another Scottish international, George Graham, and in the second half of extra-time Charlie George beat Clem with a tremendous shot from outside the box. It was one of the most memorable Cup Final-winning goals and TV coverage of Charlie lying flat on his back with his arms and legs outstretched is still shown to this day.

Shanks and several of the players who played in the Arsenal match were desperate to get back to Wembley and walk up the famous thirty-nine steps as Cup winners. When the third-round draw paired us with Doncaster Rovers, everyone at Anfield was confident that the home draw would ensure a comfortable passage to the fourth round. Liverpool players were never disrespectful to their opponents and there was no way Shanks would have allowed complacency to creep in, but no one expected Doncaster to give us much trouble. I mean you only had to look at the statistics – Liverpool were the reigning First Division League Champions and starting to put a decent run of results together after a poor start to the league campaign, whereas Doncaster Rovers were languishing some eighty-five places below us in the bottom half of the English Fourth Division. But as everyone knows, league form goes out of the window in the FA Cup and many a big club Charlie has been humbled by lower league opposition over the years. That's what is called 'the magic of the Cup'. Magic if you are the minnow taking the big team scalp, a nightmare if you play for or support the 'giant' who has just been slain.

To say defeat never entered my head as I trotted onto the park with my Liverpool team-mates on 5 January 1974 would be an understatement, but by half-time, if not a reality, defeat by Doncaster was certainly very possible. The Doncaster players had set about us from the kick-off and their quick tackling stopped us playing with any fluidity. It didn't help us that Tommy Smith was out due to injury, as I am sure Smithy would not have allowed the Doncaster players to intimidate us in the manner that they did. The accuracy of the BBC Grandstand teleprinter, that for years relayed the football results on a Saturday afternoon, must have been doubted in many households up and down the country when it showed Doncaster leading 2–1 at Anfield after the first forty-five minutes. But it wasn't a printing error. Rovers were leading at half-time in the FA Cup and Shanks made it clear in the interval that if we didn't shake ourselves from our lethargy we would be on the end of one of the biggest upsets in FA Cup history. 'I can assure you, lads, that is one bit of English football history I don't want Liverpool Football Club associated with,' he told us in no uncertain terms in the half-time teamtalk.

He also did say that our full-time training should stand us in good stead in the second half and if we played with our heads, making the Doncaster players chase the ball, they would tire as the second half wore on.

Not for the first time Shanks was proved correct but whilst the Doncaster players did run out of steam we could only manage to score one goal from Kevin Keegan that saved us from a very humiliating defeat. The 2–2 draw meant a replay four days later at Doncaster's Belle Vue stadium which was packed to overflowing with 25,000 fans. However, everyone at Anfield was ready for the return match and we were all determined to make amends for the Saturday performance. Steve Heighway settled early nerves and silenced the vociferous Rovers fans when he opened the scoring after fifteen minutes and I added to the scoresheet with a second goal thirty minutes from full-time. Job done, 2–0, and we looked forward to the next round. In the fourth round we were drawn at home again, this time to Second Division Carlisle United. After the 'brown trousered' scare we got in the previous round nobody at Anfield was taking Carlisle lightly and whilst our performance was much improved Carlisle battled and fought their way to a 0–0 draw. In truth I came off the park at the end wondering how we never managed to score but the Carlisle keeper Alan Ross must have had the best match of his career that day and the Kop gave him a standing ovation at the end of the match. That was one of the things I loved about the Liverpool supporters. They appreciated football ability first and foremost even if it was to the detriment of their team.

I picked up an injury in the first match and failed a fitness test to play in the replay. The Kopites might have been generous in their praise of the Carlisle players and their keeper in particular but before the replay I sat in the dressing room listening to Shanks telling the Liverpool players that their generosity ended on the Saturday and that they were to show no mercy at Brunton Park. That was easier said than done given the full-to-capacity stadium and icy pitch which made playing football very difficult. In the end the Liverpool players, inspired by Tommy Smith, just rolled up their sleeves and got stuck in, winning 2–0, with goals from my replacement, Phil Boersma and Tosh. I still wasn't 100 per cent fit for the league match the following Saturday and was on the bench for the game at Anfield against Norwich City.

After coming on at the start of the second half I managed to score the only goal of the game in sixty-three minutes to secure another two important league points. By the time of the fifth round FA Cup tie against Ipswich at Anfield on 16 February I had secured my place back in the team with the newly-acquired number five jersey on my back. I was relieved the draw had paired us with tough First Division opponents as there was no way anyone at Anfield would be in any doubt that we would have to be at our very best to beat Bobby Robson's Ipswich to qualify for the quarter-final. Another home draw was a big advantage, as was the fact that Ipswich liked to play open attractive football which suited our quick counter-attacking style. Two goals in either half gave us another 2–0 victory and afterwards Shanks said that the 'performance and result would prove to be a turning point in our season'. Once again he was not wrong.

The quarter-final draw gave us an away tie at Second Division Bristol City who had produced the shock of the fifth round when they drew with league leaders Leeds United and then beat them in a replay. Shanks didn't need to warn us of complacency after that result, and we managed to overcome City at the first time of asking when a goal from Tosh early in the second half secured a 1–0 win. Up until then I had pushed to the back of my mind any thoughts about going all the way to Wembley. I had learned over the years not to get too far ahead of myself as football has a habit of reality bringing you crashing back down to earth with a thud. I had suffered several semi-final disappointments at Hibs and one Scottish League Cup Final appearance that I'd rather have forgotten but the prospect of an FA Cup semi-final against Leicester City meant that I was one game away from achieving one of my boyhood ambitions of playing in an FA Cup Final at Wembley.

I know it might seem strange to many people for a boy brought up in Leith to dream about playing in the English Cup final, but Wembley had a special magic all of its own – especially since live television coverage had propelled it into one of Britain's biggest sporting spectacles of the year. It was up there alongside The Grand National, The Open Golf Championship and Wimbledon. Playing in the FA Cup Final was unquestionably top of the 'to do' list of every professional footballer and before the game against Leicester at Old Trafford I was starting to dream of getting to the Cup final.

*

The weekend before the semi-final the *Sunday People* published an article by Leicester City striker Frank Worthington under the headline 'You'll be sorry Shanks'. Frank clearly still had a big chip on his shoulder for Shanks not signing him two years earlier after he twice failed his medical after Huddersfield Town agreed to sell him to Liverpool for £150,000. Frank's misfortune led to my salvation and whilst Shanks never mentioned Frank's *Sunday People* utterings in the run-up to the semi-final the Liverpool players were determined that we would make sure he would eat his words.

Over the years there have been very few great Cup semi-final games and our match against Leicester proved to be no different. This is mostly put down to the fear of losing at the penultimate stage of the competition and I could relate to that after my experience at Hibs. We dominated the first semi-final against Leicester but England's goalkeeper Peter Shilton was in inspired form and for the second time in the competition that season the opposition goalie prevented us winning the tie at the first time of asking. The only positive was that Phil Thompson made sure Frank Worthington never got a sniff of the penalty box in the ninety minutes and the only person 'kicking himself' after the match was Frank for opening his big mouth to the papers the week before.

Whilst we were playing out a scoreless draw Newcastle were waiting in the final after disposing of Burnley in their semi-final match. Before the replay Shanks told us in the Villa Park dressing room that if we put in the same performance as we did in the first game we would win and that is exactly how it turned out.

We again took the game to Leicester and opened the scoring through Brian Hall. But just when we thought that we were on our way to Wembley we had to start all over again after Leicester equalised. Even when Leicester did score, thankfully it wasn't Frank Worthington that did the damage but fellow forward Keith Weller. Our response to the setback spoke volumes about the character of our team and we went on to perform at the highest level, earning plaudits that it was one of the finest semi-final displays for many a year in the FA Cup. John Toshack created a goal for Kevin Keegan, which he took brilliantly with a controlled half volley from the edge of the box to put us 2–1 ahead. Then with Leicester chasing the game I slipped the ball to Tosh and he put the game beyond doubt with a third goal near full-time. I have to admit that I had never felt so elated at the end of a football match. The fact that it had been such an exhilarating performance to get to the FA Cup Final probably added to my excitement but it was just a great feeling to know that 'Wembley here we come'.

The build-up to the Cup Final was a fantastic experience and the outcome was even better than I had dreamed as a youngster growing up in Leith. The Liverpool squad travelled down to London a few days before the final and stayed at The Seldon Park Hotel on the outskirts of the city. I was sharing a room with Kevin Keegan, as we did when we played abroad, and a couple of days before the final Kevin injured his back in a five-a-side match at the end of the training session.

Ironically, Kevin was injured in a clash with the manager, after Shanks' knee collided with his back when they went for a fifty/fifty ball. It might have been a couple of days before a Wembley final but it didn't dampen Shanks' exuberance in the five-a-sides. On the eve of the match Kevin was still struggling to breathe properly and asked me if I thought he should tell the boss. My view was that he should wait until the last minute rather than worry Shanks and added, 'He's got enough on his plate contemplating his team selection and coping with all the media demands. A good night's sleep and you'll be fine in the morning,' I said to try and put his mind at rest.

In any event, Shanks was indeed up to his eyes. On the eve of the match, the BBC arranged a live link to both teams' hotels where Jimmy Hill interviewed the managers live on TV. Shanks was a natural in front of the cameras; however, the Newcastle manager Joe Harvey was anything but, and Joe sat shifting uncomfortably in his seat for the duration of the interview. Shanks put in a masterful performance talking up the Newcastle team, complimenting their players and deflecting as much pressure as he could of his own men. But he left his 'coup de grace' until the very end of the broadcast. Just as Jimmy Hill was thanking both managers for their comments Shanks pulled off his head-phones and turned around to someone out of camera shot, saying, 'Jesus Christ, Joe's a bag of nerves.'

The Liverpool players watching the live broadcast in the hotel lounge burst out laughing at his comment. It was another example of Shanks' managerial genius. His apparent off-the-cuff remark had boosted the Liverpool squad's morale and very likely sowed seeds of doubt in the Newcastle camp. For us, it was like being given a goal start before a ball had been kicked. What he said on TV to Jimmy Hill was the exact opposite of what he had been telling us in the run-up to the match, and the Liverpool players sat transfixed, listening to him talk up the opposition, fully engrossed watching the master at work.

The Liverpool players also knew that what Shanks was saying in the interview was all part of the mind games he loved to indulge in with the opposition.

A few hours before at our final training session, Shanks had pinned up newspaper cuttings of Newcastle players mouthing off to the world at large what they were going to do to Liverpool in the final. Their centre forward, Malcolm MacDonald, was the worst offender, appearing in nearly every newspaper and on TV, saying how he would run rings around Phil Thompson and Emlyn Hughes. He clearly never learned any lessons from Frank Worthington's mistake prior to the semi-final.

'SuperMac' became 'Supergob' and Shanks' response the day before the final was to use the boasts of the Newcastle players to his and Liverpool's advantage.

'There you are, lads. I don't need to say anymore – it's all been said by the Newcastle players,' was Shanks' only comment as he pinned the press cuttings up in the hotel before our usual Friday get-together. If playing in an FA Cup Final was not motivation enough, the Newcastle players' public utterances of what they were going to do to us at Wembley were added incentives for all the Liverpool players.

I remember Tommy Smith being particularly wound up. Smithy had established himself at right back and Newcastle's nineteen-year-old left back Alan Kennedy was quoted in the press saying that Tommy was 'past it'. Come three o'clock on Saturday 4 May 1974, Tommy Smith and the rest of the Liverpool players on the Wembley pitch were determined to ram the Newcastle players' boasts down their throats.

On the Saturday morning I got up at my normal time and Kevin was already awake and out of bed doing stretching exercises on his dodgy back. His prognosis was that he was fit and raring to go, and I too felt rested and was looking forward to my first Wembley Cup Final appearance. After my usual light, late breakfast (I think I had scrambled eggs on toast) I joined the rest of the players for a mid-morning stroll, partly to stretch our legs but mostly to kill time. Marion and the other players' wives and girlfriends had travelled down to London on the Friday afternoon and I telephoned her at the Waldorf Hotel. She was heavily pregnant by this time with our second child but she was well, in good spirits and more nervous than me about the match.

Earlier in the week all the players in the Cup Final squad were kitted out with a new grey suit, white shirt and club tie for Wembley. We were also gifted a choice of casual suit for the Sunday and I picked a trendy bold pinstripe number. I was fortunate that I never suffered from pre-match nerves but the adrenalin started to kick in when we boarded the team bus for the drive to Wembley. The closer we got to the stadium the more red-and-white and black-and-white decked out fans we encountered, and it was great to see the fans of both sides mixing together on their way to the match. I was amazed at the numbers of fans that were already in Wembley when we walked onto the park to inspect the pitch. It looked as if more than half the 100,000 capacity had come early to enjoy the pre-match entertainment, which included a long-distance race won by one of the northeast's favourite sons, my old pal Brendan Foster. 'That will be the only thing the Geordies will win today,' Shanks said as we started to get changed for the match.

Shanks' pre-match teamtalk was brief and to the point. In goal, Clem was to try and feed the two full backs early and their job was to get up and down the wing. Emlyn and Phil were to shackle the two Newcastle front men, John Tudor and 'SuperMac'. They were relishing the task after reading all week what the two of them said they were going to do to Liverpool's 'inexperienced' central defenders. Ian Callaghan's, Brian Hall's and my job was simple. First and foremost Liverpool's midfield trio were to win the midfield battle. Shanks saved his pièce de résistance for Kevin Keegan. 'Kevin, I want you to drop hand grenades all over their back line.' Everyone knew what the boss expected of Kevin and the wee man did not disappoint.

*

After we lined up alongside our opponents in the massive Wembley tunnel the walk onto the pitch was even more exciting than I had ever imagined. The noise was deafening and the mass of colour produced by the fans of both sides was spectacular. Shanks marched in front of the twelve Liverpool players and looked like a proud father escorting his daughter down the aisle on her wedding day. One thing was certain: None of the Liverpool players entertained the notion that they were going to end up as the Cup Final bridesmaids. Both teams and the officials lined up to meet the dignitaries led by Princess Anne, who was very friendly and relaxed. I had endured this ritual on my international appearances for Scotland and on these occasions you are just itching for the battle to commence.

The first forty-five minutes passed in a blur. Both sides were trying hard to control the midfield and all the Liverpool players were working their socks off supporting each other, but whilst we had the upper hand we were unable to create any meaningful chances. The Newcastle front two had not had a kick of the ball, mainly due to the lack of service from their midfield, but their back four had not yet been fully tested.

At half-time Shanks was the calmest person in our dressing room and told us that Newcastle could not keep that work rate up in the second half and for us to be patient and the goals would come. Early in the second half I thought the breakthrough had come when our left back, Alec Lindsay, fired in a screamer. But our ecstasy was short-lived when the referee disallowed the goal for offside. I have watched re-runs of this on countless occasions and I am still at a loss as to why Alec's goal was chalked off.

Undeterred, we continued to outplay Newcastle and started to totally outrun them in midfield. Our two full backs, Smithy and Alec, were pushing further and further forward and it was from a cross from Tommy that we opened the scoring. The ball from Smithy found Kevin Keegan on the edge of the box and almost in one movement Kevin killed the pass and fired it beyond Iam McFaul in the Newcastle goal. I was one of the first to jump on Kevin and after celebrating the goal, I could see the confidence and hope drain away from the Newcastle players.

A second goal wasn't long in coming and Steve Heighway doubled our lead. After that we totally dominated the game and where the Liverpool players had an abundance of energy, the Newcastle lads were tired and laboured. I loved every minute of it and near the end we scored a magnificent third goal following a flowing eleven-pass move. It was right up there with Brazil's fourth goal in the 1970 World Cup Final. As we knocked the ball about to run down the clock, Kevin Keegan switched play from the left with a long crossfield pass. Tommy Smith played it first time with the outside of his foot and took the return pass from Steve Heighway. Smithy then skinned Alan Kennedy and cut the ball back from the bye-line for Kevin at the back post to slide the ball home. It was the icing on the cake of a magnificent second half performance. As we celebrated the goal the BBC match commentator David Coleman said, 'Newcastle were undressed. They were absolutely stripped naked.'

Climbing the Wembley steps to the Royal Box to collect my FA Cup winner's medal from Princess Anne and getting to lift that famous trophy was a fantastic experience and one that I will savour for the rest of my life.

Mentally I had prepared myself for the experience of playing football at the highest level and Wembley 1974 did not disappoint. What I hadn't prepared myself for was the reaction of the Liverpool fans to our Cup Final success. It was great meeting up with Marion and the other players' wives and girlfriends at the Waldorf Hotel on the Saturday evening where the club had organised a post-match celebratory party – or 'banquet' as they liked to call it. The highlight of that was a live TV interview that Shanks conducted with Jimmy Hill for *Match of the Day*. Shanks was in the middle of the players – the king surrounded by his courtiers. He was in imperious form with some lively banter from the merry players to supplement Shanks' natural charm and wit.

The following day a large Liverpool contingent of players, management, directors and their partners left London on a mid-morning train that arrived at Allerton Station just after two-thirty in the afternoon. The champagne was flowing on the journey north and the closer we got to Liverpool the more fans that appeared in stations and on bridges to try and catch a glimpse of the Cup. It was great to be climbing the steps of an open-topped bus for the second year in succession to parade silverware in front of Liverpool's loyal fans. The police estimated that over one million people turned out, four times the number from the previous year, which shows how important a part the FA Cup has in the hearts and minds of English football supporters. I recall seeing one female in the Old Swan area lifting her skirt to reveal a red pair of knickers embroidered with the Liverpool club badge, and in Kirkdale a local Orange Lodge band belted out 'You'll Never Walk Alone'. I don't think that was a regular part of their weekend repertoire but it went down a storm with players and fans alike. The victory tour ended at Picton Library where the players and Shanks climbed onto the sanctuary of a makeshift stage.

All the players received an ecstatic cheer when they were introduced to the crowd with the Cup, but the loudest cheer of all was rightly reserved for Bill Shankly. One banner proclaimed 'Shanks for Prime Minister' and he milked the audience like the experienced orator that he was.

'We have had many proud moments at Liverpool, but today I am prouder than I have ever been before,' he said to rapturous applause.

Nobody present on that euphoric and emotional afternoon on Sunday 5 May could have guessed that Bill Shankly's next public pronouncement just over two months later would be the announcement of him retiring as manager of Liverpool Football Club.

Before that, I was shocked to get called into the Scotland squad heading off to West Germany for the finals of the 1974 World Cup. My performance for Liverpool at Wembley had won me a surprise recall after three years in the international wilderness at the expense of Newcastle inside forward Jimmy Smith. I had just achieved one boyhood ambition by playing on the winning side in an FA Cup Final and I was now on the verge of playing for Scotland in a World Cup Final tournament. It would mean not being around for the birth of our second child, but Marion was adamant that I should go to the World Cup. She was aware how much it meant to me, but if I knew how things were going to work out in Germany I would have stayed at home and watched the Scotland matches from the comfort of my front room and been there when my son Peter was born. Still, the disappointment of not playing for Scotland in West Germany when I was at the peak of my game did not knock my confidence or dampen my enthusiasm to build on two fantastic years at Liverpool as I looked forward to the new season. But Shanks' decision to retire came as a bolt from the blue to Liverpool players and fans and sent shock waves throughout the football world.

Once again a football father figure I had grown to know and love was deserting me, but unlike when Jock Stein left Hibs for Celtic when I was eighteen years of age, I was now an experienced football professional who had encountered enough ups and downs in his career to know that no matter who replaced the great man, my football future lay in my own hands.

When Bob Paisley was handed the reigns at Anfield I was sure that he was the right man for the job but Bob went on to exceed my expectations, and if truth be told, he would have probably been the first to agree.

10

ON THE MARCH IN EUROPE

Whilst Hibs were in the vanguard of British clubs' participation in Europe, Liverpool's first taste of competitive European football came after First Division title success in 1964.

Like Hibs, Liverpool reached the semi-final of their very first European Cup adventure but lost in controversial circumstances to Inter Milan. Easter Road may have borne the physical scars of the 1961 Fairs Cup encounter with Barcelona but Shanks carried around the mental scars of that first European Cup experience.

Shanks was not the only one who still harboured a grudge about the manner of Liverpool's exit at the penultimate stage of Europe's biggest club competition in 1965. Tommy Smith, Ian Callaghan and Chris Lawler played in both matches and every so often they would regale team-mates with events of the second leg match in Milan.

In the first leg at Anfield, Liverpool claimed a two-goal lead after winning 3–1 on the night. But even that result could have been better as Chris Lawler had a legitimate goal chalked off and Ian St John hit the woodwork late on in the game. Tommy Smith in particular recalled the hostile atmosphere from 90,000 excitable and noisy Italians in the San Siro stadium in the second leg. Smithy was adamant that the Spanish referee had been got at by the Italian club. 'Bent as a five-bob note,' was how Tommy would always describe the referee and even Shanks, who very rarely criticised match officials, was convinced that the referee had been bribed. Inter won the match 3–0 with the first goal, early in the match, being scored direct from a free-kick that the referee had signalled was indirect. The second goal shortly after was scored after a forward knocked the ball out of keeper Tommy Lawrence's hands and fired it home. To rub more salt into Liverpool's wounds, Ian St John had a goal disallowed near the end of the match that would have taken the game into extra-time. At Hibs I had experienced firsthand some dodgy refereeing performances in Europe but Liverpool's experience in Italy in 1965 put those in the shade. There was such an outcry following the match in Milan that UEFA conducted an enquiry into the referee's performance, but surprise, surprise, no evidence of wrongdoing was found and the result stood.

The following season 1965/66, Liverpool qualified for the European Cup Winners' Cup as FA Cup holders and after disposing of continental opposition in the earlier rounds were drawn to play Celtic in the semi-final. I well remember the excitement the tie generated on both sides of the border and this was the first of many subsequent England versus Scotland club European matches that were to be billed as a 'Battle of Britain'. There was an added incentive for both teams as that year's final was taking place at Hampden Park. It was also the first, and as things would turn out, only time that Bill Shankly and Jock Stein sat in opposing dugouts in a competitive match.

Once again the second leg of the semi-final was to end controversially. Celtic had won the first leg 1–0 at Parkhead with a goal from Bobby Lennox and tens of thousands of Celtic fans made the journey to Anfield for the deciding second game. Tommy Smith and Geoff Strong gave Liverpool a 2–0 lead. A few minutes from full-time Celtic's centre forward Joe McBride headed the ball down for Bobby Lennox to score, but the officials ruled it offside. When I played with Joe at Easter Road he often mentioned the 'good' goal that was disallowed at Anfield but Smithy's recollection of the incident had more to do with the reaction of the Celtic fans to this decision.

'They went fucking mental, Barr!' he told me. The Celtic fans were packed in the Anfield Road end and after the goal was disallowed they threw hundreds of bottles and beer cans towards the pitch, injuring many of their own fans in the process. The match was held up while the police tried to restore order and when play resumed the referee hardly played any stoppage time despite the hold-up. I had seen firsthand Celtic and Hibs fans hurling bottles and cans at each other in the Cowshed at Easter Road, so I had a good idea what the scene must have been like that night at Anfield. It was Celtic's turn to feel cheated about the semi-final outcome and Smithy, Ian Callaghan and Chris Lawler recalled Jock Stein going 'berserk' in the tunnel after the match. Big Jock was convinced it was Celtic's destiny to win the Cup Winners' Cup at Hampden that year and he was as bitter leaving Anfield as Bill Shankly had been heading home from Milan a year earlier. As it turned out, Liverpool lost their first European Final 2–1 after extra-time to a Borussia Dortmund side that contained four players who would go on to star for West Germany a few months later at the World Cup in England.

By 1973 Shanks had formed the view, with sound reasoning, that the UEFA Cup was the hardest of the three European trophies to win. Nowadays that is not the case, with the Europa League being a poor cousin to the Champions' League, but back then each country had one representative in the European Cup and the European Cup Winners' Cup respectively, whereas three or four top clubs from the European leagues qualified for the UEFA Cup, which had only recently changed its name from the Fairs Cup. Many people scoffed at Shanks when he said this, but I knew from my time at

Hibs just how right he was. During my eight years at Easter Road I had played against Valencia, Napoli, FC Porto, Leeds United and Hamburg. All excellent teams in their respective domestic leagues that were full of experienced internationalists.

Liverpool had not missed a season of European competition since qualifying for the European Cup after winning the league in 1964 and Shanks was convinced going into the 1972/73 season that he had a squad of players capable of winning Europe's toughest competition. Newcastle, Leeds United (twice), Arsenal and Tottenham Hotspur had previously lifted the trophy and Bill Shankly and his backroom staff in the Boot Room were convinced that Liverpool now had the right balance of youth and experience to go all the way in Europe.

When I signed in the summer of 1972 it hadn't crossed my mind that Liverpool had qualified for the UEFA Cup. In my two seasons at Nottingham Forest the only 'foreign games' I played were pre-season warm-up games in Europe and an unforgettable trip to Airdrie in deepest Lanarkshire for a Texaco Cup tie. Three days after my goalscoring home debut against Wolves I ran out at Anfield for a UEFA Cup first round first-leg tie against German club Eintracht Frankfurt, the side that had participated in that memorable European Cup Final with Real Madrid in 1960. A goal in either half from Kevin Keegan and Emlyn Hughes gave us a two-goal lead to take to Germany. Our tactics for the second leg were to defend in depth and try to catch Frankfurt out with quick counter attacks. Our rhythm and fluency was disrupted when Tommy Smith went off with a calf injury but we battled our way to achieve a satisfactory goalless draw. The second-round draw paired us with Greek side AEK Athens but fortunately the first-round tie was again at Anfield. I had established myself as first choice number eight by then and notched our second goal in twenty-eight minutes after Phil Boersma had given us an early lead. AEK never threatened in that first leg tie and Tommy Smith gave us a comfortable 3–0 lead to take to Athens when he scored a penalty ten minutes from time. Shanks and Bob Paisley warned us before we left for Greece that we would be in for a hot reception in more ways than one from the volatile AEK fans, but two goals from Crazy Horse and a late strike from Phil Boersma gave us a comfortable 6–1 aggregate victory.

Three weeks after our trip to Athens we faced a trip behind the Iron Curtain to play Dynamo Berlin. Unlike my previous trip to East Germany with Hibs, at least Liverpool were able to fly direct to Berlin, although the facilities at the hotel were still as spartan as I remembered from my previous visit. Another efficient hard-working performance enabled us to take a goalless draw back to Anfield. The return leg came at a good time for me four days after my sending-off at West Brom. I was determined to show my gratitude to Shanks, my team-mates and the Liverpool fans, and whilst I didn't get on the scoresheet I more than played my part in a comfortable 3–1 win. Phil Boersma continued his good goalscoring run in Europe, notching our opening goal in the first minute, and Steve Heighway doubled our lead midway through the first half. An early second half goal from Tosh secured a comfortable 3–1 win and a quarter-final tie against another East German side.

Dynamo Dresden were not only one of the best teams in East Germany they were one of the favourites to lift the UEFA Cup that season. When the first leg at Anfield came around I was unavailable, still recovering from the injury I sustained in the FA Cup replay at Manchester City. Brian Hall wore my number eight shirt, and 'Little Bamber' notched our first goal after twenty-five minutes. Phil Boersma notched his fourth goal in the competition after sixty minutes to double our lead. Despite our 2–0 first-leg victory nobody at Anfield was under any illusion that we would be in for a tough match in the return leg in Dresden. I made my comeback in the first team on the Saturday before the second leg tie away at Stoke City where Brian Hall's late goal gave us a vital 1–0 win.

When we arrived at our Dresden hotel the day prior to the match we were met by hundreds of noisy and intimidating locals. None of us were too keen at the prospect of a restless night and Shanks decided to take the bull by the horns. Armed with nothing more than a friendly smile and bagfuls of Liverpool goodies, Shanks breezed into the middle of the noisy crowd, handing out Liverpool lapel badges and signing autographs for the football-mad Germans. It was a fantastic piece of PR and took the heat out of what was a potentially difficult situation. What was initially a large hostile crowd eventually melted away to give us a peaceful evening prior to the match.

Shanks decided to put me in for Tosh with Brian Hall at inside right for the game in Dresden. After studying the Germans, Shanks felt that by filling the midfield we would make it very difficult for Dresden to play their normal fluid attacking game. The stadium was packed with 33,000 noisy Germans but Shanks' actions at the hotel had won Liverpool many friends and we put in our best European away performance, controlling the game throughout.

Less than ten minutes into the second half Kevin Keegan scored a precious away goal to put the tie out of Dresden's reach and we held out for a comfortable 3–0 aggregate victory. Following the match many of the British football journalists said that our performance in Dresden was one of Liverpool's best ever in Europe.

Our quarter-final win meant that we joined Spurs, Dutch side Twente Enschede and the crack West German outfit Borussia

Moenchengladbach in the semi-final draw. As luck would have it, the two English teams were the first names out of the hat with the first leg tie at Anfield. Spurs had knocked us out of the League Cup earlier in the season and we knew we were going to face two very hard matches against the North London club. We didn't do ourselves any favours when three days before the first match we lost 2–1 at Birmingham, our first defeat in two months. This was the week after our 1–1 draw at Anfield with Spurs, where Pat Jennings saved two penalty kicks. Shanks worked his magic in the pre-match talk before the semi-final first leg and all the players were fired up as we walked down the steps touching the 'This is Anfield' sign for luck. We went right at Spurs from the kick-off and left back Alec Lindsay scored in the seventeenth minute. Despite us dominating the match we could not get another goal, but on the plus side we hadn't conceded in the home tie and were confident that we could score at White Hart Lane. The return match was played two days after our League Championship winning match over Leeds where I had picked up an ankle injury, which ruled me out of the game in London.

England World Cup winner Martin Peters scored two first-half goals to give Spurs a 2–1 aggregate lead. At half-time Shanks fired up the players by telling them that they had the chance to make English football history as League Champions and European trophy winners and the players came out firing on all cylinders in the second half.

Ten minutes in, Steve Heighway scored after a great run and pass from Kevin Keegan and despite a final twenty-minute onslaught from Spurs, the Liverpool players held out to go through to the two-legged final. It had been a nerve-jangling ninety minutes for me, watching the game from the White Hart Lane centre stand. In truth, it was more exhausting than being on the pitch as I had cleared every Spurs attack and fired all Liverpool's shots at goal.

Our opponents in the final would be Borussia Moenchen-gladbach, who had demolished Twente Enschede 5–1 on aggregate. Borussia had scored over thirty goals on their way to the final and nobody at Anfield was under any illusion that Liverpool would be facing a quality team who were dangerous in away legs and formidable on their own ground. After the semi-final victory my priority was to ensure I would be fully fit for the first-leg match at Anfield on Wednesday 9 May.

In the run-up to the final lots of nice things were written in the press about Liverpool following our League Championship success. Leeds manager Don Revie said, 'When I congratulate Liverpool I do so sincerely. I'm delighted for them that they have won the championship. If it could not have been Leeds there is no one else I would rather see on top.' Certainly given the animosity between Revie and Brian Clough I am sure the Leeds manager was relieved that Cloughie's Derby had not followed up their title success from the previous season. Former Liverpool idol Ian St John added, 'To win the League Championship in any season is an achievement. Now I fancy them to win the UEFA Cup. One thing the old team never won was a European trophy and it would be a great thing for the boss for the present team to win one.'

In an article in the *Liverpool Echo* on the Saturday before the UEFA Cup Final, Shanks said, 'Peter Cormack, whom we bought last summer, has more than fulfilled what I hoped he would do. I thought he'd score ten to fifteen goals for us and he's done that. He'd have scored more if he hadn't suffered a few injuries. He has been brilliant in his shielding of the midfield and the back four as a semi-defender and I have never seen him beaten in the air.'

Typical of the man, Shanks had something positive to say about every Liverpool player and it was a great confidence booster for the team going into the UEFA Cup Final. I was certainly pleased to have got into double figures in my first season at Anfield and my ten goals was only three behind Kevin, Tosh and Phil Boersma who shared thirteen apiece in all competitions.

Fortunately my ankle had responded to treatment and come the Wednesday I was raring to go in the first leg of the final. Shanks decided to leave out Tosh and we played with a front two of Kevin and Steve Heighway with 'Little Bamber', Ian Callaghan, Emlyn and me making up a midfield quartet in front of our usual back four of Chris Lawler, Smithy, Big Larry Lloyd and Alec Lindsay. As usual Clem was between the sticks.

We met during the day as normal at Liverpool's Holiday Inn, but it would have been easier canoeing my way from home to the hotel such was the volume of rain that was falling. It was the kind of monsoon-type deluge that I had only ever seen before when I was on tour with Hibs in Nigeria and Ghana. In the coach on our way to Anfield most of the roads were more like rivers. In my four years at Liverpool I never seen the pitch as waterlogged as it was that evening, but because it was the UEFA Cup Final and was being beamed across Europe on live TV, pressure was put on the referee to declare the pitch playable. Conditions for water polo were perfect but there was no way Anfield was fit for football that evening. It was really difficult to concentrate in the run-up to the kick-off as I couldn't help thinking that it was ridiculous the game was on and the farcical conditions were not a good advert for a major European final.

I remember someone saying as we waited in the Anfield tunnel before we ran out onto the park, 'Here we are for final of *It's a*

Knockout,' imitating commentator Eddie Warings' voice. All the Liverpool players burst out laughing and the Germans looked at us as if we were mad. It certainly relieved the tension minutes before kick-off. As I took my position in midfield I couldn't see my boots as the muddy water was up to my ankles. Things didn't improve once the match got underway and neither side could pass the ball any further than a couple of yards. I have never been so happy to hear a final whistle blown less than thirty minutes into a game that should never have started in the first place. Both clubs agreed that the match should be replayed the following evening but little did the Germans realise that there was no one happier with the turn of events than Bill Shankly. In the little play that had taken place, Shanks and the backroom staff could see that the West German team were weak in the air in the middle of their defence. The Borussia side contained several West German internationals, including right back Bertie Vogts and midfield general Gunther Netzer, but in that farcical thirty minutes Shanks had spotted a weakness that Liverpool could exploit.

On the Thursday evening John Toshack was back up front with Kevin and Brian Hall was relegated to the bench. This completely wrong-footed the Germans and Tosh caused mayhem all night. Kevin opened the scoring halfway through the first half and two goals in the second half by Lloydie and substitute Brian Hall gave us a tremendous 3–0 lead to take to Germany. Our clean sheet was down to Ray Clemence who saved a penalty from Heynckes near the end of the match. Clem had watched a video recording of Borussia's semi-final where Heynckes had scored a penalty by shooting the ball to the keeper's right. When the German repeated the placing of the spot-kick at Anfield, Clem's pre-match preparation helped second-guess where it was going and his save was to prove priceless.

*

All the Liverpool players were confident that the 3–0 first-leg result was more than enough to guarantee that we would lift the trophy, but Shanks told us that this was only half-time and to expect to face a different team in the return leg.

Publicly he said, 'That was an international class game. Really tremendous. I'm not making predictions about the second leg but Liverpool have a distinct advantage because we did not give away a goal.'

The second leg in Moenchengladbach on 23 May was Liverpool's sixty-sixth match that season and my fifty-second. Shanks had prepared us to expect an onslaught from the Germans but I never expected the backs-to-the-wall titanic battle that we ended up enduring for virtually the whole ninety minutes. Heynckes more than made up for his Anfield penalty miss by scoring twice in the first twenty minutes. The Germans totally outran and outplayed us in the first half, and it was only the inspirational leadership of Tommy Smith that kept us in the game. At half-time Phil Boersma came on for Steve Heighway and Kevin and Tosh were brought back to shore up the midfield.

Smithy was even more magnificent in the second half, crunching into tackles and snarling at the rest of us to keep working and fighting for every ball. Tommy would go on to lift the European Cup for Liverpool in Rome four years later but for me his greatest-ever game for Liverpool was that night in Germany when he won the UEFA Cup almost single-handedly.

As soon as the final whistle went the tiredness in my legs disappeared and I was swamped by ecstatic Liverpool fans who had charged onto the pitch. After we received the trophy and our medals on the pitch I went on my first lap of honour as a Cup Final winner. After eleven years as a professional footballer it was a fantastic feeling of satisfaction, especially after my European disappointments at Hibs. Later in the dressing room amongst all the mayhem and madness I compared the feeling of elation to the night Hibs had beaten Napoli 5–0 at Easter Road. But that was a false dawn as Hibs had gone out to Leeds in the next round.

I looked over at the UEFA Cup, which had been placed on the physio's table in the middle of the dressing room, wondering if I was dreaming. Then Kevin Keegan sprayed me with champagne and I realised that this was the real deal. I had achieved more in my first season at Anfield than I had managed in ten previous years and I was hungry for more success. But before looking too far forward there was still the small matter of an open-top bus tour on the Friday following our return to Liverpool.

The players and their wives met at Anfield at tea time on the Friday and were joined for the ten-mile bus tour to the centre of the city by Liverpool boxer John Conteh. John won the Commonwealth and British lightweight championships on the Tuesday evening prior to our second-leg tie with Borussia and he had the Lonsdale Belt to show off from the bus along with our League Championship trophy and the UEFA Cup. As the bus set off from Anfield the only trophy on display was the Lonsdale Belt. In all the excitement the League Championship and UEFA Cup had been left in the dressing room! Tosh and Alec Lindsay were dispatched to retrieve the trophies for the city tour. Conteh also had the loudest checkered jacket of the bus party but nobody was going to criticise him for his dress sense and I was certainly in no position to slag off anyone's attire.

The Liverpool fans were out in their droves and the atmosphere throughout the ten-mile journey can best be described as chaotic, both on and off the bus. At fifty-five pounds the

UEFA Cup was a handful for a lightweight like me and I much preferred to show off the championship trophy during the two-hour tour, although at one point Steve Heighway and I both managed to prop the UEFA Cup on the front of the bus. The only time the noise of the crowd quietened was when Shanks was introduced. After initial euphoria he raised his arms like the great messiah and the noise of the crowd subdued. 'This is the greatest day of my career. It is difficult to find words. If there is any doubt that you are the greatest fans in the world then this is the night to prove it. We have won something for you and that's all we are interested in, winning for you. The reason we have won is because we believe and you believe, and it is faith and interest that have won us something. I have no more words to say.'

But Shanks being the great orator that he was did have a few final words for his adoring fans. 'Thank God we are all here. You don't know how proud we are, you don't know how much we love you.' And then he led the thousands of fans who were crammed in front of Picton Library in a rendition of 'You'll Never Walk Alone'. It was unbelievable watching grown men cry with tears of joy streaming down their faces. I'm not ashamed to say I also had a lump in my throat at the emotional scene, which I will never forget. Bill Shankly was of the people and always for the people and he never let any of his players or the media forget that.

It was a fantastic climax to my first season at Anfield and I couldn't wait for pre-season training to begin in July. But before that Marion, Donna Lee and I headed for a quiet relaxing holiday to Torremolinos on the Costa Del Sol. It would be Donna Lee's first holiday abroad and I was looking forward to splashing about in a pool for two weeks with my three-year-old daughter who had no idea what all the fuss of the open-top bus tour had been about.

That is the great thing about kids – they have a wonderful way of making sure adults keep things in perspective.

As the first Liverpool team to win a European trophy, Shanks was convinced that we had all the right credentials to win Europe's biggest prize played for by the League Champions of each country. The Liverpool manager and the club's football-mad fans were desperate to emulate the feat of Manchester United and become the second English side to lift the European Cup. In those days there wasn't a nasty edge to the rivalry, simply a desire by both sets of players and fans to come out on top each season. Whilst Man United may have the upper hand at the moment in the Premier League, they still have a long way to go to eclipse Liverpool's five European Cup victories. That is probably one record too far for the mighty Fergie.

The year before United's 1968 European Cup success Liverpool needed a play-off to overcome Petrolul Ploesti from Romania in their second tilt at the trophy. Tommy Smith recounts the trials and tribulations of the Romanian experience in his excellent autobiography *Anfield Iron*. Although Liverpool scored an away goal in a 3–1 defeat after winning 2–0 at Anfield, in those days a drawn match went to a third play-off game at a neutral venue. The match was played in Belgium and Liverpool ran out comfortable 2–0 winners.

In the second round Liverpool were drawn against Dutch champions Ajax of Amsterdam and in the first leg in Holland Liverpool suffered their worst-ever European result, losing 5–1. A young Johann Cruyff was the main architect of that defeat and a 2–2 draw in the return leg saw Ajax progress to the quarter-final 7–3 on aggregate. Later that season Billy McNeill lifted the European Cup when Celtic became the first British winners after defeating Inter Milan in Lisbon. Bill Shankly was there to see his great friend Jock Stein guide his Celtic team to European Cup glory and afterwards in the dressing room told Big Jock, 'John, you are now immortal.'

Despite playing in Europe in successive seasons, success had eluded Liverpool until the UEFA Cup campaign in 1972/73. After overcoming the German giants of Borussia everyone at Liverpool was convinced that we could go one step better the following season and bring the European Cup to Anfield.

After two weeks in the Spanish sunshine with Marion and Donna Lee I returned for pre-season training with my batteries fully recharged and raring to go. Unlike the injury nightmare I endured twelve months earlier I was flying in our two tour games against Hertha Berlin and Anderlecht. I was in the number eight shirt for our opening league match against Stoke City at Anfield and retained my position up until our first European Cup match away to Jeunesse d'Esch from Luxembourg. I was disappointed to be on the subs' bench for our first European Cup tie and Bob Paisley told me that Shanks wanted to protect me for the long season ahead. Despite drawing 1–1 in Luxembourg I was still wrapped in cotton wool for the return game at Anfield, which we won comfortably enough thanks to an own goal and a second from John Toshack.

In the second round we were drawn against Red Star Belgrade and I played the full ninety minutes in the first leg tie in Yugoslavia. Red Star won 2–1 but everyone in the Liverpool camp was confident that we would overcome them in the second leg at Anfield especially as Chris Lawler had given us an all important away goal, which now counted double in the event of a draw. On the Saturday before the return leg I was on the bench for our league match against Arsenal at Highbury and

was given the final three minutes after Tosh had given us a
2–0 lead. The following Wednesday I sat beside Tommy Smith
on the subs' bench as Red Star gave Liverpool an abject lesson
in how modern football was developing. It was not the light-
ning-quick 'total football' pioneered by Ajax and the Dutch
national team, but every Red Star player was comfortable on the
ball and they deployed two centre backs who liked to play their
way out of trouble.

The Yugoslavs won the second leg 2–1 for a 4–2 aggregate victory.
Whilst Shanks publicly lambasted their style of football as negative, in truth it was a learning experience that was not lost on
Shanks or the other members of the Boot Room. A few months
after our early European Cup exit, Larry Lloyd got himself injured
in a league match against Everton at Goodison and Phil
Thompson was brought in to partner Emlyn Hughes in the heart
of the defence. Phil had played in several positions up until that
point but he quickly established himself alongside Emlyn in the
heart of the Liverpool back four. That was the start of Liverpool
playing without a recognised centre half, the first English club
to adopt such a system. In subsequent years great centre back
pairings such as Thompson and Hansen, Hansen and Lawrenson
through to Sammy Hyypia and Jamie Carragher resulted from
that game against Red Star in November 1973. European silverware may have eluded Liverpool that season but winning the
FA Cup was a fantastic consolation prize and gained us entry
to the European Cup Winners' Cup the following season.

Whereas in season 1973/74 the players suffered a hangover from
doing the double in my first year at the club, the 1974/75 season
was Bob Paisley's introduction to the manager's hot seat and
despite his reluctance to take the job Bob took to it like a duck
to water.

After all the media speculation in the weeks following Shanks' shock announcement, the players were just glad that a manager had been appointed, and whilst some might have had reservations as to whether Bob Paisley was the best appointee, the vast majority were happy that it was someone we knew well and respected. Prior to our Cup Winners' Cup first-leg tie at Anfield against Stromsgodset from Norway we had taken eleven points from a possible twelve in our opening six league matches. The Norwegian part-timers didn't know what hit them at Anfield and they returned home with their tails between their legs after an 11–0 drubbing. I was rested for the return match two weeks later, which was a lot easier to take after contributing to finishing the tie off in the first-leg match. The same could not be said about my mood for the second round first-leg match against Ferencvaros at Anfield. I was very disappointed to be left out but was sent on after ten minutes of the second half. Kevin Keegan had given us a first half lead. As the second half progressed, Ferencvaros came more into the game and they scored an equalising goal midway through the second half. I was again on the bench for the return match in Hungary, and although I was thrown on with twenty minutes remaining, we couldn't manage to score and Ferencvaros's away goal at Anfield saw them progress to the next round. It was another very disappointing second round European exit for Liverpool and it mirrored our fortunes in all the competitions that season.

A week after returning from Hungary we lost 1–0 at Anfield against Middlesborough in the League Cup and were defeated by the same scoreline at Ipswich in the fourth round of the FA Cup in January. To crown my first season at Anfield without winning silverware Derby County, with fellow Edinburger Dave Mackay in charge, won the First Division Championship, pipping us by two points. Liverpool had won twenty league games but the eleven draws and eleven defeats meant that Derby won their second championship in four seasons.

Second place meant that we qualified for the UEFA Cup in season 1975/76 and the first round draw paired Liverpool with my old club, Hibs. For the start of the season I was back in my number five shirt and was eagerly looking forward to the first-leg tie at Easter Road. The previous season Hibs' manager Eddie Turnbull had signed Joe Harper from Everton and it was Joe who scored the only goal of the first leg in front of 20,000 fans. Ironically, Hibs did a 'Liverpool' on us by scoring with a quick counter attack. The margin of the Hibs victory could have been greater as they had a goal chalked off and Ray Clemence saved a John Brownlie penalty ten minutes from time. Once again Liverpool were grateful to Ray Clemence's penalty-saving skills for keeping our hopes alive in Europe.

Whilst Clem was the Liverpool hero in the first leg it was John Toshack who was the star of the return leg at Anfield.

Eddie Turnbull surprised everyone by leaving out Pat Stanton for the return match at Anfield at the end of September, and Pat's experience was badly missed as Liverpool tore at Hibs right from the kick-off. Tosh had a goal disallowed as early as the fifth minute but our pressure paid off when he scored with a header from a Kevin Keegan cross. However, our lead only lasted ten minutes and my old pal from the 1963 Scottish Amateur team, Alex Edwards, scored with a tremendous volley to gave Hibs a 2–1 aggregate lead and more importantly an important away goal.

We went straight at Hibs again at the start of the second half and fortunately Tosh quickly got us back into the game with another header in fifty-four minutes. He then completed his hat-trick of headers in sixty-five minutes, and despite dominating the rest of the game, there were no more goals and Liverpool went through to the next round 3–2 on aggregate.

The Hibs players were staying at the Prince of Wales Hotel in Southport and Pat Stanton and John Blackley incurred Eddie Turnbull's wrath by breaking the team curfew after the game. Pat was pissed off at being left on the bench and 'Sloop John B' was pissed off at the result and both of them decided to stay out and drown their sorrows.

Later that season, Pat moved to Celtic after twelve years' loyal service to Hibs and I was delighted for him that he ended his career on a high when Celtic won the League Championship and Scottish Cup.

In the second round of that season's UEFA Cup we were drawn against Real Sociedad and killed the tie-off in the first leg in Spain, winning 3–1 with goals from Steve Heighway, Ian Callaghan and Phil Thompson. I missed the second leg due to injury and along with the Liverpool fans watched a great Liverpool performance where we hammered the Spaniards 6–0. I was back on the subs' bench for both games in the quarter-final against Polish club Slask Warsaw. Once again Liverpool won the two legs, 2–1 in Warsaw and 3–0 at Anfield. I was given a run-out in the second half of the game at Anfield and returned to the first team in the number five shirt the following Saturday where we thumped Spurs 4–0 at White Hart Lane.

I retained my place in the first team for the remaining games of 1975, but after the turn of the year Ray Kennedy took over my place in midfield and he stayed there for the rest of the season as the team went on to repeat the League Championship and UEFA Cup double from 1973.

As I recovered from knee surgery for the remainder of the season, Liverpool defeated Dynamo Dresden 2–1 on aggregate in the quarter-final of the UEFA Cup and were rewarded with a semi-final draw against Spanish giants Barcelona.

The Barca team included the two top Dutch players from the 1974 World Cup, Johann Cruyff and Johan Neeskens, but Liverpool put in a fantastic performance in front of 70,000 noisy Catalans in the first leg and went home with a 1–0 win. Tosh scored the only goal of the game in the thirteenth minute.

A 1–1 draw at Anfield, thanks to a Phil Thompson goal, saw Liverpool qualify for their second UEFA Cup Final. After beating Barcelona everyone at Anfield was confident of beating Bruges in the Final but that looked seriously in doubt after the first forty-five minutes of the first leg at Anfield. Bruges totally outplayed Liverpool with their brand of quick passing and counter-attacking football and went in at the break with a deserved 2–0 lead. In the second half the Liverpool players just rolled up their sleeves and scored three times through Ray Kennedy, Kevin Keegan and Jimmy Case to take a 3–2 lead to Belgium for the second leg.

Two weeks before that game, three goals in the last fifteen minutes at Wolves in the final league match of the season saw Liverpool win the English First Division Championship. Although it was my second championship medal in four years at Anfield, the fact that I hadn't played since the end of December meant that my mood was in sharp contrast to that first championship at the end of April three years earlier. I just couldn't get excited because I was not out there on the pitch but there was no doubt the manner of that championship win, pipping QPR by one point in the last game of the season was far more dramatic than the first time around. Our last game of the season against Bruges in the second leg of the UEFA Cup Final was almost a repeat of the second leg against Borussia in the Final three years earlier. This time Kevin Keegan equalised an early Bruges goal after fifteen minutes and for the remaining seventy-five minutes Liverpool absorbed everything that Bruges could throw at them.

It was a tremendous team effort led again by captain courageous Tommy Smith, and I had another UEFA Cup winner's medal to add to my growing medal haul.

I may have won two medals that season but unlike 1973 I went into the close season deliberating about my football future. In my absence Ray Kennedy had taken over the number five shirt and had proved himself to be a very accomplished midfield player.

Ray was Bill Shankly's last ever signing for Liverpool and Shanks had bought him from Arsenal as cover for John Toshack. When Bob Paisley threw Ray into midfield after I got injured it proved to be one of Bob's shrewdest moves. Kennedy revelled in the role, scoring regularly from midfield and showing a tremendous appetite for hard graft. Ray's renaissance had cost me a regular first team place but I resolved over the summer to knuckle down and fight to get back in the side at the start of the season.

It wasn't to be, and after a few months I got the chance to kick-start my career at Bristol City, who had just been promoted to the First Division. Unlike my two previous transfers I agonised for a long time, as I was very reluctant to leave Anfield. The pull of the 'pool was still very strong but eventually the chance of regular first team football at newly-promoted Bristol City won out. I can honestly say that walking out of Anfield for the very last time as a Liverpool player was the hardest decision I ever made, and my four years there were the happiest of my football career. I was very fortunate to arrive at Anfield at the start of a new era for Liverpool and I had the privilege of playing under both the best manager in the history of the club and then the most successful one. Liverpool Football Club had been Bill Shankly's calling in life and Bob Paisley followed in Shanks' footsteps by taking the club onto bigger and better things.

Being part of a squad that won two League Championships, the FA Cup and the UEFA Cup twice was not a bad haul in four years at Anfield. Just as importantly, I had played in a team with great players, some of whom became lifelong friends. But there is an old football saying that 'you are only as good as your last game' and I was still hungry to prove that I could cut it with the best of them in the English First Division.

11

THE BOOT ROOM LEGACY

On 27 December 1975 I played my final first team match for Liverpool and scored our only goal after sixty-one minutes in a 1–0 away win against Manchester City. Amazingly, it was the third time in my four seasons at Anfield that I scored our only goal in 1–0 wins away from home on the last match of the calendar year. Coincidence or what?

Despite my match-winning performance I never appeared in the first team again for the remainder of season 1975/76 and to use one of Shanks' old mining sayings, 'my jaicket was on a shoogly peg'.

People still come up to me today and ask if I know why Bill Shankly decided to retire so unexpectedly from the Liverpool manager's job in July 1974. Over the years many conspiracy theories have been put forward in newspaper articles and books, but all of these theories have been just that – theories. The truth is no one who was at Liverpool at the time knew why Shanks decided to call time on his managerial career when he was at his peak, but we all accepted the reason he gave without question. Like the day President Kennedy was shot, I remember exactly where I was when I heard the news that Bill Shankly had retired as manager of Liverpool Football Club. I should have been at Melwood for Liverpool's first day of pre-season training but because I had been on World Cup duty with Scotland in West

Germany I was given a few extra days off. Marion and I had taken Donna Lee and baby Peter, who was less than a month old, to the Lake District for a couple of days' break and it was whilst we were driving down the M6 to Southport that we heard the announcement on the car radio.

It was the leading news story, and when I heard the report my heart sank. It was like being told that the Boss was dead and I was in a state of shock for the remainder of the car journey. If mobile telephones had existed I would have exhausted the battery speaking to team-mates trying to find out what the hell was going on. As soon as we arrived back in Southport I literally dumped Marion and the kids at the house with the luggage and drove straight over to Melwood where I knew the players would be doing a double training session on their first day back.

On my way to the training ground I started to convince myself that Shanks would change his mind. After all, it wasn't the first time he had threatened to quit and in the past the board of directors would play it low-key and then convince him of how much the club needed him. Following our FA Cup win two months earlier, Shanks said that this Liverpool team were on the verge of greatness so the timing of his retirement made no logical sense.

By the time I arrived at Melwood I was certain that he wouldn't leave, indeed I even thought that he'd have already withdrawn his resignation. The players were just finishing their second training session and they were just as shell-shocked as I was. Apparently Shanks had gathered them all together at the start of the morning session and told them of his decision to retire. He wanted to tell them face-to-face before he met with the Liverpool board at lunchtime. Most of the guys were certain that it was just another one of Shanks' bluffs for whatever reason and that may well have been his initial intention. But once it became the main item on the national news networks the story of Shanks' shock retirement grew arms and legs. The media began speculating on who was going to replace The Boss at Anfield and once that started I think it made it very difficult for both Shanks and the directors to back down, even if one party or the other had wanted to.

In researching the story of my football career I came across an article in my scrapbook that appeared in the *Daily Express* on 15 February 1974, five months before Bill Shankly's announcement. It helps shed some light on Shanks' mindset, and with hindsight, when you read what he was saying at the time, his resignation should not have come as such a shock.

Headed 'Shankly wins freedom of Anfield' the journalist Derek Potter wrote:

> Bill Shankly was made Freeman of Anfield yesterday when he was offered a unique new contract as manager. It will run from next June when his present agreement expires, for as long as Shankly wants it to run. 'As far as we are concerned we want Bill to be with us forever,' said chairman John Smith.
>
> And Shankly, 59, veteran of over 14 glittering years as manager of Liverpool, has no idea how long he wants to remain in charge – yet.
>
> 'It's something I want to talk over with my wife and then decide,' Shankly told me. 'It may be another year or two or even three.
>
> 'But one day I will say – that's it, I've had enough. My career as a manger will have an abrupt end. It will be a complete break. Then I shall get out my tracksuit and sweater and jog round the streets and fields and people will laugh at me.
>
> 'They will think I'm a mad man. But some of them will

drop dead the next day and I will have the last laugh because
I know I will die a healthy man.'

'That, in a few of his own colourful phrases, is Bill Shankly:
forty-one years in football, dedicated, determined and at
times dogmatic.'

Derek Potter then asked: 'What keeps Shankly spinning along
the savage soccer road?'

I think it's my age – 25. You are only as old as you feel and
that is vital. It is a hard game to keep up your motivation.
As a player you strain to prove yourself, but as a manager
it is a bigger strain because you have to depend on others.
'You get great pleasure in the team winning things for our
wonderful people. Now this gesture to me is flattering. I
am inwardly glowing that they want my services to
continue.'

Shankly will recommend his successor to the board before
he finally decides to quit.

'That's a bridge I hope we are a long way off crossing,'
said chairman Smith.

As Shanks alluded to in the article, on 12 July 1974 he walked
into Anfield and told the assembled players, 'That's it, I've had
enough.' He then repeated that to the Liverpool board of directors and a subsequent lunchtime media conference. Whether he
had sat down and discussed 'chucking it' with his wife Nessie,
I don't know. I also don't know if he did recommend his successor
to the board. But knowing how closely he had worked with Bob
Paisley from his very first day at Anfield, I would be astonished
if he hadn't recommended Bob to take over from him.

When Bill Shankly was appointed manager of Liverpool in
1959 Bob Paisley was already part of the furniture at Anfield.

Bob signed for Liverpool from Bishop Auckland in May 1939 and shortly after the Second World War he helped Liverpool to their first League Championship win in twenty-four years. When he retired from playing in 1954 Bob Paisley became the club's physiotherapist and after Bill Shankly arrived as manager he became an integral part of Shanks' backroom team, subsequently known as The Boot Room.

Tommy Smith used to tell me about Shanks and Bob setting about the renovation of Anfield single-handedly (or should that be double-handedly?). Long after the players had gone home after training the two men would repair the plumbing in the toilets at the back of the terracing or paint crush barriers. Any odd job needing done at Anfield or Melwood was, more often than not, done by them. They did all of Liverpool's DIY long before B & Q arrived on the scene. Shanks not only wanted Anfield to be a fortress for visiting teams, he wanted it to be a fortress Liverpool players and fans could be proud of. I had a lot to thank Bob for, although it was his job to play bad cop to Shanks' good cop. More often than not, it was Bob who was left to break the news to players that they were dropped, whilst Shanks would simply ignore players dropped or injured. But Bob was a self-taught master at diagnosing players' injuries and he had helped me return to fitness and playing quicker than other trainers I had seen previously. It was also Bob and Doc Reid who convinced the FA Disciplinary Committee of the severity of my injuries after I had got myself sent off against West Brom in my first season at Liverpool.

There was no question that everyone in the club liked and respected Bob but there were not many around Anfield that pre-season in 1974 that thought he could fill Bill Shankly's boots. In fact, I'm pretty certain that was also Bob's view. In the days and weeks following Shanks' resignation there was not a day that went by that some manager's name appeared in the newspapers linked with the vacant job. If Shanks did recommend Bob as his successor, the Liverpool board took a hell of a long time acting on it. Bob Paisley took responsibility for team selection in our pre-season friendly against Kaiserslautern in Germany but he had still not been appointed manager by the time we played Leeds United in the infamous Charity Shield match at Wembley on 10 August – a full four weeks after Shanks resigned. Although Bob picked the team that day it was Shanks who walked proudly in front of the players at Wembley alongside Brian Clough leading out Leeds for the very first time.

When I look back on that time gap, it makes me wonder if the so called 'Boot Room Legacy' happened more by accident than design. Subsequent Liverpool managers' appointments from within the club were made almost immediately, the incumbent having been groomed for the job, but in Bob Paisley's case the board prevaricated for a very long time.

When Bob was eventually made manager he gathered all the players together and told us that he didn't really want the job and that it would probably be a short-term appointment. His authority was not helped when Shanks started appearing every day at training. When we stepped off the bus taking us to Melwood from Anfield, Shanks would be waiting in his tracksuit to join in the training. None of us did it to undermine Bob but automatically we would refer to Shanks as 'Boss' and he would laugh and joke with the players as if he was indeed still in charge. This went on for several weeks and eventually someone on the coaching staff was handed 'the black spot' to tell Shanks to stop coming to training. I would chat with Shanks at training and to me he was a lost soul after he retired. He just couldn't change the routine he had known all his adult life and after getting the cold shoulder from Liverpool he spent his week-days training with Everton at their Bellefield ground, which was close to his home.

After such a difficult start in the job Bob quickly grew into the manager's role, proving to be just as shrewd a manager as Shanks and in time, a more successful one. He had Shanks' knack of spotting players' strengths and weaknesses, but he also trans-formed players' careers by subtle positional changes. Although his elevation from physio to the Liverpool manager's hot seat came more by accident than design he recognised the true value of The Boot Room's worth and he, more than anyone else, laid the foundation for his successors.

When I signed for Liverpool in July 1972 The Boot Room at Anfield had a mystique all of its own and I was determined to discover its secrets. When I asked my team-mates I was told that The Boot Room was where Shanks and his backroom staff discussed Liverpool players' fitness and performances and where they analysed opposition teams' strengths and weaknesses. But in truth it was much more than that. After a couple of years at Anfield, when I started thinking about coaching and football management after I stopped playing, I was allowed into The Boot Room's inner sanctum. Most Sunday mornings players would report to Anfield to get injuries looked at or enjoy a relaxing massage. It was also when The Boot Room would conduct their post mortem into the previous day's game and start planning for Liverpool's next match. For months on end I would absorb everything discussed like an information-hungry student study-ing for a football degree. It was a footballing education at the best soccer university in the world.

For a start, details of every training session and all Liverpool matches were meticulously recorded and regularly referenced. Dossiers were kept on every player at the club and if someone's form dipped the dossiers were pored over to try and establish a reason for the loss of form. For instance, before I arrived at the club, The Boot Room noticed that the team's performance consistently dropped in matches in London. At the time the Liverpool squad travelled to London on a Friday afternoon and The Boot Room came to the conclusion that players were overeating on the train journey south. The solution was to change the time of the train journey to enable the players to have their normal Friday night meal prior to the match.

The Boot Room's interest was wider than just Liverpool players. After every game opposition managers and coaches were invited into the hallowed place for a friendly post-match cup of tea and a convivial chat about the game. But those occasions were much more than just hospitable niceties. During the course of these conversations The Boot Room members would elicit information on opposition players and try to find out if the club had any promising up-and-coming youngsters about to break through.

If Anfield was a spacecraft, then The Boot Room was Mission Control, monitoring and guiding everything that was going on. Week by week I was getting to understand the club's methods for success which centred on simplicity in training and getting players to apply common sense away from the club. Players were encouraged to play to their individual strengths and no matter what position you played the team ethic was 'pass and move, pass and move'. At times Shanks would ask for my opinion on an incident in a past game or on an opponent we were about to face. I'm convinced the question was put to test whether I was learning the Liverpool craft.

Long before I left Anfield I became a fully signed-up disciple to their training methods, confident I could put the knowledge to good use after I stopped playing. By the time I left Liverpool I was certain I knew all I needed to take with me into football management and possessing The Boot Room's secret formula would ensure that I could step into the manager's hot-seat, confident that I would succeed.

The challenges Bob Paisley faced and subsequently conquered in that first season in charge at Anfield was probably what made him into Liverpool's most successful manager. Although he had not been appointed manager for our first competitive game of the 1974/75 season, the fall-out from the match was considerable.

Kevin Keegan's sending-off for fighting with Billy Bremner, where they both threw their shirts to the ground, cost Kevin an eleven-game ban. It was tough enough for Bob stepping into Shanks' shoes but doing so minus our star player for eleven games was a monumental challenge. Then at the beginning of November in the space of one week Liverpool went out of the European Cup Winners' Cup, lost 3–1 at home to Arsenal in the league and the following mid-week were knocked out of the League Cup at Anfield by Middlesborough. I had been struggling with an injury just before our season hit the buffers and whilst I did not play in the Ferencvaros and Arsenal games I was back in the number five shirt for the defeat against Middlesborough.

Thereafter I only missed three more matches that season where we ended up finishing second in the league to Dave Mackay's Derby County side. I ended my third season at Anfield having made forty starts, was sub on six occasions and scored four goals. The following season I was back in the centre of midfield for our first league game at QPR, which we lost 2–0. I played from the start in nineteen out of the first twenty games and came off the bench for the second half in a 3–1 home win against Birmingham. I then missed six weeks through injury from the start of November and returned to the team for a 4–0 away win at Spurs. By this time the travel issues to play in London had been well and truly sorted and the team put in their best performance of the season up to that point with Kevin Keegan, Jimmy Case, Phil Neal and Steve Heighway all getting on the scoresheet. Little did I realise when I scored my first goal of the season to win the match against Manchester City at Anfield on 27 December that it would be my last goal for Liverpool and my last appearance in the first team.

At the start of 1976 I required a cartilage operation. In my absence Bob Paisley gave Ray Kennedy the number five shirt and he was transformed from a bustling forward into a hard-working, cultured midfield player. Like me in my first two seasons at Liverpool, Ray also came through from midfield to score important goals. The move may have been inspired on the part of the manager but it signalled the end of my career at Anfield. Whilst Liverpool repeated their 1973 double success of League Championship and UEFA Cup I made only twenty-two starts and started five games on the subs' bench. My feeling of frustration at the season end was in complete contrast to the elation I had experienced three years previously. Despite completing an injury-free pre-season my only involvement with the first team at the start of the 1976/77 season was as sub in the Charity Shield match against shock FA Cup winners Southampton. When Bob Paisley called me into his office in early November to tell me Bristol City were interested in signing me and that Liverpool had agreed a £50,000 transfer fee I have to admit I had mixed emotions about leaving Anfield.

It was a completely different situation to my two previous transfers and although Bristol City had only just been promoted to the First Division Marion, and I talked long and hard about agreeing to the move. Bristol manager Alan Dicks had assembled a good squad of players and he promised me regular first team football as long as I stayed fit but it was a wrench to leave Liverpool. They were the best club in England and had just started competing in that season's European Cup. But the football reality was that events had conspired to put me completely out of the picture and as well as the rejuvenated form of Ray Kennedy, Jimmy Case and Terry McDermott were starting to knock regularly at the first team door. The battle for places in the Liverpool midfield was fierce. It was with a heavy heart that I left Anfield as a Liverpool player for the last time. Three weeks later I walked through the players' entrance at Anfield with the Bristol City squad, apprehensive about the reception I would receive from the Kop. I should have known better than to think I had anything to worry about.

In my four years at Anfield I enjoyed a completely different lifestyle to what I experienced at Hibs and Nottingham Forest. Those first two seasons playing for Liverpool were without doubt the best two years of my football career. Shanks was, and still is, a football legend, but as well as the boss the team was graced by great players. Ray Clemence was one of the most consistent goalkeepers in the English league and after a long and distinguished career at Anfield went on to perform at the highest level for Spurs for seven years from 1981. Chris Lawler had been a great servant to Liverpool before I arrived and he continued to hold down the right back spot until a knee injury cost him his place and he played his last match for Liverpool in 1975 in the UEFA Cup against my old team Hibs.

Alec Lindsay was a solid, dependable left back who could also score the occasional goal. It was a standing joke at Anfield that when Liverpool signed Alec from Bury in 1969 they actually signed the wrong player. Liverpool scouts had been impressed by a Bury midfield player who had the same blond curly hair as Alec and that's who they thought they had signed. It is hard to believe, particularly given how meticulous The Boot Room went about things that they could fork out £67,000 for the wrong player, but that's exactly what they did in Alec's case. Still he made a great contribution to Liverpool and ended his Anfield career sitting on the subs' bench in Rome at the 1977 European Cup Final.

In that memorable first season at Anfield the defensive spine of the team was Larry Lloyd and Tommy Smith. Larry was a commanding centre half who gave no quarter but Smithy was the inspiration in the team. Even when the team captaincy was given to Emlyn Hughes, Tommy was the man all the players looked up to. He was a total professional dedicated to the cause and was the best tackler I've ever seen. But there was much more to Smithy's play than just aggression. He was a great reader of the game, an excellent passer and all-round great guy to have in your dressing room. It spoke volumes that the first player picked at five-a-sides was always Smithy. He was an asset to your team and nobody enjoyed playing against him.

Ian Callaghan was a great role model for youngsters starting out in the game, who ended up making 859 first team appearances for Liverpool, still a club record that will likely never be broken. Cally was skilful, quick and could score goals, and he would constantly relieve pressure off his team-mates by taking the ball for a walk. On the other wing Steve Heighway was lightning quick but a better finisher than Cally. I quickly developed a good understanding with Stevie and scored many of my goals from his passes.

Up front John Toshack and Kevin Keegan developed a tremendous understanding. Each seemed to know where the other would be and defences couldn't take their eyes off either of them for a minute. With his height Tosh obviously caused more damage in the air but he scored his fair share of goals with either foot. When I arrived at Anfield and for the four years I was there Kevin was without doubt our star man. Although small in height he had a tremendous physique and his work rate at training and in games was second to none. It was no accident that many of his goals were scored in the last ten minutes of games, as he was the fittest man on the pitch week in and week out. It was Kevin's class that got us to the 1974 FA Cup Final with his two goals in the replay and he repeated that goalscoring feat in the final, despite getting injured by Shanks in the run-up to the match at Wembley.

In those first two seasons Phil Boersma and Brian Hall made great contributions to the team's success although neither of them enjoyed the luxury of a decent run in the side.

Then after Larry Lloyd got injured Phil Thompson came into the back four and with Emlyn Hughes formed a partnership and established a style of play that became the hallmark of Liverpool's domination of English and European football for the next twenty years. In my last two years at Anfield Phil Neal, Jimmy Case, Terry McDermott and 'super sub' David Fairclough started to break through and they would go on to make considerable contributions for Liverpool in subsequent years.

As well as playing with the best team in England during my four years at Liverpool I also enjoyed some unusual perks of being a professional footballer. Within a couple of weeks of being at Anfield I was recruited by a publicity agent who promised me great riches away from football. Now this guy was more Del Boy Trotter than Eric Monster Hall, Shanks wouldn't have had any time for today's football agents – theirs would not be a meeting of minds. Anyway, my publicity agent was kept well away from Anfield and the ever watching eye of the Boss. In fairness his marketing strategy was knocked off track after I was injured on my debut in Bochum. Nevertheless, he had Del Boy's tenacity and around the time I made my competitive debut at Derby I was told that 'Peter Cormack Football Boots' were at design stage with a launch plan of early in the New Year.

Around the same time Kevin Keegan was approached by Hummel to emulate Alan Ball and wear white boots. Whilst Kevin was offered the princely sum of £2,000, my agent advised me that he could get me £100! Needless to say I was not overly impressed but undeterred I told him about 'The Peter Cormack Female Fan Club' that was started when I was at Hibs. This encouraged him to create the 'Liverpool Peter Cormack Female Fan Club' and over five hundred teeny-boppers signed up as members. A local printer produced t-shirts and membership letters were issued but I reckon my entrepreneurial agent made more out of the fan club than I ever did.

After my first season at Anfield I took stock of my off-field activities and decided 'Peter Cormack PLC' needed a new agent. My new PR man enthusiastically set about my new venture of designing and modelling clothes. I realised it was a big step but I had previously put my artistic skills to use dabbling at clothes design ideas and when the chance came to get some 'Cormack Creations' onto the catwalk, it seemed like a great idea at the time. To complete the look I grew a trendy moustache in the close season and just after the start of the new season my 'collection' was launched in a blaze of publicity.

I now look back at the array of press cuttings that appeared in the newspapers with a mixture of pride and embarrassment. Whilst the papers reported that my designs ranged from men's suits to swimwear, most of the accompanying photographs had me either in an unbuttoned denim shirt or showing off a three-quarter length brown leather coat, cream flares and multi-coloured polka-dot Cuban-heeled boots. Unfortunately the colour photographs from the modelling shoot highlighted the multi-coloured spots on the boots. I just can't believe they didn't catch on! Fortunately I was not asked to model the swimwear for the photo shoot. I also sensibly said, 'Nobody need think that because I'm getting into fashion that I'm giving football up.' I don't think the fashion designers in Paris and Milan felt they had anything to worry about there. After the stick I got from team-mates and opponents I decided to put the clothes designing and modelling on ice until my playing days were over. It is still in cold storage.

The final straw came after Donna Lee kept pestering me to shave off the 'Omar Sharif' moustache. I had an inconsistent start to the season and when Shanks dropped me for an away league match at Arsenal and the home Red Star Belgrade match that ended our involvement in the European Cup I decided the 'tache had to go. The hairless top lip may have brought a prema-ture end to my modelling career but, more importantly, I got my place back in the first team and stayed there for the remainder of the season that culminated in Liverpool's FA Cup success at Wembley. As I said previously, footballers are a superstitious bunch.

My final venture in my second season at Anfield was an assault on the pop charts. Well, assault might be a little strong; prob-ably it would be more accurate to say I cut a record.

Liverpool had spawned The Beatles and Gerry and The Pacemakers to name but two of the many musical talents that came out of Merseyside, and I had always fancied myself as a bit of a chanter. My PR man teamed me up with Les McGuire who did the arrangements on 'You'll Never Walk Alone'. Despite the superb efforts of Les, my version of the Rolling Stones classic 'Route 66' didn't threaten T Rex, Rod Stewart and The Osmond's at the top of the hit parade and I had to put my singing career on hold until karaoke arrived in the UK from Japan. My unsuccessful attempt on the music charts was not lost on all of my team-mates, although Kevin Keegan had the good sense to wait until he played for Hamburg before making a record. After seeing and joining in the stick I got from all the Liverpool players, the fact that Kevin played and lived in another country probably limited the abuse he got from team-mates when he released 'Head Over Heels in Love' which got to number thirty-one in the charts in 1979. Unfortunately for me, 'Route 66' started badly and then fell away when it was released in the summer of '73.

Over the years I've often wondered if I left Anfield too soon and maybe I should have kept plugging away in the Liverpool reserves and at training in the hope that I'd get another chance to establish myself in the first team. I especially wondered about that when I sat at home with Marion watching Liverpool win the European Cup later that season. I wouldn't be human not to think that but for the grace of God and my dodgy knees I might have played a part in that wonderful achievement. Whilst a little bit of me was envious that I wasn't there as part of Liverpool's first European Cup success against Borussia Moenchengladbach, I was absolutely chuffed for the lads and proud of the way they won the final. It was a fitting end to a fantastic career at Anfield for Smithy and a great way for Kevin to leave the club.

I may have left Anfield with a heavy heart but I have always been a Red after four fantastic years as a player at Liverpool. In my four seasons I played in one hundred and eighty-six first team games and scored twenty-six goals. Two memorable strikes came in my first season at Anfield – the header from Steve Heighway's cross to win my first Merseyside derby and the first goal in the 2–0 defeat of Leeds at Anfield in my fiftieth match that sealed the League Championship. But my most memorable game was the 1974 FA Cup Final at Wembley when we blew Newcastle away with a sublime second half performance. To win the FA Cup in style was extra, extra special and something I will treasure for the rest of my life, even more so as it turned out to be Bill Shankly's last game in charge.

12

ROCKING WITH THE ROBINS

Bristol City is not one of England's most fashionable club sides. I'm sure even the most diehard Robins fan would not argue with that statement. But for four seasons in the late 1970s they went toe-to-toe with England's footballing elite and won a trophy – in one of only four competitions they competed in. From a personal point of view, I loved my time at Ashton Gate and being part of that exciting adventure was a fun-filled challenge. Formed in 1897, Bristol City has only ever played in one FA Cup Final, finishing up as losing finalists to Manchester United in 1909. City's one and only Cup success prior to me joining the club was in 1934 when they won the Welsh Cup. Even that must have raised some eyebrows given that they are in England. The River Severn separates Bristol from Wales but the club must have been buying a lot of Welsh lamb the year they won the Welsh Cup. In 1967 Bristol City appointed Alan Dicks as manager and after years of hard graft City gained promotion to the First Division in nine years later. The last time Bristol City had played in England's top flight was in 1911 – it had been a long sixty-five years' wait for Bristol City's loyal fans.

When I first met Alan Dicks I was immediately struck by his honesty and straightforwardness – not a trait you always associate with football managers. After a whirlwind start to the season – City had beaten Arsenal 1–0 at Highbury in their first match back in the First Division and then taken four points from their next three games – they quickly slipped into the relegation zone after losing six of their next seven fixtures. Dicks didn't pull any punches in my first meeting with him. 'Peter, I'm not going to kid you on that life at Ashton Gate will be anything like what you have been used to at Liverpool. We have good players but the majority of them lack First Division experience and that is where you come in. I need quality players with the necessary experience and who are prepared to roll up their sleeves and battle.'

After my injury problem the previous season and my struggle to get back into the Liverpool team, Dicks' frankness impressed me. I liked the fact that he was a strong character who didn't suffer fools, and he assured me that the Bristol City board gave him a free hand in team matters. Bristol were also prepared to increase my basic wage from what I was getting at Liverpool to £240 a week and pay me a £10,000 signing on fee. All of these factors, along with the chance to get back playing first team football, were very persuasive arguments. However, the icing on the cake and further proof that Bristol City and Alan Dicks were deadly serious about staying in the First Division was that two weeks earlier they had signed Norman Hunter from Leeds United. The chance of playing alongside Norman rather than against him convinced me to sign on the dotted line. From the first time I played against Norman for Hibs in the Fairs Cup he seemed to pick me out for his first 'freebie' tackle in a match. Norman said that defenders were always given the benefit of the doubt with their first foul, no matter how bad it was, and it just so happened that whenever I played against him previously for Hibs, Forest and Liverpool I seemed to be the one who got his 'freebie'. When I first met the Bristol players Norman came up to me and recalled our previous encounters but I was just happy that we would both be in the same side and some other poor bastard would be in receipt of his 'freebie'.

I also thought that if Alan Dicks was able to persuade 'Bites Yer Legs' to leave his beloved Leeds United after sixteen years then he was deadly serious about doing everything he humanly could to ensure that Bristol City didn't yo-yo back down to the Second Division.

By 13 November, City were occupying twentieth place in a league of twenty-two teams, with their last win having been against Sunderland over two months earlier. I replaced fellow Scot Gerry Gow in the side that played Tottenham Hotspur at White Hart Lane. Gerry was sidelined following a cartilage operation – ironically the same problem that brought about a premature end to my time at Liverpool. I was encouraged before the game when I read Norman Hunter's comments in the local newspaper: 'We can get something tomorrow. Spurs are having a bad time at the moment and the crowd are giving them a bit of stick, so we should at least get a point.' Norman not only talked a good game, he always gave his all on the park and that day at Spurs was no different. I played left midfield and the whole team grafted for ninety minutes and through sheer hard work we took maximum points on my debut. Keith Fear scored the only goal of the game and that victory meant we overtook Spurs in the relegation zone. That win was also especially sweet for me because it was the first time in my career that I had been in a winning side on my debut.

On the Saturday evening Alan Dicks led the celebrations and, as I was to discover, the manager loved to party after a Bristol City victory. We followed up that first win in over two months with another victory in our next game, beating Norwich City 3–1 and just like I did at Nottingham Forest and Liverpool I scored on my home debut at Ashton Gate. There were fewer than 20,000 fans there but the local support was tremendous and they could see that all the players were giving 100 per cent to the cause. The two back-to-back victories had lifted team morale in the dressing room but I was nervous about our next match – Liverpool at Anfield.

After I signed for City I agreed with Alan Dicks that I would continue training at Liverpool until Marion and I had sorted out accommodation in Bristol. Bob Paisley was happy for me to train with the Liverpool lads three days a week but it was strange training at Melwood in the run-up to the match knowing that I would be lining up against Liverpool on the Saturday. Whilst Bristol were beating Norwich, Liverpool were drawing 1–1 with Arsenal at Highbury but still flying high at the top of the league. The banter at training was sharp, with Tommy Smith winding me up, saying that my 'new pal' Norman Hunter and me would be in for a rough reception from the Kopites.

I knew Norman would get it tight from the Liverpool fans, he always did, but he revelled in his notoriety. However, I had always enjoyed a great relationship with the supporters on the Kop and I wondered how they would take to me now that I had left Anfield. I couldn't remember the last time I felt so nervous before a game – probably two years earlier when I walked out at Wembley before the FA Cup Final. When I arrived at Anfield after getting off the Bristol City bus I instinctively made for the home dressing room. Fortunately I managed to stop myself and turn around just as I got to the door. As we got changed I recalled the last time I was in the away dressing room at Anfield with Nottingham Forest five years earlier. That had been the day when Kevin Keegan made his Liverpool debut and since then he had become a cult hero with the Liverpool fans and was a regular in the England team.

The following day Tim Taylor wrote in one of the local Liverpool newspapers:

Peter Cormack went back to Anfield and got an ovation before a ball was kicked. But the first time Norman Hunter kicked it – an early tap back to his goalkeeper – the boos could be heard the other side of Stanley Park. Like some huge elephant, the Kop never forgets.

I got a fantastic reception from the best football supporters in the world. It gave me goosebumps. Even so, it didn't stop me doing all I could to try and win the game for my new club. I played my part in the move that gave us the lead through big Tom Ritchie, but goals from Joey Jones and Kevin Keegan saw Liverpool win 2–1. Bristol City had been beaten but not disgraced by the League Champions, and although I had not long turned thirty I felt fresh and full of running for the winter battles that lay ahead.

Not long after I signed for Bristol City, Marion and I became friends with Kelvin and Anne Hughes. Kelvin had his own building business and he agreed to build a house for us overlooking the sea in Portishead. Whilst the house was being built Marion, Donna Lee, wee Pete and I moved into rented accommodation but it was well worth the wait. Of all the properties we have owned the house at Portishead was extra special, mainly because of the fantastic views and the large park at the bottom of our garden. It was a great spot to bring up our children and wee Pete and I spent many a happy hour honing our snooker skills in the large sports room Kelvin added to the house spec.

As further evidence of Bristol City's and Alan Dicks' determination to stay in the First Division, the club signed Chris Garland at the beginning of December. Dicks was concerned that we didn't have a regular goalscorer and Chris had a proven track record in that department.

Chris was a big, strong local lad who started his football career with Bristol City but left for Chelsea in 1971. After three years at Stamford Bridge he moved on to Leicester City to team up with my old 'pal' Frank Worthington. Jimmy Mann had started the season at centre forward but only managed one goal in the league and Alan Dicks turned to Garland, given his proven track record of scoring goals in the First Division. Chris made his debut in a home match against Leeds United on 4 December but the game was abandoned at half-time due to thick fog which had descended on Ashton Gate.

I remained a regular in the side until my knee trouble came back to haunt me after we lost away at Ipswich in mid-March, which sidelined me for the next six games. During that fifteen-game run we only managed to amass twelve points from fourteen league games and were unceremoniously thumped 4–1 at Ipswich in the third round of the FA Cup.

My personal highlight in those fifteen matches was a 2–0 home win over Arsenal when I scored both the goals. The victory over the Gunners also meant that Bristol City had notched their first league double of the season and those four points would prove vital by the end of the league campaign. The local Bristol newspaper's report of the game included the following:

The hero of City's first win of the year was £50,000 signing Peter Cormack who hit both goals and had a third disallowed. He spelled out his mood early on when he headed a pass from Garland against the bar. And he was right on target in the 22nd minute when he headed an overhead kick from Fear via the bar to send City surging into the lead. Cormack, always in the action both in attack and defence, should have scored again ten minutes later. He headed a centre from

Merrick just wide of the post. Then in the 36th minute he had the ball in the net again. Referee Morris Baker ruled that Sweeney was offside although the linesman kept his flag down . . . In the 63rd minute a cunningly flighted corner was hammered home by Cormack – again off the bar.

Two things stand out from that report. The first is that the ref wrongly denied what would have been my one and only hat-trick in ten seasons in the English First Division and secondly, players today don't seem to know how to deliver 'cunningly flighted' corners or free-kicks. It must be these new balls! My only other goal in that spell came from the penalty spot in a 2–1 home defeat by Everton which saw us hit bottom spot in the league for the first time that season.

In the six games I was out injured the team picked up five points from a possible twelve. Although we beat Spurs at Ashton Gate on my return, City still propped up the table. I was delighted to be back playing and made my comeback all the sweeter by scoring our only goal from the penalty spot. I scored again in our next match on 16 April at Norwich but we still ran out losers by the odd goal in three. That same day an article appeared in the local *Bristol News Green 'Un* about my injury predicament. Under the headline 'Bombshell by key player Cormack' it reported that I did not expect to be fit for more than half the club's remaining eight league games. I told the paper that, 'My knee simply won't stand up to the pressure. The combination of the hard grounds and two matches a week is causing it to blow up after each game.' The article mentioned the cartilage operation I had at the beginning of 1976 and I commented, 'I don't think I got my muscles built up enough in the close season before my move to Bristol. I don't expect any problems next season because I shall concentrate on building up my leg in the summer with a lot of weight training. The trouble now is time. I just haven't got enough rest between matches to get myself right for each game.'

At the end of April City were still firmly rooted at the foot of the league and the bookies were giving long odds on us staying in the First Division. Three of our remaining five games were at home – but against Manchester United, Leeds and Liverpool. I missed all of these games because of injury, but amazingly the team took five points out of a possible six. Chris Garland more than repaid his transfer fee, scoring our only goal in the 1–0 defeat of Leeds and both goals in the 2–1 defeat of the Reds. Fortunately for us the Liverpool match was one week before the European Cup Final in Rome and Bob Paisley rested several key players for the game. I replaced Chris at centre forward for a battling away draw at Middlesborough and I was substitute for the final league match away to Coventry City on 19 May.

It was still mathematically possible for any three from six teams to get relegated, depending on the final day's results. Going into the game Coventry, Sunderland, Stoke City, West Ham and ourselves had thirty-four points and Spurs were bottom with thirty-three. In all my years in football I had never known nervous tension like it before a match and it was twice as bad watching from the subs' bench. To make matters worse, our kick-off was delayed for fifteen minutes to enable the larger-than-normal crowd to get into the ground.

The omens were not good for us when Coventry held a two-goal lead with less than half an hour remaining, but then Gerry Gow pulled one back for us and shortly after Donny Gillies equalised. With fifteen minutes remaining the final scores from the other matches were relayed to all the players. Sunderland had lost, which meant that if our match stayed level, Coventry and ourselves would remain in the First Division. Without a word being spoken between opposing players, the game became a training match where the object for the team with the ball was to keep possession without attempting a shot at goal. It was funny and nerve-wracking at the same time. Fortunately I never had to experience that situation ever again.

At the final whistle Coventry and Bristol City fans celebrated their survival in England's top football flight and Alan Dicks' gamble in signing Norman, Chris and myself had paid off. I was delighted for Alan, who had invested his heart and soul in firstly getting City promoted and then keeping them in the First Division. I was also really chuffed that after a summer of building up my knee I would hopefully be fit and ready for the start of the new season.

Unlike Liverpool, Bristol City had a good representation of Scots in the first team squad and apart from me all had been recruited from Greenock Morton. Gerry Sweeney, Gerry Gow and Don Gillies had helped City win promotion and their first season in the First Division had been a great learning experience for them. Norman Hunter christened us the 'Scots Mafia' and it made for some interesting end-of-training Scotland versus England five-a-side matches. It got to the stage that the manager banned the matches less than two days before Bristol City games, such was the competitive nature of the fives.

On away trips I always roomed with Norman and he used to moan that he thought that he had got away from the 'Scots Mafia' at Leeds only to find that the backbone of the Bristol City team was made up of Scotsmen. But Bristol and Leeds were no different from every First Division club at the time, in that respect. Nowadays there are only a handful of Scottish players gracing the English Premier League. In fact there are more Scottish managers than there are Scottish internationalists. The conveyor belt that saw hundreds of Scottish players move to the top teams in England in the 60s, 70s and 80s is no longer there and that is a sad reflection on the current standard of the game in Scotland. It also reflects how cosmopolitan the English Premier League has become with hundreds of players coming from all over the world to play in the richest league in the world.

On one occasion fellow Scots Gerry Sweeney, Donnie Gillies and I were out for a meal with Norman and we decided to wind him up. When the bill for the meal arrived I made an excuse to go outside and was quickly followed by Gerry and Donnie. We hid behind a car across from the restaurant and after what seemed like ages the door burst open and Norman went running down the street in the direction of our hotel. To be honest, we had never seen him run as fast before in games or at training and we bolted after him. When we caught up with him at the hotel he called us all the dirty Scottish so and so's but it just goes to show that Yorkshire men are just as careful with their cash as us Scots. There was no way 'Bites Yer Legs' was paying the bill and he did his one and only runner from a restaurant at the back of us.

Most of the Bristol players were good pros and what they lacked in top-flight experience they more than made up for in hard work, skill and determination. I could see in our summer tour of Scandinavia that all the players had learned a great deal from their first year in the First Division which would stand them in good stead for season 1977/78. Whilst Spurs and Stoke had been relegated with Sunderland, my old club Nottingham Forest had been promoted from Division Two along with Wolves and Chelsea. Our first league match was against newly-promoted Wolves. And for the only time in my ten years in England I scored two penalties but despite this we lost 3–2. We fared no better in our next league match back at my old stomping ground in Nottingham, losing 1–0. Our first win didn't arrive until the sixth game of the season when we defeated West Ham 3–2. Three weeks later Norman Hunter inspired us to another 3–2 win over his old team Leeds scoring his first goal for City in the process. It would seem that 'Hell hath no fury like a good, old football pro spurned'.

Despite managing to put in a full pre-season at training, which included strengthening work on my knee, I missed half a dozen games during the first half of the campaign because I was still having problems with my knee. My absence included a 1–1 draw at Anfield with Gerry Gow equalising an early Kenny Dalglish strike. The team's goalscoring problem was resolved with a vengeance with the arrival of Joe Royle at the end of November. Joe arrived at Ashton Gate on loan from Manchester City and in his first match scored all four goals in a 4–1 defeat of Middlesborough. 'Josie', as I called him, was a strong, skilful goalscoring centre forward who had spent most of his career at Everton before moving to Maine Road in 1974, and I marvelled at his debut for City from the subs' bench. Josie's addition to the squad proved to be another inspirational acquisition by Alan Dicks.

By half-time in the First Division season, Bristol City had managed to position themselves above the relegation dog-fight zone and at one stage sat at the lofty height of twelfth. There were two personal highlights for me in league matches that season. The first came on 8 February when I scored Bristol's only goal in a 1–1 draw with Manchester United. Old Trafford was still to become the Theatre of Dreams but over 43,000 fans saw me score at the Stretford End against a United side that contained fellow Scots Arthur Albiston, Martin Buchan, Joe Jordan and Lou Macari. It was a great feeling, greeting the boos and abuse of the United fans with a Denis Law, arm raised salute, after equalising Gordon Hill's goal, and it also let my Scotland peers see that I could still play a bit. My second highlight came against Liverpool at a packed Ashton Gate on 15 April when I equalised Steve Heighway's opening goal. Unlike the previous season's relegation threatened battle for survival game, this time we were well clear of the drop zone.

Nevertheless, scoring the equalising goal and drawing against my old team gave me a lot of personal satisfaction. I was also relieved that the dropped point had not dented Liverpool's championship-winning aspirations – those had already been spoiled by Brian Clough's Nottingham Forest who had run away with the league in Forest's first season back in England's top flight. Still Liverpool would have the consolation of a second European Cup win a few weeks later against Bruges at Wembley.

My last game of the season came in Bristol City's penultimate league match against Manchester United at Ashton Gate, which we lost 1–0 to a Stuart Pearson goal.

Following our final league match, City ended the season in seventeenth place on thirty-five points – ironically exactly the same number of points we achieved the previous season but where we had taken ten points from our last eight games to stay up in 1976/77, City only managed four points from the remaining eight games a year later.

My second season at Bristol City saw us winning the Anglo-Scottish Cup. I had played in the inaugural tournament in my first season at Forest and I had formed the view that this competition meant a lot more to Scottish clubs and their supporters than it did to the English clubs' fans. The competition did not excite them the way it seemed to resonate with supporters of clubs north of the border. This was reflected in attendances where matches in Scotland attracted decent crowds, whereas only a small fraction of supporters of English club sides turned out for

Anglo-Scottish Cup matches. But in season 1977/78 Bristol City went all the way to the final, eventually defeating St Mirren over the two legs played. Part of the reason for that success was down to the Scottish players who played for City – I have no doubt about that. It meant a lot more to us Anglo-Scots going back to play against Scottish club sides – our professional pride was at stake and we had a point to prove to players and fans in Scotland desperate to take a Sassenach scalp.

The same could be said for players at Scottish clubs who were just as determined to bring these ex-pat Scots down a peg or two. It made for some interesting and bruising encounters. After some changes to the initial format, the competition started in early August when City played the first of three group matches against our Bristol Rovers neighbours. Despite it being a local derby, the game at Ashton Gate only attracted 5,500 spectators and we ran out comfortable 3–1 winners thanks to a Tom Ritchie hat-trick.

Our next two group matches were both away from home and in the first game we defeated Plymouth Argyle 2–0 where I managed to grab our first goal. In our final game we drew 1–1 with Birmingham at St Andrews, which enabled us to top the group.

In the quarter-final Bristol City were drawn against Partick Thistle and I played in the first leg match at Firhill on 13 September which Thistle won 2–0. I was left out of the return match at Ashton Gate a fortnight later, which City won 3–0 thanks to two goals from my replacement Jimmy Mann, with the winner coming from Clive Whitehead.

Having disposed of Thistle, City then faced my old club Hibs in the semi-final.

Again the first leg was in Scotland and it was not a match for the faint-hearted. *Scotsman* journalist Ian Wood's report of the game began: 'In a match which might better be charted by submissions and falls than goals, Hibs and Bristol City fought out a torrid draw at Easter Road last night which saw two players sent off, two booked and a penalty for Hibs missed.'

I was looking forward to returning to my old stomping ground, having last played there for Liverpool two years earlier, but I was not expecting the physical battle that transpired.

Donnie Gillies fired us ahead just before half-time but for most of that first half I was getting lumps kicked out of me by Des Bremner. Des was a big, strong lad from the Highland league who would go on to star for Aston Villa in their League Championship and European Cup-winning side but that night he was determined to make his mark on me. Every time I got the ball Des was snapping at my ankles and the longer the game wore on the more annoyed I got with Scottish referee Ian Foote's leniency to the fouling.

Hibs equalised right at the start of the second half, which gave them and their fans a huge lift. Norman Hunter was then sent off for a tackle on Ally MacLeod with about fifteen minutes left and then a few minutes later I too saw red. Bremner caught me late again and my boot came flying off. When the referee waved play on, I turned around and hit Bremner, laying him out. The old Sparta Boxing Club training had not deserted me. It was my first sending-off in five years although it was not such an unusual sight for Hibs supporters who remembered my four red cards when I played at Easter Road.

The excitement didn't end there. Foote awarded Hibs a penalty with five minutes remaining but justice was done when John Shaw saved Ally MacLeod's spot-kick.

Fortunately the return match was played while I was out injured and I watched from the safety of the stand as Bristol beat

Hibs 5–3 at Ashton Gate. After the excitement and drama of the first match over 6,000 City fans turned up for the second leg despite it being a horrible wet night and they were treated to a five star performance from the City team.

The 6–4 aggregate victory set Bristol City up for a two-legged final against St Mirren, managed by a young, up and coming Alex Ferguson. For the third tie running our first game was away from home but we left Love Street with a 2–1 lead after Kevin Mabbutt and I grabbed a goal apiece. Unfortunately I got injured in a league game at Coventry two days before the second leg but was part of a 16,000 Ashton Gate crowd that watched City draw 1–1 to win the final 3–2 on aggregate.

It may have only been the Anglo-Scottish Cup but City supporters and players celebrated as if it was the European Cup. Given it was the club's second trophy in its eighty-year history we had every reason to be happy. St Mirren got ample revenge in the next two seasons knocking City out at the quarter-final stage both times.

I made thirty-three first team appearances in my second season at City, was sub on two occasions and managed nine goals. That proved to be my best season in my three and a half years at Ashton Gate. In 1978/79 the club finished thirteenth, their highest league position in their four-year run in the First Division. I only managed fourteen league starts and scored three goals, two of them from the penalty spot and the other in a five-goal hammering of Coventry where Joe Royle grabbed a hat-trick.

Joe and I became good friends, and Marion and Joe's wife Janet also hit it off. One summer we took our families on holiday to Morocco which proved an eventful trip. Our respective children were around the same age and the kids really got on well together which as every parent knows is half the battle on family holidays. The problem wasn't looking after the kids, though, it was more the kids needing to keep a beady eye on their parents. It was one of those all-inclusive holidays where local alcoholic drinks were free. The Moroccan beer was passable, which is more than could be said for the local wine which tasted as if the wine makers had kept their socks on when treading the grapes. After a few days we discovered that mixing the red and white together produced a drinkable rose that we enjoyed with lunch and dinner.

One afternoon after a pleasant, relaxing lunch, Joe and I joined in a 'take-on' between guests and staff at the hotel. Unfortunately what started out as a friendly football match quickly deteriorated into a battle for survival when the Moroccans realised the opposition team contained a couple of ringers from the English First Division. Joe was big and ugly enough to look after himself but one waiter wanted to make a name for himself by kicking lumps out of me whether I had the ball or not. Either that or he wasn't happy with the tips I had been giving him, but after countless late tackles and digs off the ball the red mist descended and I hooked him whilst play raged at the other end of the park.

Thinking back, it was very reminiscent of the Cagliari match in my second North American tour with Hibs and within seconds of taking the law into my own hands I was surrounded by angry Moroccans seeking retribution for their comatose team-mate. Thankfully the US Cavalry was close at hand in the shape of big Joe Royle and he ushered me back to the safety of my hotel room. On the way there he asked me, 'What was that all about, Peter?' to which I replied, 'I'm sorry, Josie, but that wee Moroccan had one sneaky kick too many.' Joe had never seen my dark side before and he said, 'Well, remind me never to get in your bad books at training. With Norman and you in our side I'll fancy City's chances in a battle against anyone.'

Fortunately for us when the hotel management heard of the altercation they sent the waiter to our table at dinner that night to apologise. To be honest, I felt embarrassed when he appeared sporting a black eye that was getting darker by the minute and the following day I bought a Liverpool shirt at the local market and signed it for him. He was made up and we enjoyed five-star service at meal times for the rest of the holiday.

Season 1979/80 was to be my last season at Bristol City and it would also be City's last season in the English First Division. I'll leave you to draw your own conclusions from that statement of fact. I was only picked to start one match that season, and ironically it was against my old team Nottingham Forest on 22 September at Ashton Gate.

Only a few months earlier Forest had won the European Cup for the first time. Brian Clough had performed miracles at Nottingham Forest but that Saturday in Bristol they could only manage a 1–1 draw after being behind at half-time to a Jimmy Mann goal.

Jimmy had taken my place in the team's left midfield berth and I was drafted into the Forest match to play alongside Jimmy to strengthen our midfield. I was frustrated at not getting a regular first team game and the guys started to give me stick at training after I appeared with a large holdall. In truth, the kit bag was a present from Marion and it contained all my lotions, potions, shampoo and conditioner. It even included a portable hairdryer for my coiffured dark locks, which only increased the mirth and merriment from my team-mates. The Bristol players used to joke that I'd nicked Kevin Keegan's complimentary Brut aftershave samples but when the manager asked me one day what was in the bag I snapped back, 'It's a fucking bomb making kit for you. I'm pissed off at being left out of the team.' Whilst the players saw the funny side of my comment the manager was not amused and needless to say my reaction did not get me back into the side. I pulled a Bristol City shirt on for the last time when I was picked as a substitute for an away match against Norwich on

15 December 1979. The 2–0 defeat left us in nineteenth place and a week later the team dropped to twentieth spot following a 1–0 home defeat by Southampton. City would never be out of the relegation zone for the remainder of the season, finally finishing in twentieth place and getting relegated along with Derby County and Bolton Wanderers.

Just after the turn of the year Alan Dicks told me that he would be happy to let me go if I could find another club. In my three and a half years at Bristol City I played in eighty-six matches and scored nineteen goals. As well as making a significant contribution in my first two seasons at the club, which helped keep City in the First Division, I made many great friends in my time at Ashton Gate.

I am sure, like me, there are many Robins fans who fondly remember the team's great adventure for the four successive seasons they graced the English First Division. Alan Dicks did a superb job as manager and he was very fair to me when he thought I could no longer make a contribution for the team. At the start of 1980 I certainly hadn't envisaged that my next football move would be back to where my career had started almost eighteen years earlier and I certainly never expected to join up with a living football legend.

13

BYE, BYE BRISTOL, HELLO BESTIE

I enjoyed three and a half good years at Bristol City. The team held its own in the English First Division and had won the Anglo-Scottish Cup. Marion and I lived in a beautiful house and Donna Lee and young Pete were growing up happy and contended. We had also made many good friends inside and outside the Bristol football family but as the old saying goes, all good things must come to an end. By the start of 1980, injuries and more than six hundred first team games in eighteen years of top-flight foot-ball had taken their toll. Bristol could not have been fairer and the manager said the club would not stand in my way if another team were interested in acquiring my services.

At this time many British football professionals saw out the end of their career in the burgeoning North American Soccer League. Football was trying to gain a foothold in the States with world famous professionals such as Pelé and Franz Beckenbauer selling the football 'product' to the sport-mad American audi-ences. I was approached by Tulsa Roughnecks who dangled a very tempting five-figure carrot to go and play for them, but whilst Marion and I were deliberating the pros and cons for our young family of a move to Oklahoma, the Hibs manager Eddie Turnbull telephoned me and asked if I would be interested in returning to Easter Road.

*

Like one of my favourite singers Gene Pitney, 'I was twenty-four hours from Tulsa' when Eddie's call came to rejoin the Hibees. Eddie Turnbull was a legend with Hibs fans. Not only was he a member of the great Famous Five team from the 1950s, as manager of Hibs, he had built one of the best teams in Scotland during the early 1970s. Eddie had taken over from Willie McFarlane a few months after I left Hibs in 1970 and guided the team to Scottish League Cup success in 1972. He was from the Bill Shankly and Jock Stein school of football managers and didn't suffer fools gladly. He was small in height but his stature was huge. I had the utmost respect for Eddie, who ruled the dressing room with an iron fist. Although I had spent ten years playing in the English First Division, our friends in Edinburgh regularly regaled us with tales from behind the scenes at Easter Road. The funniest story I remember happened at half-time in a game when Eddie reprimanded the Hibs centre forward Alan Gordon for not following pre-match instructions. Alan was a very good centre forward and a chartered accountant to boot, and during Eddie's half-time tirade he turned to Alan and said, 'The trouble wi' you, Gordon, is that all your brains are in yer fuckin' heid.' Apparently big Alan sat non-plussed whilst the rest of the players rocked with laughter.

But in February 1980 Eddie's Hibs team were having a tough time of it, propping up the Scottish Premier League and odds-on favourites to be relegated at the end of the season.

To the casual observer it may seem odd that I turned my back on a big payday in the United States to return to Hibs but there were also two big football incentives for me choosing Easter Road. The first was that Eddie Turnbull said he wanted to groom me to take over for him as manager when he finally decided to call it a day. The second was that a few months earlier, Hibs chairman Tom Hart had brought George Best to play at Easter Road.

In 1979 George was playing for Fort Lauderdale Strikers in the NASL after intermittent spells with Dunstable Town, Stockport County, Los Angeles Aztecs, Cork City and Fulham, with his pal Rodney Marsh. In November that year Hibs' chairman Tom Hart offered Bestie £2,000 every time he turned out for Hibs. That was ten times more than the average Scottish professional player's weekly wage and when news broke that George Best was wanted by Hibs many people, including me, were sceptical. I had played against George several times when he was in his prime with Manchester United and was in awe of his footballing talent. I had been fortunate to play against all the footballing greats from that era and in my book Bestie was right up there with Pele, Johann Cruyff and Eusebio. He had everything – two good feet, lightning pace, was excellent in the air and a demon tackler. If truth be told, I often fancied myself as the Scottish Bestie but my ex-Hibs team-mate Peter Marinello was given that tag after he signed for Arsenal in 1970.

When George made his debut for Hibs at the end of November against St Mirren it was national news and I received telephone calls in the run-up to the game from many friends in Edinburgh who said that they were going to Love Street to see Scottish football history being made. The following week just over 20,000 people turned up at Easter Road to see Bestie make his home debut against Partick Thistle. That was double the average gate at this time. When Marion and I sat down and looked at my football options in early 1980, the offer to go back to Edinburgh and rejoin Hibs won hands down. Although Hibs couldn't compete with Tulsa in money terms, Tom Hart dug deep in his pocket and I received a healthy signing-on fee to sweeten the deal.

The thought of playing in the same team as Bestie really excited me, and the longer-term opportunity of honing my coaching skills with a view to replacing Eddie Turnbull as manager at Easter Road clinched the deal. Marion and I were also looking forward to bringing up our two children in our home city beside family and long-standing close friends. I had no sooner informed Hibs and Bristol City of my decision when two things happened to put a spanner in the works. First, Willie Ormond agreed to become assistant manager at Hibs. Willie and I had not parted on the best of terms when he was manager of Scotland and chose not to play me in any of the Scotland games at the 1974 World Cup. He had subsequently left the Scotland job to manage Hearts but was given the bullet by them following their relegation to the First Division the previous season. Hibs had first approached Willie to become the assistant to Eddie Turnbull a few weeks before I signed but he had knocked them back. But at the end of January Willie had a change of heart and decided to accept a second approach by Hibs to become Eddie's right-hand man at Easter Road. Good timing for me it was not.

Whilst I had no desire to be a player-coach at the time, I was not looking forward to teaming up with Willie again after my depressing World Cup experience. The second factor to put a damper on my return to Hibs was that Bestie managed to get himself suspended by the club after failing to turn up for a home match with Morton and then going on a drinking bender with the French rugby team who were in Edinburgh for a Five Nations international against Scotland. When Marion and I returned to Edinburgh in mid-February all the newspapers were full of George's suspension and stories of him being on the razz with the French rugby player Jean-Pierre Rives. Although Hibs had suspended Bestie he was still holed up at the North British Hotel, now the Balmoral, with the paparazzi and unscrupulous journalists from the tabloid press for company.

The weekend before I made my Hibs debut, the team, minus Bestie, beat Ayr United 2–0 in a Scottish Cup tie. Whilst Hibs were marching on in the Cup, George spent the afternoon sobering up in his hotel room, and not for the first time in his life he had glamorous female company. I arrived at Easter Road in the middle of a media storm and one player told me that when club officials eventually got into George's room on the Sunday lunchtime he was lying in bed with a scantily clad 'bird'. When they asked Bestie if he was fit for the game George's reply was pure Bestie: 'What would you rather do – spend the afternoon in bed with her or play against Ayr United?'

That was the final straw for Hibs chairman Tom Hart, who was personally funding Bestie's pay-per-game arrangement and he announced that George was sacked. As you could imagine, the newspapers during the week prior to my debut at Dundee United were full of George's antics, which certainly helped take the spotlight off my return to Easter Road. Unfortunately it didn't take any pressure off the rest of the players and we lost 1–0 at Tannadice to continue the team's run of having lost every away league game that season. More seriously, it meant that we were now seven points adrift from the next team above us in the league who, ironically, were Dundee United. In truth I thought the 1–0 scoreline flattered us and we had our goalkeeper, Jim McArthur, to thank for not suffering a far heavier defeat.

After my first game and a couple of training sessions I thought there were enough good players in the squad to save the club from relegation but it concerned me that heads seemed to drop as soon as we went behind. The squad had good, experienced players in Tony Higgins, Jackie McNamara, George Stewart and Arthur Duncan along with some promising youngsters in Craig Paterson, Ally Brazil, Willie Jamieson and Gordon Rae.

In my ten years in the English First Division the one striking feature I noticed with every team was that players continued to follow their pre-match instructions even when they went a goal behind. In that first match back at Hibs I thought too many players lost their positional discipline as well as their confidence when United took the lead.

As I rested on the Sunday following the game this was uppermost in my mind, particularly as the following week we were away to Rangers at Ibrox – a daunting task at the best of times but a huge mountain to climb with the team's confidence at rock bottom. In the run-up to the Rangers game Tom Hart announced that he was going to give George Best another chance and Bestie arrived at Edinburgh Airport on the Wednesday with his wife Angie for company (or more likely to try and keep him on the straight and narrow). I and several other Hibs players made a point of meeting George outside the ground on his first day back at Easter Road to let him, the media and fans see how much we valued having him as a team-mate. The last time I had seen George was when I was playing for Liverpool when we beat Man United 2–0 at Anfield in December 1973. It was around this time that Bestie's football career started to take a nosedive, and a few weeks after that match he walked out of United for good. That was also the season they were relegated from the First Division.

I arrived at Hibs in the short time George had been gone following his brief suspension, and after shaking hands Bestie pulled me to one side and told me that my signing was one of the reasons he had returned.

I was genuinely chuffed when he said, 'Peter, you are a footballer's footballer and it will be good playing with somebody who is on the same wavelength as me.'

Coming from a guy I had always admired I was indeed flattered, but part of me was also thinking that given the number of games in our legs and the injuries we both endured over the years we had a tough job on our hands. George and I were the same age and at thirty-three our best playing days were definitely behind us. But Bestie's compliment was yet another reason for me to admire George the man as opposed to the image the media painted of him, and I couldn't wait to team up with him on the Saturday at Ibrox.

As we took to the pitch I was at right half, playing wide midfield and George was wearing his customary number eleven shirt with a roving commission to pick up the ball, take on defenders and spray passes. Unfortunately due to a combination of his four-week lay-off and the anti-alcohol treatment he had started, George was a shadow of his former self and struggled to get into the game in the first half. I think Eddie Turnbull decided to save George from further embarrassment and abuse from the Ibrox faithful and substituted him early in the second half. However, whilst the team played well after George's early departure we still lost 1–0 to keep our abysmal away record intact.

I teamed up with George the following week for a quarter-final Scottish Cup match at Berwick Rangers but Bestie was again anonymous in the game and this time he was left in the dressing room at half-time. We managed to grind out a 0–0 draw with the Wee Rangers to force a replay back at Easter Road which we won 1–0 the following Wednesday. George was again withdrawn at the break because of a mysterious injury he allegedly picked up and we were grateful to Ally MacLeod for netting our winner, which set up a semi-final tie with Celtic.

During this period Bestie was training full-time with the club following the breakdown of his previous arrangement, which had been to turn up on the Friday before a game and play on the Saturday. All the players, myself included, loved working with George in training and I admired his determination to get fully fit. Part of my remit with the club was to coach the young players in the afternoon and I persuaded George to join in these coaching sessions. To be honest, he appreciated being asked, as a major part of George's problems lay with him getting bored and up to mischief away from football. The young lads also loved having George at training sessions and he would play one-twos off their shins and bet them on the number of times he could nutmeg them.

He never once lost a bet and was the only player I ever saw who could put a ball through a player's legs after telling him that he was going to do it. The kids used to moan to me that he was just lucky and I would have to keep telling them that no one is that lucky – it takes natural football ability to do what George did at training day-in and day-out and Bestie had that by the bucketful.

After the French rugby weekend debacle, George committed himself 100 per cent to getting fit and laying off the booze. Initially Hibs relocated him to the Caledonian Hotel on the west side of Princes Street and then the club rented a flat for Angie and George in the city's West End when she decided to join him permanently in Edinburgh. The week before Angie arrived, George stayed with Marion and me in our house. He loved nothing better than playing with our two children and wee Pete used to hurry home from school to get changed into his Hibs strip and play football in our garden with his dad and 'Uncle George'.

Bestie and I would also sit for hours talking about previous games we had played in and I recall one conversation where we discussed defenders we had come up against. Bestie said that Liverpool's Tommy Smith was the hardest defender he faced, not just because Tommy was a great tackler but because he could read a game and after breaking up an opposition attack launch a counter-offensive from deep in defence with the accuracy his of passing.

The one thing we both agreed on was that Chelsea's Ron 'Chopper' Harris was the dirtiest defender we encountered in the English First Division. Chopper's eyes just glazed over when he looked at you and you daren't have your back to him with the ball arriving at your feet because invariably you would end up on your arse. George said that although Harris was the 'maddest and baddest' defender in England he always enjoyed playing against him, as no matter how hard Chopper tried to kick him Bestie would keep going back for more to let him see that he wasn't going to be intimated. That let me see that Bestie was not just an awesome football player but he was also tremendously brave.

After Angie arrived to stay with George in Edinburgh, Marion and I went out regularly for meals with them and it was on these occasions that they talked to us about starting a family. Marion and I were delighted when young Calum was born in February the following year. Whilst George was quite content drinking Perrier water, he was excellent company and to anyone that didn't know him, of which there were very few, they would never have known about his battle with the demon drink.

It was a privilege for me to get to know George Best at this time and I just wish our combined football experience could have got Hibs out of the dire predicament they were in. Near the end of March, Bestie turned in his best performance in the seven games I played in the same team as him when we beat Dundee 2–0 at Easter Road. Despite some brutal tackling from ex-Hibs player Eric Schaedler, George pinged passes all over the park and as well as running the Dundee defence ragged he scored the first goal and set up the second in a 2–1 win. Dundee were managed at the time by my ex-Nottingham Forest team-mate Tommy Gemmell and after the match Big Tam asked me what Bestie had been on that day, given the press reports of his 'battle with the booze'. When I told him it was down to hard work at training and drinking Perrier water Tam said that he was going to order a case of the stuff for his players if that's what it does for you. But that was as good as it got for Hibs, Bestie and me. We only managed one more win in the league for the remainder of the season and were thumped 5–0 by Celtic in the semi-final of the Scottish Cup.

I was none too happy at being dropped for that semi-final, and the Tuesday after the Hampden hammering Eddie Turnbull was sacked as manager and replaced by my 'pal' Willie Ormond. The following night we travelled to Aberdeen for a league match and Willie carried on where he left off in West Germany by leaving me out of the team, which only darkened my mood even more. Aberdeen were battling it out with Celtic for the league title and Bestie was at his imperious cheeky chappy best, upsetting the Aberdeen players and fans with some long pass-backs and mazy dribbles which helped earn Hibs a 1–1 draw and our first point away from home that season. The Aberdeen players thought they had blown their league chance and after the game their captain Willie Miller sought out Bestie and after exchanging a few 'pleasantries' the two of them ended up brawling in the tunnel.

The following Saturday I was on the bench for Bestie's last match of the season at home to Dundee United. I came on for Gordon Rae midway through the second half but the 2–0 defeat was a repeat of the scoreline from only a couple of weeks earlier. With George gone back to the States on his travels, we managed to double our away points tally for the season in a hard-fought 1–1 draw with Morton at Cappielow.

With us doomed for relegation to the First Division, Alex Ferguson's Aberdeen team rolled up to Easter Road on 3 May and hammered us 5–0 to give Fergie's Dons their first Scottish Premier League Championship trophy. Hibs chairman Tom Hart made himself popular with Fergie and the Aberdeen players when he had a case of champagne delivered to their dressing room after the match. Unbeknown to them, it had been left over from the previous season's Cup Final defeat to Rangers and after our semi-final defeat and relegation to the First Division, Tom probably felt that Hibs would not have much use for the bubbly in the near future.

It had been a real eye-opener return for me at Easter Road and I brooded over the close season at the turn of events. When I decided to sign for Hibs at the start of the year it was on the basis of a foot in the door to the manager's job and playing alongside Georgie Best. Now the man who had said that he saw me as his 'heir apparent' was gone and his replacement was the manager who put paid to my Scotland career six years earlier. As for Bestie, he had returned to North America to play in the NASL for San Jose Earthquakes and true to previous form he went AWOL as soon as his plane touched down in the US.

Of the sixteen games I played in the previous season for Hibs, George Best played in seven of them and in truth the team's relegation fate was sealed before Bestie slipped on a Hibs shirt at the end of November, and long before I made my debut three months later.

Still, none of this consoled me during the close season and I can't honestly say I was looking forward to starting my nineteenth season as a professional footballer in the Scottish First Division.

Unlike when I was at Nottingham Forest, there was no Bill Shankly to rescue me from my predicament and when the season kicked off on 9 August with Hibs at home to Raith Rovers, I was in the starting line-up. The chairman had told the players and the fans that relegation was going to cost the club in excess of £200,000 and as a consequence several members of the first team squad were released in the summer. Despite the economic impact of relegation, Hibs had splashed out £60,000 installing under-soil heating, the first club in Scotland to make such an investment. Once again the club showed that they were ahead of all other Scottish clubs when it came to investing in the future even though relegation had cost Hibs the shirt sponsorship deal they had negotiated three years earlier with sports firm Bukta.

The omens were not good in that first league game with Raith when we conceded a last-minute goal in a 1–0 defeat. The following Saturday I scored my one and only goal in my second spell at Easter Road when we put Stirling Albion to the sword 2–0 at their Annfield stadium. It was somewhat ironic that what turned out to be my last senior goal was my 100th competitive goal in a Hibs shirt and it was at the other Annfield.

I played in three more matches in August but got injured in the 1–1 home draw against Alloa. As a consequence of the reduced number of players at the club the team faced an injury crisis early in the season, and Tom Hart once again turned to George Best to help the club out of their predicament. Bestie duly appeared in an away league match at Dundee and although his return to Scottish football was much more low-key than ten months earlier, his appearance did help us to a 2–1 win. George made another five appearances for Hibs that season, finally bowing out in a 2–0 victory over Falkirk on 11 October where he was made team captain for the day.

I only managed another four matches that season, unfortunately none of them coinciding with appearances by Bestie. I played my final match for Hibs in a 2–0 home defeat in the quarter-final of the Scottish League Cup on Wednesday 23 October 1980. After drawing 2–2 in the first leg at Somerset Park the return match was played on a horrible, rain-drenched evening and just over 5,000 hardy souls defied the terrible conditions where we gave a performance to match the weather.

I was a month short of playing eighteen years in top-flight football, with almost half the 650-plus matches in the green and white of Hibs. The Hibs team for my final match was in goals Colin Kelly, 2 Stephen Brown, 3 Arthur Duncan, 4 Ally Brazil, 5 Craig Paterson, 6 Ralph Callachan, 7 Willie Jamieson, 8 Gordon Rae, 9 Ally MacLeod, 10 Peter Cormack and 11 John Connolly.

I had heard of and read about other footballers who dreaded hanging up their boots and when the time came for me to retire from playing I shared that fear and uncertainty. As I got older it took longer to recover from injuries and aches and pains following matches. In the first few months of the 1980/81 season my body was calling time on my football career and I had to consider where my future lay. Given I had been involved in professional football since signing for Hibs just after my sixteenth birthday, my options were pretty limited. I had always fancied having a go at football management and felt that I had a lot to give back to the game that had given me so much as a player. I had been lucky enough to play under two of Scotland's greatest managers, Jock Stein and Bill Shankly, and wanted to use their training methods and their approaches to playing the game as I developed my own style of football management.

I had gone back to Hibs to cut my coaching teeth under Eddie Turnbull but his plans for handing me the managerial reins evaporated when he was given his P45. One thing was certain: I had no chance of working as an understudy to Willie Ormond and in truth I wouldn't have wanted to even if he had offered. Then once again the good hand of fate came to my rescue when, a couple of weeks after my final match, Hibs sacked Ormond and brought in former Celtic Lisbon Lion Bertie Auld. Bertie ended his playing career at Easter Road and had been making a name for himself as manager at Partick Thistle. Tom Hart, the Hibs chairman, decided he was the right man for the manager's hot-seat at Easter Road after Willie Ormond was sacked following a 3–3 draw with Hamilton on 15 November.

As a former Hibs player and Celtic legend, Auld was a popular appointment with the vast majority of Hibs fans. The cigar-smoking Bertie was also a good appointment for me, as his departure from Thistle gave me a chance to go straight into football management.

Whilst Bertie was driving his Jag eastwards on the M8 towards Easter Road, I was driving in the opposite direction heading for the manager's chair he had vacated at Firhill, firmly believing that I could make my mark in football management. It was a challenge I was looking forward to and I had every confidence that my football experience and know-how would stand me in good stead. I was determined that the old adage that 'the only certainty in football management is that at some point you will be sacked' would not apply to me. Well, there's nothing like being optimistic in your first management job, is there?

14

SCOTLAND HIGHS AND LOWS

When I look back at my playing career the biggest regret I have is that I never managed to play at a World Cup Finals. I was lucky enough to be part of Scotland's first trip to a Finals in sixteen years when we qualified for West Germany in 1974, and whilst being part of the squad was a great experience, it was frustrating watching all three games from the subs' bench. It still rankles with me almost forty years on that when I was at the peak of my game Willie Ormond denied me the chance of playing at the World Cup. West Germany was also to be my last involvement with the Scotland national team, and it was a disappointing end to my international career and in such stark contrast to when I won my first cap against Brazil in June 1966.

As every Scotsman knows, to his cost the 1966 World Cup held in England was won by the host country. Like Denis Law I spent the afternoon of the Final playing golf rather than watching England and West Germany battle it out at Wembley. It's not that I am anti-English – far from it; some of my best friends from my football days are ex-England Internationals – but in professional sport you never want your oldest rival getting one over on you. If England were going to win the World Cup, I couldn't bear watching them do it, so playing eighteen holes of golf at Torphin Hill Golf Club seemed like a good alternative, especially as it was a nice sunny July afternoon. Although Scotland had not managed to qualify for the 1966 Finals after going down 3–0 to

Italy the previous December, the SFA organised two glamour friendly matches at Hampden against Portugal and Brazil. At the beginning of June I received an official letter from Willie Allan, SFA Secretary, which contained the pool of players selected for the two friendly matches, along with the timetable and arrangements for the squad members. My name sat proudly between Charlie Cooke of Chelsea and Bobby Ferguson, the Kilmarnock goalkeeper. Also included in the squad was my boyhood hero Alex 'The Golden Vision' Young.

I still have Willie Allan's letter and as well as the team squad, meeting arrangements and training timetable it states that 'those who possess golf clubs should bring them along' and that 'training sessions will be arranged at the discretion of the team manager'. In those far-flung days players had to provide their own boots, gym shoes, spare studs (to guard against possible changes in the weather) and shinguards. Still, the letter advised me that players would receive a sixty-pound fee for each match they took part in and reserves would get thirty-pounds. Finally the letter stated that 'players are forbidden to comment upon matches in press reports, or on radio or television after the game'. Changed days indeed from today, when players are pounced upon by pitchside reporters seconds after the final whistle.

After getting my first international call-up I couldn't wait to join the Scotland squad at Glasgow's North British Hotel on 13 June before we made our way by coach to the Queen's Hotel in Largs where we were based prior to both matches. Now for those cynics amongst you who think that this was a nice wee summer jaunt I can assure you that all the Scotland players in the squad were consummate professionals and trained hard for the matches against two of the best teams playing in the World Cup Finals a few weeks later.

The Scotland manager John Prentice wouldn't have tolerated anything else, and I learned more in those two weeks with the Scotland squad than I had previously learnt in three years as a professional at Hibs. Prentice had been appointed part-time Scotland manager in March following Scotland's unsuccessful attempt to qualify for the '66 World Cup but had a disappointing start to the job after Scotland lost 4–3 to England at Hampden in early April. That was followed up in May with a 3–0 drubbing by Holland at Hampden. I was very impressed with the new Scotland manager's coaching abilities as he was a perfectionist in every aspect of the game and worked the players extremely hard on the training ground at Largs.

For the first match against Portugal the manager decided to play a team of experienced internationalists and as it would turn out, Alex Young made his final Scotland appearance in the 1–0 defeat. Portugal were a very good team and it was no surprise to me when they later reached the semi-final of the World Cup, only losing out to two Bobby Charlton goals at Wembley. They had the star of the tournament in Eusebio and their centre forward Torres was good in the air and also comfortable with the ball at his feet. It was a goal from Torres midway through the second half that beat Scotland in the first friendly match. I was on the bench for that match and I loved the atmosphere of a packed Hampden Park, little thinking at the time that the following Saturday evening it would be me on the park making my debut against the reigning World Champions.

Following the Portugal match John Prentice worked the players twice as hard at training in the run-up to the Brazil game. He was especially focused on creating a disciplined system that would make us hard to beat and that players could become comfortable with. For too many years he felt that Scotland teams were too gung-ho in their approach to games, happy to lose by the odd goal in a high-scoring game. Prentice wanted to change that mentality and two days before the Brazil game he told me the role he wanted me to perform in the number eleven jersey. Playing at inside left was the legendary Jim Baxter, and 'Slim Jim' was given licence to pick the ball up and run at the Brazilians. I was expected to cover back for him in midfield, whilst Billy Bremner was given the monumental task of trying to shackle the undisputed best player in the world, Pelé.

Brazil were heading to the World Cup as favourites to lift the trophy for a third consecutive time but in my first international at just nineteen years of age I was an integral part of a Scotland side that outplayed and out-fought the World Champions that June night at Hampden. Writing his report of the match, football journalist Hugh Taylor said:

> Modern planning, a style from tomorrow's football text-book, and good old-fashioned spirit, gave Scotland the greatest result for years – a magnificent draw with World Champions Brazil. Be proud of our international team. Don't let us damn our brilliant players with faint praise. It was a wonderful result. I never thought it would happen. How could I? HOW COULD ANYONE?
>
> But it did and it wasn't a fluke – and indeed Scotland were unlucky not to beat baffled Brazil.

The headline on the back page of *The Scotsman* the following Monday read 'Scots show spirit, discipline and method'.

It really was a dream international debut for me. Celtic's Stevie Chalmers put us ahead in the first minute, and although Brazil equalised fifteen minutes later through Servillo, with Bremner marking Pelé out of the game, Jim Baxter ran the show in midfield for most of the match. What I lacked in experience I more than made up for in effort and I don't think I'd worked as hard or covered as much turf in a game up until that match. At the final whistle I swapped jerseys with the famous Brazil inside right Gerson and it still has pride of place in my trophy cabinet at home. I had hoped to get Pelé's shirt but given the man-marking job done on him by Billy Bremner I think wee Billy already had Pelé's jersey long before the referee blew his full-time whistle.

After the match John Prentice was fulsome in his praise of all the Scotland players but in the dressing room afterwards he took me to one side and told me that I had a long Scotland career in front of me. I certainly had a longer career to look forward to than he did. Three months after the Brazil game Prentice resigned to take up the full-time manager's job at Falkirk, and it would be another two and a half years before I would win my second Scotland cap.

Throughout my football career, representing Scotland always meant a lot to me. Today top British pros' commitment to their national side is often questioned by the media and fans, which I think is unfair. I am certain that playing for their countries means just as much to them as it did in my day, but today's players have far more outside pressures and influences to contend with. For one, I think club managers often resent having to release players for what they regard as meaningless international friendly matches. At the root cause of the problem is the vast sums top players are now paid in wages. Clubs now exert much more influence on their players and the football associations than ever before, creating tensions between players' loyalties to their employer and turning out for their country. I don't see that dilemma being resolved anytime soon.

Whilst at Hibs my biggest problem was breaking the monopoly Old Firm players seemed to have over Scottish managers and selectors. I have no doubt that if I had been playing for either Celtic or Rangers in the 1960s I would have won a lot more

Scotland caps than the four I did get. There were plenty of other Scottish club players in the same position as me, but that was just the way it was at the time.

Before making my full international debut in June 1966, I had represented Scotland at Youth International, Secondary Juvenile and Scottish Amateur level. I had also played twice for the Scotland Under-23 team. My first Under-23 game was in 1964 shortly after I had established myself in the Hibs first team under Jock Stein. I was picked to play on the right wing in a young Scotland team that included Billy Bremner, George Graham, Charlie Cooke and Spurs left winger Jimmy Robertson, and we ran out 3–0 winners over Wales at Rugby Park. I managed to bag the second goal and laid on the third for wee Billy.

A few months later I was picked to play outside left for Scotland Under-23's against England. The game ended in a 0–0 draw and following that match the Under-23 series of matches was suspended in the run-up to the 1966 World Cup.

I played a further three times for the Scotland Under-23 side. Early in 1967 I was picked to play inside left in a team including my Hibs team-mate Pat Stanton, Leeds' Eddie Gray, my ex-Scotland amateur pal Alex Edwards from Dunfermline and a future full international team-mate Jim McCalliog, who at that time played for Sheffield Wednesday. We hammered the Welsh Under-23's 6–0 at Wrexham's Racecourse Ground and a couple of months later we beat England 3–1 at St James Park in Newcastle. Whilst I didn't manage to get amongst the goals in the Welsh match, I scored our decisive second goal in the England game – a screamer from twenty-five yards – just a few minutes after my future Liverpool team-mate Tommy Smith had equalised for England. I seemed to revel in international matches in the north-east of England and the Under-23 game came almost four years after the Scottish Amateur team won the FA's Centenary tournament at Sunderland's ground.

The Scotland Under-23 match against England was the new full-time manager Bobby Brown's first competitive match in charge following his appointment after John Prentice's short reign, and the young Scotland team's victory was a prelude to the full international side's famous 3–2 victory at Wembley the following month. Unfortunately whilst the Scotland 'big team' were handing the World Champions their first defeat since winning the World Cup the previous year, I was playing for Hibs in a league match against Ayr United at Easter Road. My Scotland Wembley debut would have to wait another four years.

Twelve months later I came within a whisker of winning my second full international cap after I received a telephone call from Bobby Brown at midnight on the Thursday before the Scotland vs England match at Hampden. Scotland striker Alan Gilzean was injured and his place in the team was in doubt. When I joined up with the Scotland squad at Largs on the Friday morning, the manager informed me that it was between Celtic's 'Yogi' Hughes and me if Gilzean didn't make it. Then on the Friday evening prior to the match Brown gave me the bad news that he had decided to play Hughes up front. To say I was gutted is an understatement and I had gone from the high of getting called up to be told I would not be playing all in the space of twenty-four hours. I didn't even get the consolation of sitting on the subs' bench. Because the match was a European Nations Cup tie only goalkeepers could be substituted, so I had to suffer watching the match from the centre stand at Hampden, which was never an enjoyable experience when you thought you should be out there on the park. Ironically sitting next to me in the stand was wee Jinky Johnstone who was even more pissed off than me that he wasn't in Brown's starting line-up. In fairness to the manager, Yogi scored Scotland's only goal in the 1–1 draw but that was of no consolation to me at the time.

Still, it wasn't all doom and gloom. My flying visit to Largs and watching the match from the centre stand earned me thirty pounds with a pair of new Adidas Santiagos, worth all of a tenner at the time, thrown in for good measure. The SFA still outlawed players speaking to the press after the game, so it was left to my mum to voice my displeasure.

When I was asked by the *Edinburgh Evening News* if I felt I'd have been picked if I played for Celtic or Rangers it was a straight bat, 'No Comment,' and 'I only wanted to get back to Edinburgh after the game.' My mum was less diplomatic and she told the paper, 'Peter's dad and I watched the game on TV. We're sure Peter would have made all the difference to Scotland's attack. If he hadn't been an Edinburgh boy he would have walked into the team.'

So there you have it, a totally impartial, unbiased opinion, which the journalist John Gibson neatly summed up, saying, 'It's true what they say: Mother knows best.'

I don't know if it was down to my mum's unofficial lobbying but I was included in the next Scotland squad for a friendly against Denmark in Copenhagen in October 1968. On the same evening, Manchester United were drawing 1–1 with Estudiantes at Old Trafford in the second leg of the World Club Championship. This international was the first time Billy Bremner captained his country, and he would go on to lead Scotland at the World Cup Finals in West Germany six years later. Unfortunately I only managed to make the substitutes' bench in Copenhagen, whilst my Hibs team-mate Colin Stein wore the number nine shirt. The match was a warm-up for Scotland's first World Cup qualifier against Austria at Hampden, but like most friendly matches neither team excelled and Scotland scrambled a 1–0 win, thanks to a seventh-minute goal from Celtic's

Bobby Lennox. I managed to earn my second cap and made something of an international record at the time when I was sent on for the final ninety seconds after Jim McCalliog suffered severe cramp. My ninety seconds apparently cost the SFA a monumental thirty-seven pounds ten shillings (or thirty-seven pounds fifty in new money). As well as doubling my match fee from thirty pounds to sixty pounds because I entered the field of play, the insurance premium for my fragile bones jumped to seven pounds ten shillings. Whilst the Scottish football writers thought it funny that my second cap cost the SFA twenty-five pounds per minute, the observant amongst you will have noticed that although I had not played for Scotland for two and a half years, appearance fees had remained the same. One thing's for sure – the football professionals who were laying their bodies on the line playing for Scotland were not doing it for the money!

My fleeting ninety-second appearance in Copenhagen did nothing to enhance my Scotland international chances, and I was not included in the first World Cup Qualifying game against Austria at Hampden three weeks later. In fact, my international career resembled a football version of the *hokey cokey* over the next twelve months.

After Scotland opened their campaign with a 2–1 victory over the Austrians I was recalled to the squad for the next qualifier away to Cyprus. Unfortunately my services were not called upon in the 5–0 victory, and I was left out of the next two qualifying matches at home to West Germany which we drew 1–1 and the 8–0 demolition of the Cypriots at Hampden, where Colin Stein banged in four goals. Then the month before the crucial World Cup qualifying match against West Germany in Hamburg I was recalled to manager Bobby Brown's starting line-up for a warm-up match against the Republic of Ireland. The match took place on a Sunday afternoon and twenty-four hours earlier I played the full ninety minutes for Hibs in a 3–1 home win over Raith Rovers.

Still my ninety-minute run-out was a doddle in comparison to the six Old Firm players in the Scotland starting eleven who had battled it out in the first Celtic vs Rangers match of the season. Whilst I was delighted to be included in the team and to win my third Scotland cap, as preparation games went it was a total waste of time. I recall Celtic left back Tommy Gemmell having to retire to his hotel room at eleven a.m., so exhausted was he after the early morning flight to Dublin. Although Big Tam made the kick-off four hours later, he had to be subbed at half-time. My Hibs team-mate Pat Stanton was playing in midfield and struck up a good understanding with Billy Bremner. I was given a roving role at inside left and we played with two wingers, Willie Henderson of Rangers on the right and Celtic's Yogi Hughes wide left.

The 1–1 result was totally incidental and by the time of the crucial qualifier with West Germany four weeks later the Scotland starting eleven had five changes from the team that had taken to the field in Dublin. This time I had the number eight shirt on my back and up front Jimmy Johnstone replaced wee Willie Henderson on the right wing, Eddie Gray of Leeds took over from Yogi Hughes on the left wing and Alan Gilzean joined Colin Stein in attack which meant that Pat Stanton was relegated to the bench. I felt sorry for Pat, as he had played well in the Republic of Ireland match and deserved to keep his place in the starting line-up. Manager Bobby Brown knew that our only chance of qualifying for the World Cup Finals in Mexico depended on us beating West Germany, and he put an attacking Scotland team on the park to try and achieve that result.

This was the Germans' final qualifying match, but we still had to travel to Austria for our last game. West Germany sat only two points ahead of us in the group table with a slightly superior goal difference and every Scotland player took to the Hamburg pitch determined to give our all in this 'do or die' match.

It made no difference to us that the West German side contained many of the players who had lost out in the final to England in extra-time three years earlier. As far as we were concerned, it was eleven against eleven and the German players' reputations meant nothing as we lined up on the Hamburg pitch for the national anthems. The 'Tartan Army' had not yet been born but there were thousands of Scots fans in the stadium, many of them serving with the British Army stationed on the Rhine. We got off to the perfect start when Eddie Gray fired in a shot from twenty-five yards that goalkeeper Sepp Maier could only parry and the on-running Jimmy Johnstone fired high into the West German net. Midway through the first half I thought I had scored when I curled a shot past Maier, but it slid the wrong side of the post. As the half wore on the West German players started to become very physical, with Jimmy Johnstone the target of some scything tackles and the Swiss referee ignoring a blatant kick on Colin Stein but booking John Greig and Tommy Gemmell for complaining about his leniency. The Germans equalised after thirty-seven minutes when we needlessly gave away a corner kick and we went in level at half-time.

Bobby Brown impressed upon us the need to retain possession in the second half and we began strongly, controlling play in midfield but lost a second goal after sixty minutes when Gerd Muller hooked a shot past Jim Herriot in goal. After the match the Scotland manager pointed out to the press that our centre half Billy McNeill was punched in the face when he went to tackle Muller before he scored. This injustice only increased the Scotland players' resolve and within three minutes we were level. I was fouled in midfield and Billy Bremner played the free-kick square to Ronnie McKinnon, who crossed for Alan

Gilzean to head the ball into the German net. My abiding memory is of 'Big Gillie' swinging on the crossbar after the goal as the Scotland fans in the crowd went wild. Following the equaliser we went for a winner and hit the crossbar twice. The West Germans were hanging on by their fingernails, but with ten minutes left their right winger Libuda raced away from Tommy Gemmell and fired an unsaveable shot past Jim Herriot. To add insult to injury, Big Tam was sent off near the final whistle after chasing Helmut Haller half the length of the pitch to kick him up the arse in retaliation following a nasty foul by the German forward. The remaining ten Scots left the pitch with their heads held high and the German players knew they had been given the fright of their lives.

As well as the World Cup qualifier in Germany being the most important international I played in during my football career, it was also my best performance in the dark blue shirt of Scotland. I received rave reviews in the press after the match and glowing compliments from both managers, Bobby Brown and Helmut Schoen. But the stark fact was that Scotland were out of the World Cup and the West Germans went on to Mexico to knock out England in the quarter-final after being 2–0 down. West Germany lost 4–3 in the semi-final to Italy, who themselves lost 4–1 to Brazil in one of the best ever World Cup Final matches. Two weeks after the West German defeat Scotland lost 2–0 in Austria to end the group in second place on seven points – four behind West Germany and one ahead of the Austrians.

When the Home Internationals came around in May 1970 I was serving my twelve-week SFA suspension that had resulted in my hasty move to Nottingham Forest. Unfortunately in those days domestic football suspensions also applied to international games and whilst my indiscipline at Hibs may have fast-tracked my departure from Easter Road, it also ruined any chance I might have had of playing in the Home International Championship games that season. A double-edged sword indeed! My next cap arrived later that year when I was on the bench for Scotland's first European Championship qualifier against Denmark at Hampden, and like my previous appearance against the Danes I came on very late in the game after an injury to the Scotland centre forward John O'Hare. Only 24,618 Scotland fans braved a cold, rainy November Glasgow night to see a header from O'Hare squeeze through the Danish goalie's legs in the first half to give Scotland a 1–0 win. Five months later I was selected at inside left for Scotland's third European Nations' Cup qualifier against Portugal in Lisbon.

In between the Danish and Portuguese match, Scotland had lost 1–0 to Belgium and defeat from Portugal would make qualification for the 1972 finals virtually impossible. Unfortunately Eusebio, Baptista, Nene and Simoes controlled the midfield and my Scotland team-mates and I spent most of the ninety minutes chasing shadows. *The Scotsman* back page headline the following day summed it up neatly with 'Eusebio and Co. make it yet another lament for Scots'. In reporting on the 2–0 defeat *The Scotsman* football writer John Rafferty said:

> Yet another Scotland defeat has to be reported and with it almost certain elimination from the European Nations' Cup. But this was no Liege where the effort was suspect. Scotland were beaten by better footballers. They can be admired for their spirit but spirit evaporates and what was needed was more bone in the middle of the team.

Just over three weeks after the Portuguese game I won my seventh cap in a 0–0 draw against Wales in Cardiff. In truth, the match was a lottery and should never have gone ahead. Torrential rain turned what was a bone-dry pitch a couple of hours before kick-off into a quagmire, making football impossible.

The following Tuesday I was rested for the Home International match against Northern Ireland at Hampden where Scotland lost 1–0. On the Wednesday morning the Scotland squad travelled down to London to prepare for the final Home Nations match against England, and after a training session on the Thursday Bobby Brown told me that I would be playing on the Saturday. Despite injuries to some established internationalists, Bobby Brown picked an attacking team in a four-three-three formation, with Jimmy Johnstone, Hugh Curran and myself in the forward line. The build-up to the match was totally different from any other international I had played in before, and the fact that there were more Scots fans in the Wembley crowd made it seem like a home match. When the referee blew his whistle to start the match it was the beginning of one of my boyhood dreams turning into a nightmare.

In truth England played us off the park that May Saturday afternoon and could have won by a lot more than the final score-line of 3–1. They scored early on and although we equalised just afterwards this only seemed to annoy them. It was one of those occasions when the last place I wanted to be was on the pitch that day and our performance and the result spoilt the rest of my summer. My mood didn't improve any on my first day back at pre-season training at Nottingham Forest, as the English boys took great delight in reminding me of the Wembley drubbing.

The match didn't do Bobby Brown any favours either. Losing badly against England is never good at any time, but the 3–1 defeat also meant that Scotland had finished bottom of the Home Internationals table with a miserable one point from the three games played.

The knives were out for the manager following the game and Brown duly resigned and was replaced by the former Chelsea manager Tommy Docherty. The Doc was one of football's first pundits, always available with a cutting comment or funny remark, which went down well with the media. In December 1971 I won my ninth and final cap when The Doc brought me off the subs' bench with just over twenty minutes remaining in a friendly against Holland in Amsterdam. The Dutch were developing their 'total football' style that would take them to the World Cup Final in 1974 with Johann Neeskens and Johann Cruyff at the heart of their team. When I was given my chance it was one apiece. Johann Cruyff had opened the scoring for the Dutch after five minutes, but George Graham equalised with a header ten minutes before I got on. Five minutes from full-time Archie Gemmill nearly put Scotland ahead but the ball ran agonisingly the wrong side of the post and two minutes later Holland scored their second goal.

What turned out to be my final Scotland cap happened to coincide with the debut of Kenny Dalglish. Kenny had established himself that season as a prolific goalscorer with Celtic and The Doc was determined to build his Scotland team around the up-and-coming star. It may sound churlish to say forty years on given what Kenny went on to do at Liverpool and latterly for Scotland, but the truth is Kenny struggled for Scotland in the early part of his international career. I just wish I had been given the support and shown the loyalty Kenny was given by the three Scotland managers I played for. I thought that might change after I established myself in the Liverpool first team in 1972 but despite winning the First Division Championship and the UEFA Cup in my first season at Anfield the call from The Doc never came. On reflection, that's not exactly true, Tommy did write me a nice letter saying that I was 'in his plans'. Unfortunately Manchester United scuppered those plans when they lured Tommy to Old Trafford for a rumoured £300 a week.

*

After Tommy left the Scotland manager's job in 1973 I hoped that Willie Ormond would give me a recall to the Scotland set-up. Perhaps my cause wasn't helped by the fact that I was the only Scot at the time in the Liverpool team but this was more than made up by Shanks regularly singing my praises in the Scottish media and pressing my case for a Scotland recall.

Ironically, the international comeback door opened just before Scotland left for the World Cup Finals in West Germany in May 1974 when I was called into the squad as a late replacement for Jimmy Smith. A few weeks earlier I had played in the Liverpool side that had comprehensively beaten Jimmy's Newcastle team 3–0 at Wembley in the FA Cup Final. But I was as surprised as everyone else when Willie made me the only change to his successful Home International squad. Still, I wasn't complaining at getting the chance to play for Scotland in the World Cup in West Germany. Unfortunately the late call-up meant that I missed out on singing with the squad and the Bay City Rollers on the World Cup song 'Easy Easy'. Given my subsequent karaoke career I am convinced my singing abilities would have greatly enhanced the record. At least if I had appeared on the record I could have said I made a contribution to Scotland's World Cup campaign!

But the biggest frustration for me that summer was not getting the chance to play in any of Scotland's three World Cup games. For the first match against Zaire the manager stuck with most of the players that had got Scotland to the Finals for the first time since 1958. I was not the only one frustrated at being left out, and in truth Jimmy Johnstone and Tommy Hutchison probably had more reasons than me to be pissed off. Tommy made his Scotland debut in the side that beat Czechoslovakia at Hampden the previous September to guarantee qualification for West Germany, but injuries in the run-up to the tournament had cost him his place in the team. On the other hand, Wee Jinky had been the star man for Scotland in the 2–0 defeat of England in the team's last competitive match before the tournament. Jimmy's problem was that he had appeared all over the Scottish papers just before the England game, when the Clyde coastguard had been called out to rescue him after he drifted out to sea in a rowing boat. Jinky may have redeemed himself with his performance against England but he then blotted his copybook by getting bevvied in Oslo after a pre-World Cup friendly match against Norway.

Jimmy was not the only player who got pissed in Oslo. Team captain Billy Bremner and Jinky waltzed merrily into a pub full of Scottish journalists who were only too happy to tell the Scottish public about their lack of discipline prior to the tournament. Willie Ormond's response to public calls for the two players to be sent home in disgrace was to ban the media from having anything to do with the Scotland team. After two years working with Bill Shankly at Liverpool, I was appalled at the lack of professionalism in the Scotland camp. The training sessions were not well organised and I thought the manager carried no respect with the senior, experienced players in the squad.

Ormond stated publicly that I had been called into the squad 'on grounds of current form' and he was absolutely right. I had just completed my second season at Liverpool and although we finished runners-up in the league to Leeds we had won the FA Cup in style. I was in the best form of my career and after an indifferent Scotland performance in beating the inexperienced African team 2–0 I was confident that I would get picked for the following match against Brazil. The Brazilians were a shadow of the magnificent team that had won the World Cup four years earlier in Mexico, but Willie Ormond decided to put a team on the park that wouldn't lose when a little flair, creativity and imagination could have unlocked the Brazilian defence. As a consequence, chances at both ends in the ninety minutes were few and far between and both teams settled for a 0–0 draw.

Brazil also had the dirtiest player in the tournament in right back Luis Perreira. He put in at least four challenges on Scotland players that today would be automatic sendings-off but the lenient referee never even showed him a yellow card. Fortunately he got his comeuppance against Holland when he was sent off for scything down Johan Neeskens.

In my opinion, Willie Ormond's big mistake was to allow himself to be influenced in team selection and tactics by senior players' opinions – none more so than team captain Billy Bremner. When Scotland needed an 'up and at them' approach, like the one adopted against West Germany in 1969, we went for caution. The media and Scotland fans were crying out for a gung-ho effort against the South Americans but what they got was a team that was set up not to lose. And that is how both teams played.

Following the Brazil match I had a set-to with the manager at the training camp at Erbismuhle where I told him that I would rather go home to my wife, daughter Donna Lee and newly-born son Peter, who had arrived whilst I was in Germany, than simply make up the numbers in his squad. In some respects, I felt sorry for Willie who in truth was out of his depth and he allowed himself to be manipulated by players who should have known better. After my heated exchange with Ormond, other players and the trainer Ronnie McKenzie persuaded me to back down but I couldn't see the point of hanging around to watch the last group match from the subs' bench. Still, my loyalty to Scotland won out and part of me thought that I might get a chance if we qualified from our group. Everyone in the Scotland camp knew that a win against Yugoslavia in our final group match would take us through to the second round phase but again caution won out in our formation and we could only manage a 1–1 draw. Scotland finished third in their group, eventually losing out to Brazil and Yugoslavia on goal difference, and went out of the competition. The support by the Scotland fans in West Germany had been fantastic and their loyalty deserved much more than they got from the Scotland team that had a squad of players good enough to have qualified from the group.

After West Germany defeated Holland 2–1 in the final it meant that Scotland were the only unbeaten team in the tournament but that meant nothing given our first round exit. Brooding at home afterwards I knew, following my disagreements with the manager, that my international career was probably over but I consoled myself knowing that I was with the best club in England and playing under the best manager in Bill Shankly. Little did I know that Shanks was about to announce his resignation a few weeks later.

Looking back, I wish I had won more Scotland caps than the nine I did get, but factors were at play which were outwith my control. For too long managers and selectors had a West of Scotland bias towards Celtic and Rangers players and I was never given a consistent run in the Scotland set-up. Perhaps things might have been different if John Prentice hadn't left in 1966 after just six months in the job, but looking back, I can understand why he wanted to move on. He was a part-time manager and didn't even have the luxury of picking the players in the squad – that fell to a group of selectors with the SFA.

I may have only won nine Scotland caps but I was lucky enough to play against the World's greatest players at the time. Getting on the same park as Pelé, Eusebio, Bekenbauer and Cruyff was an experience I will cherish for the rest of my life. My biggest regret is I never got the chance to play and make a contribution for Scotland at the 1974 World Cup. Hindsight is a wonderful thing, and after the birth of my son whilst in West Germany I was on a high and I know I would have made a difference for Scotland in those so-near-yet-so-far matches against Brazil and

Yugoslavia, but it was not to be. In football you have to learn to take the rough with the smooth but I can't help thinking that my Scotland international career could and should have been better.

Still, whenever I think back on playing for Scotland and what might have been, I look at Gerson's number eight jersey in my trophy cabinet at home and remember how lucky I was to win my first cap against the Brazilian World Champions. Now there are not many players who can say they have played against the most famous international team in the world, never mind it being your international debut as a wet-behind-the-ears teenager.

15

FIRHILL FOR THRILLS

Hibs Chairman Tom Hart didn't hang around after Willie Ormond handed in his resignation following the 3–3 draw with Hamilton Accies. In many ways Bertie Auld's appointment within twenty-four hours of the news of Willie's departure was very similar to Jock Stein's introduction to Easter Road sixteen years earlier. I would be amazed if Bertie and Partick Thistle chairman Miller Reid hadn't had their cards marked about the manager's job at Hibs before it became public knowledge. Bertie had been in charge at Partick for six years and was a popular personality with the media and Scottish football fans. However, Bertie wasn't my type of football manager and as I was soon to discover Partick Thistle fans were pretty much split down the middle on Bertie's football philosophy. Tom Hart and Bertie Auld were very similar characters, both single-minded and headstrong, but at the press conference announcing his appointment Tom Hart said that Bertie would be allowed to run the playing side of things without interference and he had his full personal backing. In years to come, that kind of statement from a chairman has usually been a poisoned chalice but I am certain Tom meant every word of that commitment to Bertie.

Within a couple of days of moving into the manager's office at Hibs, Bertie brought my old Hibs team-mate Pat Quinn from Partick to be his assistant at Easter Road. I was confirmed by Bertie as Hibs' third team coach but Willie Ormond's departure, following so soon after the end of my playing career, had me keen to move into football management. Whilst I was still only thirty-four, I had secured my coaching qualifications in Scotland and England and I was impatient and hungry to succeed. Whilst Hibs moved swiftly to appoint a new manager, Partick were in no hurry to find a replacement for Bertie. With Pat Quinn also leaving Firhill for Easter Road the Scottish media were not slow to start speculating on who was going to take over. Tommy Docherty and his former assistant at Manchester United, Pat Crerand, were early front-runners. Then Billy Bremner was touted for the job. Partick announced they were advertising the vacancy and Marion set to work crafting my application for the manager's job at Firhill. A short time later Miller Reid said in the Scottish press that applications had been received from a West German coach and an English manager who was working in the North American Soccer League. I began to think my chances of becoming the new manager at Thistle were disappearing like 'sna off a dyke'. But two weeks after Bertie left Partick for Hibs I was appointed to the managerial hot-seat at Firhill. I was delighted when Bob Paisley agreed to provide a recommendation on my managerial credentials to the Firhill board and following an interview I was offered a three-year contract.

When I was introduced to the media as Thistle's new boss I said, 'I won't be happy until the side are in Europe and I'd like to see Thistle there next season. In the short term I plan to sit back and weigh up the playing situation at the club but the chairman has told me that money is available for me to strengthen the squad.' Miller Reid pointed to my achievements as a player and said,'Partick Thistle have appointed a football winner to take over from Bertie Auld.'

The majority of the Partick first team were full-time and I knew I was inheriting a good squad who had established themselves in the Scottish Premier League. I was moving from a team in a lower division, although I was confident Hibs would return to the Premier League at the end of that season, and I knew Partick would be a good start for my career in football management.

If there was a prize for the most inoffensive football club in Scotland then Partick Thistle would be one of the leading contenders. Sandwiched between Glasgow's two oldest rivals Celtic and Rangers, Thistle epitomise everything that is good about Scottish football. Like Bristol City, the Partick trophy cabinet was not weighed down with years of success – in fact, despite being formed in 1876 Thistle had never been crowned First Division Champions and had only won the Scottish Cup once, in 1921. However, Thistle made history in the 1971/72 season when they won the Scottish League Cup, beating Jock Stein's Celtic side 4–1 in the final at Hampden. It was reported at the time that when the 4–0 half-time score reached the BBC Grandstand studio in London, presenter Frank Bough at first refused to read out the score, believing that someone had made a mistake or was playing a practical joke on him. Frank subsequently relented but after reporting the shock half-time result added, 'I'll bring you the correct score as soon as I have it.'

Partick Thistle fans had the last laugh that day and when I took over as manager many of the diehards loved recounting the day they humbled the mighty Celtic in the League Cup Final.

My predecessor, Bertie Auld, took over from the League Cup-winning manager Davie McParland and won Thistle promotion to the Scottish Premier Division in 1976. Whilst the club had survived in the Scottish Premier Division the Thistle fans were divided over Bertie's defensive tactics. He made no bones over the fact that his number one priority was keeping Partick Thistle in the top division and if that meant sacrificing attractive foot-ball for results then so be it. When the Glasgow comedian Billy Connolly started out on his career, one of his lines was: 'When I was younger and growing up in Glasgow I used to think the team were called Partick Thistle nil'. Whilst the 'Big Yin' always got a laugh with the comment, it was no laughing matter for Thistle's loyal supporters, especially when Bertie Auld was in charge. The team may have managed to survive the battle to stay in Scotland's ten-team top flight, but the constant emphasis on 'having what we hold' meant that Thistle had become Scotland's draw specialists. Given the football philosophy I learnt in Liverpool's Boot Room, there was no way I would be following in Bertie's 'safety first' tactical footsteps.

From my very first training session with the players at Firhill I stressed that I wanted the team to play open, attacking football. That was the commitment I made in my interview, which I repeated publicly in my first press conference as manager and I was confident that the group of professionals I had to work with at Thistle would respond positively to this new approach. My introduction to football management in Scotland could not have been much harder, as my first game in charge was a home match against Celtic on Saturday 6 December 1980.

I couldn't have asked for more from the players or the fans, but Celtic ran out 1–0 winners on my managerial debut. The following week saw a repeat of that scoreline at St Mirren. Thankfully we won my third match in the Thistle hot-seat when we beat Clyde 3–1 in a Glasgow Cup tie nine days before Christmas. I breathed a sigh of relief after that game having secured my first win as a football manager. After drawing 1–1 at Firhill with Alex Ferguson's Aberdeen team, 1980 finished on a downer when we travelled to Cappielow and lost 2–0 against Morton. In my first three weeks as manager at Partick Thistle I had lost three games, drawn won and won one – 1981 could not come quickly enough. A New Year and a new dawn at Thistle started promisingly when we held Rangers to a 1–1 draw at Ibrox on 1 January. That day I could see the quality of some of the players I had inherited from Bertie Auld. Alan Rough had been the best goalkeeper in Scotland for several years and was still in his prime. Davie McKinnon and Brian Whittaker were excellent full backs who would go on to play for either side of the Old Firm. Donald Park, Ian Jardine, Kenny Watson and Alex O'Hara were good players who added quality to the Thistle side. That Rangers game was the start of an unbeaten seven-game run which included my first league win two days after the match at Ibrox when we beat Hearts 1–0 thanks to a Kenny Watson penalty kick. The seven-game unbeaten run also included beating the 'Teddy Bears' 1–0 at Firhill in the semi-final of the Glasgow Cup. Unfortunately our successful run was ended by Dundee United at Tannadice on Valentine's Day in the fourth round of the Scottish Cup.

Following our Scottish Cup exit I said to the players and fans that the focus of our attention would be the remaining Premier League games. 'A good points return from our next three games and we're in with a chance of European Competition. That must be our target now.' Whilst I genuinely believed that qualification for the UEFA Cup was a real possibility, I don't think I managed to convince all of the players of this and we ended the season in sixth spot – one place higher than the previous season. But the season did not end disappointingly as we beat Celtic 1–0 at Firhill to lift the Glasgow Cup for only the sixth time in Partick Thistle's 105-year history. The media pointed out that Celtic put out a team comprising first- and second-team players but I was proud as punch that I had won silverware less than six months into my managerial career. Whilst the Thistle players and supporters were overjoyed at our 1–0 victory, courtesy of an Ian Jardine goal, at the end of the game Celtic's manager Billy McNeill was 'beelin' at his team having lost a final. Big Billy's and Celtic's philosophy was to try and win every competition they played.

Big Billy was not accustomed to defeat as a Celtic player and he did not take kindly to wee Partick Thistle stealing his thunder in the Glasgow Cup Final. In fairness to Ceasar, thirty minutes later he sportingly accepted the defeat and was fulsome in his praise of my Thistle players. Still, the following year I took great delight in reminding him of the occasion when Marion and I met up with Billy and his wife Liz during the World Cup in Spain. We spent every evening of that holiday sitting up to the wee small hours talking football. Getting silverware in my first season as a manager was a real shot in the arm, and I assumed the Partick Thistle board would celebrate the achievement with an end-of-season party. Unfortunately, the Thistle purse-strings did not extend to such excesses so Marion and I organised and paid for the end-of-season bash to thank the players for their support in my first six months in the manager's job. Winning the Glasgow Cup also gave me a lift going into the summer break and I set about planning for the following season, hoping to guide Thistle into Europe as I had pledged on my first day at Firhill. What was it Rabbie Burns said about 'the best laid schemes of mice and men gang aft aglay'?

I wasn't the only one looking forward to the new season. Everyone at Firhill had a spring in their step in pre-season training, hoping to build on our Glasgow Cup success and improve on our sixth-placed SPL finish. I did not have the luxury of funds to splash out in the close season transfer market but one new recruit at Firhill would bring a smile to the face of Thistle fans that season and go on to make an indelible mark on Scottish football. A fresh and freckle-faced Maurice Johnston arrived in the summer of

1981, having signed from the Glasgow amateur club Milton Battlefield. From his first day at training Maurice showed he had an abundance of football ability and an appetite for hard work to match his skill. Mo also had bags of 'cheeky chappy' confidence that all really good strikers need and his bubbly enthusiasm made for a lively Thistle dressing room.

Maurice didn't figure in our first three League Cup matches at the start of the season but came off the bench to score our only goal in a 2–1 home defeat to Dundee United on 19 August. I gave Mo the number nine jersey for our following match away to Motherwell, and whilst he didn't score on that occasion he showed enough promise to give me encouragement for the league campaign ahead. I decided not to risk Maurice and went with an experienced team for our opening league match at home to Rangers on 29 August which we lost 1–0. That was the first of six consecutive defeats, which included a shock 1–0 reverse at home to Queen's Park in the first round of the Glasgow Cup. After that result I decided drastic measures were needed and I threw Mo in at centre forward for our sixth league match at home to St Mirren where we managed to get our first point on the board in a 1–1 draw.

Our first league win arrived two weeks later when a Kenny Watson goal gave us a 1–0 victory over Bertie Auld's Hibs. A fortnight later we started the second quarter of the league campaign with a 2–0 win at Ibrox. Mo Johnston and big George Clark were the goalscorers against Rangers but the whole team played exceptionally well and I genuinely thought that result would be the springboard for us to climb away from the relegation zone but sadly it was a false dawn. The Ibrox victory was our last one that year and in our final match of 1981 we lost 3–0 to Hibs at Easter Road. In the Thistle match programme for our first match of 1982 against Rangers, supporter Mark Rowantree wrote the following letter which neatly captured the mood of some of the fans, probably most of the players and was an opinion I wholeheartedly agreed with:

> In view of the recent combination of bad luck and elementary mistakes, it seems possible, if not probable, that Partick Thistle Football Club will be playing First Division football next season. Yet in spite of this, I feel that Thistle are on the verge of creating the best side seen at Firhill for a number of years. The attacking policies of Peter Cormack have certainly made the team better to watch, and his enthusiasm and ambition seem to be exactly what the club needs. Yet if the press is to be believed, if Thistle are relegated at the end of the season, all players are available for transfer. This seems to be a very short-sighted policy. Although financial considerations are important, surely the views of the support are more so. We are sick and fed up seeing good players going only to be replaced by others of a mediocre standard.
>
> Finally, maybe the worst might never happen, perhaps Thistle will win all their matches, win the league and Cup, and this time next year we'll be involved in Europe.
>
> Who said Thistle supporters don't have a sense of humour?

Many at the club thought I had something to do with Mark's letter, and whilst I don't deny there wasn't much in it I could disagree with – well maybe with the exception of the comments about going on to win the league and the Cup were a tad OTT – his prophecy came to pass. Thistle ended the season second bottom of the SPL with twenty-two points. Ironically two of our six wins came against Rangers at Ibrox as we followed up the October victory with another 2–0 win on 17 February with Tony Higgins joining Mo Johnston on the scoresheet this time. It may say something that the second win over Rangers came three days after a disco for Alan Rough's testimonial fund. It was a Sunday night bash, with tickets priced at one pound fifty, so there was no chance Roughie was going to retire a millionaire at these prices But all the players enjoyed it and it seemed to put them in a relaxed mood for the match at Firhill. I just wish they had been as relaxed in the build-up to all our games that season and, as Mark said tongue-in-cheek, Thistle might have gone on to do a league and Cup double.

Fortunately the widely-predicted mass exodus of players didn't materialise over the summer as we prepared for life in the Scottish First Division. Centre half Jackie Campbell retired from playing and became my first team coach, Andy Anderson was given a free transfer and moved to Greece, Tony Higgins retired from playing to take up the role as the Scottish Professional Football Association representative and Davie McKinnon was transferred to Rangers for £30,000. Despite having more or less the same squad as the previous season, our campaign to return to the SPL started very poorly and after eighteen games we had won only eight, lost five and drawn five. St Johnstone led the table on twenty-eight points, closely followed by Hearts two points behind with Airdrie, Clydebank and ourselves sharing twenty-one points.

The team's cause was not helped when our talisman and longest-serving player Alan Rough was transferred to Hibs in late November. My old Hibs team-mate Pat Stanton had replaced Bertie Auld in the managerial hot-seat at Easter Road and the Thistle board were happy to accept Hibs' £60,000 offer, although at the time I thought Roughie was worth a lot more. Alan had won fifty-one Scotland caps in his thirteen years at Firhill and he would go on to become a firm favourite with the Easter Road faithful, eventually leaving Hibs in 1988 after Andy Goram arrived from Oldham. Roughie's departure didn't worry me unduly as

I knew we had a good under-study in Dougie McNab, and whilst Dougie proved to be a good goalkeeper I hadn't factored in the loss Roughie would be to morale in the dressing room and with the Thistle supporters. At the end of the thirty-nine-game season the team finished fourth in the First Division on forty-nine points, six points behind the eventual champions St Johnstone, who pipped Hearts to the title by a solitary point.

Brooding over the summer prior to the start of my second full season in charge of Thistle's bid to win promotion back to the SPL, I was determined to make sure that the team improved its start to the league campaign. In that first season in Division One we lost five of our first ten games and I was convinced that was what cost us any chance of winning promotion. We gave St Johnstone and Hearts too much of a start and it was that bad start that also precipitated the transfer of Alan Rough to Hibs. I also took heart that summer from the exploits of Scotland's 'New Firm' – Aberdeen and Dundee United. Jim MacLean's United had won the SPL for the first time, and Alex Ferguson's Aberdeen side defeated Real Madrid in Gothenburg to lift the European Cup Winners' Cup. As a young manager in another Scottish provincial club I took encouragement that, with the right blend of players, support from the chairman, good coaching from me and a wee bit of luck, Partick Thistle could also make their mark on Scottish football. Unfortunately the Thistle board did not share my optimism or my ambition. In the summer of 1983 Donald Park returned to Hearts and Brian Whittaker was transferred to Celtic for a meagre £50,000. Both players were an integral part of my promotion plans and a big loss to the squad. It also meant that our playing resources were severely limited, but nevertheless the team started the season well and were unbeaten after seven games.

For our eighth game away to Brechin City on 1 October 1983 I was forced to put myself on the subs' bench and played the last twenty minutes. As luck would have it, my one and only appearance in three years at Thistle saw us lose our unbeaten streak as Brechin ran out 2–0 winners. After a run of inconsistent results, Miller Reid approached me in November to say that English First Division club Watford wanted to sign Maurice Johnston and their manager Graham Taylor had tabled a £120,000 bid. Mo had scored forty-one goals in eighty-five matches in his two and a half years at Thistle and I told the chairman that he was worth a lot more than Watford were offering. After I spoke to Graham Taylor, Watford eventually agreed to pay Thistle £200,000 for Mo's services. As it turned out it was a very good investment for Watford as the following year they sold him to Celtic for £400,000. It really would have been daylight robbery if Thistle had accepted their initial £120,000 offer. I was convinced that Mo's transfer was a good piece of business for Partick Thistle at the time, especially as I had nearly doubled the initial offer, which the chairman was prepared to accept. Miller Reid was so happy with the deal I helped negotiate with Watford that he gave Marion and me an all-expenses holiday to the US. However, there were others at the club and amongst the fans that were appalled at Maurice's transfer and who were only too happy to voice their displeasure. I could sympathise with them because the previous year Alan Rough's transfer around the same time of the season did not help the team's cause to get back to the Premier Division. However, the board, and the chairman in particular, were determined to cash in on their prized assets.

It wasn't long after Mo's departure I suffered what every football manager dreads – the sack. In my case, Thistle being Thistle, they were very civilised about parting with my services by announcing that they were not renewing my three-year contract. At the end of the day it may have been less painful than the curt, Alan Sugar, 'You're fired,' but it amounted to the same.

After three years in football management and over twenty years in professional football, I was looking for a new job, certain that I was a better manager after my experience at Firhill. Little did I think that my next job in football would be over a thousand miles away on the island of Cyprus.

16

HAVE PASSPORT, WILL MANAGE

After parting company with Partick Thistle, I was desperate to get back into football. I have never been good at sitting around twiddling my thumbs and I was not looking forward to my first period of inactivity after more than twenty years in professional football. My three years at Firhill had taught me a lot about coaching and football management, and that experience, combined with my self-confidence, convinced me that I still had a lot to offer the game. But it was all right, me thinking that I could do a job for a football club. I needed someone to put their trust and faith in me. I went to work contacting my network of football friends and acquaintances in Scotland and England, but initially to no avail. The timing wasn't good, being the second half of the football season, and in those days the managerial merry-go-round was not as active as it is now.

Then, totally out of the blue, I received a telephone call from Tim Kelly, the manager of the Grosvenor Hotel in Glasgow. At the time, the Grosvenor was owned by the wealthy Greek Cypriot Rio Stakis and Tony said that Anorthosis Famagusta FC were keen to have me as their manager. Tony told me that Willie McLean, brother of Dundee United manager Jim, was managing Pezoporikos in Cyprus and after our meeting I decided to telephone Willie to get the lowdown on the football set-up on the island. Willie gave me a glowing account of life in Cyprus and told me that the standard of football was very good. Willie also marked my card about the seedier side of Cypriot football – no, not the sex, drugs and rock 'n' roll, but the bribery, corruption and backhanders that blighted the game there. Following Willie's full and frank account and after talking the offer over with Marion, I decided I had nothing to lose in giving it a go. The worst that could happen was that I'd return to Scotland with more football experience under my belt and a good suntan to boot. As it turned out, the Cormack family spent two very enjoyable years in Larnaca. I learned a tremendous amount about Cypriot football and the psyche of Cypriot footballers and Donna Lee and wee Pete enjoyed two very productive school years at the local US academy. In our time in Cyprus we were very well looked after by everyone at the club and made many friends.

Anorthosis Famagusta FC were founded in 1911, and up until the Turkish invasion of Cyprus in 1974 their home ground was in Famagusta. After the island was divided between Greece and Turkey, Anorthosis relocated to Larnaca, and when I first arrived the club put me up in one of the best hotels on the island. As a mark of goodwill they also paid me one month's wages in advance and I got right down to work, determined to show them that I was fully committed to the job in hand. After the first couple of months on my own, Marion and the kids joined me, and the club provided us with a lovely apartment in Larnaca which became our home for two years. When I returned to Cyprus with the family in tow, just before the start of the football season, several hundred fans turned up at the airport to greet us, such was their enthusiasm for all things football related. The airport arrivals was a mass of blue and white, the Anorthosis club colours, and wee Pete in particular was awestruck when he saw the cheering, flag-waving crowd.

Because of the intense summer heat, the Cypriot football season starts at the beginning of October and finishes at the end of May.

In my first couple of months in Cyprus I learnt that trust was the most vital component at the football club. The Cypriot system is based around a president and his committee, and I quickly developed a good relationship with the Anorthosis President Stelio Frenaritis. As I quickly discovered, Stelio, like many Cypriots, was a mad keen Liverpool supporter and he told me that it was my time at Anfield that triggered their interest in approaching me to manage Anorthosis. Liverpool's reputation spread far and wide, and I was more than happy to take my Boot Room knowledge onto the training ground and pass on Shanks' philosophies to the Anorthosis players.

I also earned extra brownie points with everyone at the club when Kevin Keegan visited us for a short holiday, and Kevin being the helpful, obliging person that he is, was happy to slip on an Anorthosis jersey and line up with the squad for a team photograph. After Kevin's visit I could have told the players to run up and down the Trudos Mountains for hours in the midday sun and I'm sure they wouldn't have batted an eyelid. But I was never a great believer in that type of training regime, and anyway, the Anorthosis players were far fitter and more disciplined than your average British footballer returning from their summer break.

I was both very surprised with the Cypriot players' skill levels and their approach to training. I can honestly say that in my two years at the club the players were a joy to work with on the training ground and they showed a tremendous aptitude to learn and become better footballers. In my first couple of months at Anorthosis I formed the view that the team lacked the necessary experience to seriously challenge for honours, and I turned to good quality tried and tested pros I knew from the UK. The Cypriot league allowed teams to bring in three foreigners per season, and I managed to persuade the President and his committee to recruit three 'well kent' faces I knew from my playing days at Bristol and my managerial stint at Partick Thistle. Donny Gillies had impressed me as a solid, dependable full back at Bristol City and moved across Bristol to join Rovers after City's final season in the English First Division. It didn't take much persuading to get Donny to join me and end his playing days in Cyprus in the centre of the Anorthosis defence. It also wasn't difficult to persuade Iain Jardine and Jamie Doyle, two former players who had worked with me at Partick Thistle, to forego the dark, cold winter Scottish nights for some football in the sun. The three Scottish recruits proved to be good additions to the Anorthosis squad.

Whilst everyone at Anorthosis, from the President through to the supporters, was supportive, the same could not be said for the officials charged with refereeing matches.

In my conversations with Willie McLean he had warned me to keep an eye on players who might be tempted to throw matches and also to watch out for dodgy match officials. In my first training session I told the players that I was not in Cyprus for a holiday and that we would have to work together as a team. I played on my time at Liverpool by telling them that training would be with the ball and as an ex-player I wanted to make it enjoyable for all of them. I then hit them with what Willie had told me about players being bribed to throw games and said, 'If I find out that any of you take a back-hander to lose I will lock you in the dressing room and batter fuck out of you.'

I'm not sure if they knew what I was saying to them, but they certainly understood my message. My assistant manager Demi was an ex-captain of the Anorthosis team and later in the quiet surroundings of the local bar he ran with his English wife on Larnaca's seafront I calmly explained to him exactly what I meant with my no-nonsense teamtalk.

'You will have no problem with the Anorthosis players, Peter.

They all respect you too much to, how you say in English, take the fucking piss.'

I laughed at his reply and several Keo beers later our friendship was cemented and I was certain that I could trust him 100 per cent. My judgement on that score proved to be spot-on and we bonded into a good coaching team in our two years working together.

I had passed my first hurdle in the many and varied challenges of managing a football team abroad but I didn't have to wait long for my next test. In our opening league match I saw firsthand what Willie had warned me about before I arrived in Larnaca. During the first forty-five minutes, every fifty/fifty decision went against Anorthosis. As the teams trooped off the pitch at half-time I could see the players looking at me for a reaction and although the proverbial smoke was billowing out of my ears I tried to look as cool, calm and collected as I possibly could. As the players disappeared into the changing room I followed the referee and two linesmen into their room. Before they got a chance to speak I launched into a controlled rant about the worldwide reputation Cyprus football had for corruption and how I would have no hesitation in reporting any misgivings I had to FIFA. I never raised my voice or swore throughout my diatribe, which was a challenge in itself, emphasising my considerable playing experience in Scotland and England, but I ended with, 'And if FIFA fail to do anything about blatant cheating then I will deal with it as I think fit.'

I then turned and walked out, not giving the officials any opportunity to respond. Surprisingly, decisions were far more even in the second half and at the end of the game the players were desperate to know what I had said to the match officials at the interval, but all I told them was that I gently reminded the officials that there were two teams on the park and that the laws of the game were not open to interpretation. I know that none of the players believed me but I had gained their respect by showing that I was prepared to stand up for them.

A few weeks later I was back in Demi's wife's pub, which had become the team meeting place after training and home matches, and Stelio, the club president, informed me that following the first match word had spread like wildfire amongst the island's match official fraternity that 'Cormack is a madman'. It was a reputation I was not unhappy to cultivate if it meant Anorthosis would get more fifty/fifty decisions in their favour during the season. Unfortunately there were occasions when 'Mr Cool, Calm and Collected' went out of the window and 'Mr Angry' returned with a vengeance.

In one memorable match I completely lost the plot after the referee awarded the softest penalty I had ever seen. In those days there was no fourth official to police the dugouts and I ranted and raved for ages after the spot-kick was converted. Eventually I pushed the ref's tolerance threshold to breaking point and he stopped the game to send me to the stand. At first I refused to budge calling him the 'fucking cheating bastard that he was'. It was only when two machine gun-touting policemen stood either side of me that I realised that it was an argument I was not going to win. As they frog marched me up the tunnel I heard wee Pete, who was sitting on top of the Anorthosis dugout, shouting, 'Daddy, are they taking you to prison?' Fortunately the Cypriot polis found me a comfortable seat in the stand but they remained beside me for the remainder of the match just to make sure I behaved myself. I may have not endeared myself to the Cypriot refereeing brotherhood when I was in charge at Anorthosis, but the players, fans and club officials loved the fact that I was always prepared to argue the team's corner, even if that meant being stalked by a couple of burly-armed bobbies.

*

During my time in professional football I have heard and read many times about certain clubs being referred to as 'family football clubs'. This tag usually applies to smaller, provincial teams who spend most of their time in the lower divisions. I don't know if it applied to every club in Cyprus, but Anorthosis really was one big family. When Marion, Donna Lee and Pete joined me there would be regular get-togethers involving everyone at the club, their families and their friends. They were fantastic social occasions that went on for hours, usually late into the night, and involved eating local meze dishes and drinking copious amounts of wine and beer. I may have said I was not there for an extended holiday but we never passed up on joining in these regular get-togethers, as they were good for Marion and the kids to integrate with the local community and an excellent way for all of us to meet new friends.

I also skied for the one and only time in my life whilst in Cyprus. During one of the school holiday breaks Marion, wee Pete, Donna Lee and I drove up to the Trudos Mountains for a couple of days on the slopes. Unfortunately when we arrived there was very little snow but the next day we managed to hit the piste following some overnight snow. Marion and the children were experienced skiers and advised me to proceed cautiously, but once I set off I just kept gaining speed until I crashed into a tree. It was equivalent to getting hit by Chopper Harris, and for the remainder of the holiday I gave the pistes a miss and sat and had a few beers instead.

My skiing escapade wasn't the only dangerous moment during our two years in Cyprus. A tornado hit the island in the middle of one match that gave me one of the scariest moments of my life. I wasn't so much concerned about my own safety and thinking back on it now it seems such a surreal event. I had no idea of the impending twister, but Marion could see it approach us from the opposite side of the ground. The first I knew was when the wind suddenly picked up and the sky darkened. Wee Pete was lying on the roof of the dugout and fortunately he was too puzzled to be scared. The referee stopped the game as conditions deteriorated and I grabbed wee Pete whilst players on the park got down on all fours and crawled off the pitch, such was the ferocity of the storm. Everyone – players, officials and fans – huddled together under the stand and from the noise above us it sounded as if it was going to collapse at any moment. Fortunately after twenty or so minutes the storm subsided, but when we emerged from our shelter the devastation was unbelievable. Debris littered the pitch and the referee had no option but to abandon the match. It was my one and only experience of a tornado and I hope it will be my last.

I have to admit we had some great social get-togethers in the two years I was manager at Anorthosis and it was a great way for me to really get to know the players who always insisted on me telling them stories and anecdotes from my playing days and particularly my time at Liverpool. I also never had to worry about the fitness of the players who, although part-time, trained twice a day – early in the morning and later in the evening – after they had completed an afternoon working in their day job. In truth, I am doing them a gross injustice to say they were part-time – they trained harder than many professionals I came across in my playing days in Scotland and England. I couldn't have asked for any more from the Anorthosis players in terms of commitment, and I like to think my professional approach to the game rubbed off on them in the two years I was at the club.

Despite our collective hard work we ended the twenty-six-game 1984/85 season in third place, ten points behind league champions Omonoia FC and just one point behind Appollan Limassol.

Our record for the league campaign was won twelve, drew nine with five games lost, giving us thirty-three points. Twelve months later we managed one point less, despite winning one more match against six draws and seven defeats. Anorthosis also slipped one place in my second season, finishing fourth in the league, fifteen points behind champions Apoel FC. I have always been a great believer in demonstrating improvement in everything I do and after achieving third place in my first year at Anorthosis, I fully expected the team to improve in my second season at the club. Therefore fourth place was a big disappointment, and after much soul-searching and many late-night conversations with Marion, we decided to return to Scotland in the summer of 1986. It was a difficult decision because Donna Lee and Pete were thriving at their US school and we had made many friends in Limassol. It was also such an enjoyable and relaxed lifestyle with a near perfect climate for most of the year, although we did find July and August almost unbearable due to the oppressive heat.

Of all the decisions we have had to make during my forty-plus years in football leaving Cyprus was one of the toughest, but after we made it there was no going back – well, at least we thought that at the time, and I had to look ahead to my next job confident that my experience of coaching abroad would stand me in good stead. Little did I think that my next move would be coaching an African national side in front of the most passionate and frightening fans I have ever seen.

We returned to Scotland just as the national team were about to compete in that year's World Cup in Mexico. Alex Ferguson was in charge of the squad following the shocking death of Jock Stein in Cardiff at the end of the Wales World Cup qualifying match. Fergie's team performed well in the first match and were unlucky to lose against Denmark, and even unluckier to lose Charlie Nicholas after a bad tackle. In the second match I thought

Scotland were again unlucky to lose against West Germany, especially after taking the lead with a great piece of skill by Gordon Strachan. But despite those two defeats, Scotland could still have qualified for the next round if they beat Uruguay in the final group match. Unfortunately, even though the Uruguayans had a man sent off in the first minute, Scotland couldn't manage to score a goal and for the fourth World Cup in succession failed to qualify for the knockout stages of the competition.

Following the World Cup I received a telephone call from Craig Brown, who had just been appointed as Scotland assistant manager to Andy Roxburgh. Craig had received an invitation from the Botswana Football Association to assist their national team manager in preparing his squad for a forthcoming international friendly against Malawi. Craig asked me if I would be interested in fulfilling the six-week contract, as he was sure that my recent experience in Cyprus would prove invaluable. In truth, I was not inundated with job offers after my return to Scotland and it was a good financial deal for six weeks' work. I had no idea where Botswana was in that great African continent nor did I have any idea what standard of football to expect. Fortunately Botswana sits to the north of South Africa and could be accessed by a flight from London to Pretoria, not too far from the South African/Botswana border. I may have been in the dark about where I was going, but I can honestly say that it turned out to be the most exciting and enjoyable football experience of my entire life.

Before I set off from Edinburgh I contacted the Botswana Football Association and told them that I would require thirty balls, thirty coloured bibs and cones for the training sessions. Bibs were a no-no, and it took much explaining on the telephone to get them to understand what 'parking cones' were. I decided to take the coloured bibs and put them in my luggage, which caused great consternation amongst the customs staff in South

Africa. It took me a good half an hour explaining to the confused African customs men what the strange coloured objects in my large holdall were for. Unfortunately football was not the international language it is nowadays and at one point I thought I was going to have to call on the assistance of the British Embassy as I feared I was about to be carted off to the nearest nick. Thankfully common sense prevailed and I was eventually allowed through customs with bemused looks and shaking heads.

When I arrived in Gaborone, the country's capital city, I was met by officials from the Botswana Football Association and the national team manager Willie Seboni. I took to Willie right away. He was a real character, who appeared each day at training with a different hat, but he knew how he wanted his team to play and he made it clear to me that my job was to bring out the best in the Botswana players. On my daily taxi ride from the hotel to the training ground I quickly realised why the Botswana officials couldn't understand what I meant by parking cones as it appeared Gaborone drivers could park wherever they liked. It was a motorist's paradise, with not a traffic warden to be found anywhere.

Before I had even met, never mind seen, any of the players at training Willie told me that he wanted the Botswana team to play like the great Brazil team of the 1970 World Cup in the forthcoming match against Malawi. He also informed me that the game, on 30 September 1986, was to commemorate Botswana's twentieth anniversary of gaining independence from Great Britain, and as far as Botswanans were concerned, it was a bigger occasion than the African Cup of Nations or qualifying for the World Cup.

Later that day, reflecting back on my conversation with Willie Seboni in my hotel room, I began to wonder if I had made the right decision in agreeing to take the six-week contract. I thought to myself that the manager is expecting his players to play like Pelé, Jairzhino and Gerson in a match his countrymen regard as bigger than the World Cup – so if things go tits up it'll be the British colonial coach who'll get all the blame. Fortunately things worked out fine in the end but I had sleepless nights during my first couple of days in Gaborone wondering what I had let myself in for.

As preparation for the up-and-coming international against Malawi, the Botswana Football Association arranged four warm-up matches against local national club sides with exotic-sounding names such as Wharic Centre Chiefs, Granada Wanderers, Mahalapye Queens Park Rangers and Township Rollers. As well as the unusual club names, all the Botswana players had nicknames, which certainly made my job of getting to know them a lot easier. Like all African national teams Botswana also had its own nickname, The Zebras, and in the four weeks leading up to the match against Malawi I quickly got to grips with getting to know the squad and coaching them for the Independence Day anniversary match.

In the warm-up matches I could see that the Botswana players were extremely good athletes who were prepared to work hard at their football technique – in truth they were a joy to get to know and they made my job very easy. Still, thoughts of the implications of defeat or a poor performance in front of tens of thousands of Botswana supporters kept my mind fully focused on the job at hand. After studying the players in the warm-up games I suggested to Willie that the team needed a strong presence in the middle of the park to balance the lighter creative players on the outside of midfield. The team that took to the field had 'China' in goal, 'Defaulter' and 'Chippa' were the two full backs. In the centre of the Botswana defence were 'Rambo' (doesn't every team need a 'Rambo' at centre half?) alongside

Rodger 'Director' Chikumbudzi. The four in midfield were 'Boyo', Davis 'Mgababa' Chepete, 'Matoni' and Shadrack 'Rio' Maswabi and the two players upfront were 'Killer' and 'Paymaster'.

In all my years playing football across the globe I had never experienced the cacophony of noise that greeted the teams that September day in the Botswana national stadium and I have never heard anything like it since. Whilst the constant buzzing of the vuvuzela became familiar during the 2010 World Cup in South Africa, I had never heard it prior to the Botswana versus Malawi game in 1986, and from what I heard on TV during the South African World Cup matches these were tame in comparison to the noise that emanated from the terracing in Gaborone that day.

I was told that Botswana had a population of around two million people, but I swear half of them must have been in or around the national stadium. As well as the fantastic noise, the sight of the fans dancing throughout the ninety minutes added to the spectacle.

It was a tremendous experience and made all the better because Botswana defeated Malawi with fast, attractive, attacking football. They may not have emulated the great Brazil 1970 side but fortunately for me the fans and members of the Botswana Football Association were delighted with the contribution I made to their team's victorious performance. So much so that they invited me to extend my stay but as enjoyable and satisfying as it was, I was keen to return to Marion and the kids and hopefully another football job slightly closer to home.

The day following the anniversary match I was invited to an official reception by the British High Commissioner of Botswana that was attended by His Royal Highness the Duke of Kent. I had never attended such a lavish occasion before and found all the officialdom and formalities fascinating. Being a 'guest of honour' to a member of the royal family was also very flattering and it was a great end to my footballing adventure in Botswana. However, Botswana was not to be my last involvement of running a football team overseas.

Six years after my first spell in Cyprus I returned to the island in 1992. This time I was head hunted by Aris Limassol and I joined the side just after the Cyprus football season had started. Aris' season had started poorly and the team were rooted near the bottom of the First Division. Marion returned with me just after Christmas and the club provided a lovely top-floor flat for us to live in in Larnaca. Life was just as enjoyable in the Cypriot winter sunshine second time around, although Aris struggled to get away from the foot of the table. At the end of the season, it was incredibly frustrating to be relegated by the slimmest of goal difference margins. Relegation was a financial body blow to the club and my one year contract was not renewed during the summer. However, help was at hand in the shape of EPA Larnaca and I took over the management reins at EPA a couple of months before the start of the 1993/94 season. Again a flat was provided for Marion and me, but this time it was a dark and dingy basement and nothing like the two large apartments we had enjoyed with Anorthosis and Aris.

EPA also started the season poorly and I was frustrated that the club were not in a financial position to improve the playing squad. I soon discovered that the club had severe financial problems when my weekly wages were late in getting paid. By then Marion and I were desperate to return to Scotland anyway. Donna Lee was living with her grandma and wee Pete was knocking on the door of the Newcastle first team. The money issues were the final straw, and Marion and I returned to Scotland for good in 1994.

Whilst I was pleased that EPA managed to avoid relegation that season I was not surprised when they merged with Pezoporikos later that year. The financial reality dictated that both clubs needed to join forces to survive and AEK Larnaca FC was born out of the ashes of EPA and Pezoporikos.

In total Marion and I had four very enjoyable years in the Cyprus sunshine, the first two of which, with wee Pete and Donna Lee, being the most memorable. Cyprus is an amazing island where you can lie on a beach topping up your tan in the morning and head up to the Trudos Mountains for some skiing in the afternoon– well, people who ski can. But what made Cyprus extra special was the friendliness of the Cypriot people who made us feel so welcome throughout our stay. It is a very relaxed way of life and I can understand why so many ex-pats choose to live there. But whilst we enjoyed our four years in Cyprus the lure of Scotland was always too much too resist, especially as I was still convinced that I could make it as a successful football coach. However, I would endure more football rollercoaster rides after either side of my three managerial spells in Cyprus which would test my temperament and my push my resilience to the limit. No one had ever said to me that life was going to be easy, and managing and coaching football teams guaranteed that I would find that out first-hand.

17

SEND IN THE CLOWNS

Football history is littered with accounts of individuals whose involvement in the game had little to do with altruistic aims and objectives and was more about financial gain, massaging their massive ego or as a vehicle for their social climbing ambitions. I think it is fair to say that I had come across my share of foot-ball dodgy characters off and on the park in my playing days, but nothing prepared me for the trials and tribulations I was about to experience in the latter part of my football journey. At times I thought that I had gone from living with the *Waltons* in Cyprus to mixing with the Scottish equivalents of the Corleone family. Fortunately I was never made an offer I couldn't refuse and never woke up with a horse's head on my pillow, but it was a million miles away from the good times and fun experiences I had enjoyed during my playing days and the early part of my managerial career.

After I returned from Botswana in 1986, Alex Miller contacted me and asked if I was interested in assisting him in a coaching role at St Mirren. Alex had been at Love Street for three years and built The Buddies into a solid if unexciting side consistently achieving mid-table survival in the SPL. I had only been at Love Street a couple of months when Alex got a call from Kenny Waugh, the Hibs chairman, to take over as manager at Easter Road. My former Hibs team-mate John Blackley had resigned in mid-

November and for several weeks the media were speculating that Andy Gray, who was playing for Aston Villa, was the favourite to land the vacant manager's job. The other name mentioned in the Scottish media as a possible candidate for the Hibs manager job was Joe Jordan, who was playing for Southampton after returning to England from AC Milan. I recall thinking at the time that Gray and Jordan would have been strange appointments as neither had any managerial experience and had spent the vast majority of their playing careers in England after starting out with Scottish clubs. However both were still big names with the Scottish media and fans, but on 5 December 1986 Alex Miller was introduced by Kenny Waugh at a press conference in Easter Road as the new Hibs manager. The Hibs chairman made it clear that he wanted an experienced SPL manager at the helm and Alex Miller fitted that category perfectly. When this was reported in the following day's *Scotsman* it made mention of the fact that I was working with Alex at Love Street and I was tipped to join him at Easter Road. The article spoke in glowing terms of me 'as a former outstanding Hibs player with impeccable credentials'. My mum couldn't have put it any better!

Almost six years to the day that I'd left Hibs to become manager of Partick Thistle, I was back at Easter Road as assistant manager to Alex Miller confident that we could take the club on to bigger and better things. The one thing I can say with any certainty is that Hibs were in a far healthier position financially when I arrived at Easter Road than when I left three and a half years later. Despite the subsequent financial mismanagement of the club, I like to think I made a valuable contribution to the development of many of the players at Hibs during my time as assistant manager. I certainly brought in some additions to the playing staff that subsequently made a big impact on the Hibs team and Scottish football.

*

In our first season at Hibs our priority was to keep the club in the SPL with the playing resources that we had at Easter Road. Kenny Waugh ran a tight ship with the club's finances and there was no cash available to bring in any new faces for the remainder of the 1986/87 season. In truth that was not a problem for Alex Miller and me as it was exactly the same position we had to work with at St Mirren. In my first couple of months back at Easter Road I could see that there were several good, young players at the club who were hungry to succeed at the game. In particular John Collins, Michael Weir, Paul Kane, Gordon Hunter and Joe Tortolano stood out at training and they were dedicated professionals who were prepared to knuckle down and work hard. In that first season at Hibs Alex and I had a tough baptism, only managing to win six league games out of the twenty-two played, and we ended the season fourth bottom of the SPL, with thirty-three points. But crucially the team had avoided relegation.

In August 1987 Kenny Waugh decided to sell his majority stake in Hibs to David Duff for £700,000. Duff was a young businessman who was a qualified solicitor and had spent part of his early childhood in Bonnington Road, where I had also grown up. As I was to quickly discover, that was about the only thing we had in common. It is always easy to be wise with hindsight but I never took to David Duff from the first day I met him. Like many so-called yuppies that were around at the time, money seemed easy and talk was cheap. He breezed into Easter Road promising a new golden era of big name players that would have Hibs competing for domestic trophies and by the end of his time in charge he almost put Hibs out of business. His financial mismanagement caused mayhem at the club but thankfully Hibs survived – but only just.

The first thing David Duff did was to appoint his brother-in-law Jim Gray as full-time managing director. I always got on well with Jim and found him straightforward and relatively easy to deal with in contrast to Duff. On the playing side, the new regime was prepared to put money where their mouth was and Alex and I were told to go out and find quality players to add to the squad. Martin Ferguson, brother of Alex, was Hibs' chief scout and he was advised of Duff and Gray's brief. He scoured the country looking for the right players to bring to Easter Road. Our first signing was Neil Orr – a big, mobile defender who had spent several years at West Ham following his transfer from Morton. Neil was plucked from Upton Park for £100,000.

A few weeks later I received a telephone call from my old pal Joe Royle who was managing Oldham. Joe had read in the press that Hibs were interested in goalkeeper Ian Andrews who was at Southampton. It was true Martin had been watching Andrews and Southampton were looking for £250,000 to part with their keeper. Whilst Hibs were considering what to do about Andrews, Joe called me to say that Oldham were prepared to listen to offers for their goalkeeper Andy Goram. Hibs had played against Oldham in a pre-season tournament in the Isle of Man and whilst there was no doubt about Andy's goalkeeping abilities, he did come with a health warning. Martin Ferguson made several discreet enquiries down south and whilst every report was glowing about Andy's performances between the sticks it was not as complimentary about his antics off the park. On top of that Oldham wanted more than £300,000 for their keeper. I was tasked with negotiating with my mate and Joe drove a hard bargain. When I questioned the amount Oldham were asking for Goram, Joe reminded me that Andy was an established Scottish international having made his debut against East Germany two years earlier and he was a member of the Scotland World Cup squad that had gone to Mexico the previous summer. Joe told me that £325,000 for an established Scotland internationalist was a very good piece of business for Hibs and his final words on the matter were, 'Peter, I tell you what. If you're not happy with Andy after one month at Hibs you can send him back and we'll give you all your money back.'

I laughed at Joe's comment and fortunately Hibs never had to put his unusual offer to the test. In his second game Andy was outstanding in a 2–1 victory at Easter Road against Hearts, and four years later he would move to Rangers for £1 million where he would establish himself as one of the greatest keepers in the history of Scottish football. I don't think Hibs and Rangers fans realise how much they have Joe Royle to thank for 'The Goalie' coming to play in Scotland. Although I'm not sure Celtic fans will thank him for that telephone call back in the autumn of 1987 given the number of times he broke their hearts with outstanding performances in crucial Old Firm matches.

For a couple of years Hibs fans were drooling at the quality big-money signings that arrived at Easter Road. Scottish football had been given a much, needed shot in the arm when Graham Souness' English international imports started arriving at Ibrox and David Duff and Jim Gray seemed determined to emulate this by splashing the cash at Easter Road. Following Andy Goram's signing, in the space of a couple of years Keith Houchen arrived from Coventry City for £300,000, Paul Wright was signed from QPR for the same fee as Houchen, Brian Hamilton arrived from St Mirren and in February 1990 Hibs plucked Allan McGraw's son Mark from under the noses of Liverpool for £175,000. Martin Ferguson left no stone unturned in his search to bring top quality players to Easter Road.

One signing that gave me a lot of personal satisfaction was Pat McGinlay, who I watched play for Blackpool. Pat was only twenty-one years of age but after seeing him firsthand it took several telephone calls late into the night to secure his transfer to Easter Road. I was delighted when he went on to perform at the top level for Hibs for the next twelve years. Another youngster that went on to have an outstanding career at Hibs was Englishman Gareth Evans. Gareth was signed from Rotherham and in his first couple of weeks at Hibs wee Pete had to vacate his room at the Cormack family home for Gareth to help him acclimatise to life north of the border.

As well as these new signings, Hibs managed to get John Collins to sign a new two-year deal, despite intense interest in his services by several big clubs north and south of the border. However, the best signing of the lot was Stevie Archibald, who arrived from Barcelona via a loan deal at Blackburn in the summer of 1988. Archie was another player who came with a reputation – only his was of his love for the finer things in life such as luxury cars and designer clothes.

About the only thing Stevie had in common with his Easter Road team-mates was their mutual dislike for the club's manager, Alex Miller. In my opinion, Alex was a first-class coach who could read a game, knew when to make important changes before and during games and was very tactically astute. Alex's big problem was that he was not a good communicator with players, and when I worked with him for three and a half years at Easter Road, my main job was acting as the go-between between the team management and the players. Fortunately, this role came naturally to me and man-managing players was probably one of my biggest coaching strengths.

I relished working with Stevie Archibald during his time at Hibs, and in many ways it reminded me of when George Best was at the club. Archie had proven himself in Alex Ferguson's great Aberdeen side of the early 1980s and had gone on to star for Spurs and Barcelona. When he arrived at Hibs there had been speculation that Kenny Dalglish wanted to sign him for Liverpool, so it was a major coup to have him at Easter Road. He kept himself to himself away from the ground and rarely, if ever, socialised with the rest of the squad but at training he was a great role model for the younger players.

Like Bestie, he joined in specialised striker training sessions in the afternoons and I loved working with Archie in those sessions. In truth, it was a privilege to work with him and there was no question in my mind that even though he was past thirty he was one of the best players in Scotland at the time. His first touch was excellent, and like Bestie he was two or three moves ahead of the opposition and unfortunately on most occasions, his own team-mates. I also think working with Archie made many of the younger guys better players and I am sure the likes of John Collins, Mickey Weir, Gordon Hunter and Paul Kane learnt a lot from the football pro that was Stevie Archibald. One of the best individual performances I have ever seen in all my years in football was a master class by Stevie in how to lead an attack as a lone striker in a game against Celtic at Easter Road in October 1989. As well as helping himself to two goals in the 3–1 victory, Archie ran the Celtic back four ragged with his astute positional play, subtle lay-offs, incisive passing and clinical finishing. His performance had everything that day and I would urge coaches to look out a tape of that game and use it as a perfect example of how today's modern centre forward should lead an attack. It was nigh on perfect and a joy to watch.

Unfortunately, Stevie's relationship with David Duff and Alex Miller deteriorated after he took umbrage at being left out of Hibs' travelling party for the second-leg UEFA Cup tie in Liege. Then in early January it was 'taxi for Archibald' to make a sharp exit before a mid-week league game at Fir Park after Alex Miller dropped Stevie from the side. Archie's card was marked after that and he bought himself out of his contract at the end of January and returned to Spain to play for Espanyol. He proved to be a big loss to the team for the remainder of that season.

*

In the three years David Duff was chairman at Hibs, whilst the team's performances and results improved, Hibs didn't manage to bring any silverware to Easter Road. Our best finish in the SPL was fifth in season 1988/89 which qualified us for the following season's UEFA Cup where Hibs put in one of their best ever away European performances in beating Videoton of Hungary 3–0 before losing 1–0 on aggregate to Standard Liege in the next round. The team also managed to reach the semi-final of the Scottish Cup in 1989 but lost 3–1 to Celtic at Hampden. Mick McCarthy not only totally subdued Archie and Keith Houchen, but he also managed to score one of Celtic's goals and they would go on to beat Rangers 1–0 in the final.

During my last season at Hibs rumours began circulating around Easter Road, saying that the club's finances were not as healthy as David Duff wanted everyone to believe. Questions began to be asked by prominent supporters, shareholders and inquisitive local journalists.

In October 1988 Duff had floated Hibs on the stock exchange, the first club in Scotland to become a PLC. This initiative raised £1.6 million at the time, but within a couple of years, unbeknown to the players, the team management and fans, Edinburgh Hibernian PLC had bought a pub in Exeter for £1 million and a sports club in Devon for £400,000. Then in the early part of 1989 Duff announced a further share issue to raise £5.6 million to purchase Avon Inns, a chain of fifteen pubs and restaurants in the south-west of England.

During my final season at Easter Road there was more interest in the financial wheelings and dealings of Edinburgh Hibernian PLC than there was in the Hibs team on the football park. At one point there was talk of Hibs selling the stadium at Easter Road to help balance the books and relocating the short distance to Meadowbank. Fortunately, that idea was given short shrift by the council who owned the athletics stadium. By May 1990 the club's debts had climbed from the £880,000 they had been only eighteen months earlier to £4.5 million. The shenanigans in the boardroom were a total distraction for everyone at the club and at the end of the season I was one of several on the payroll that became surplus to requirements. Stevie Archibald had already left Easter Road in January, John Collins was transferred to Celtic for over £900,000 and I was given my P45 after the last game of the season against Dunfermline in early May.

It was in sharp contrast to my fortunes at the club only a few months earlier after I had taken over as temporary manager whilst Alex Miller recovered from a hernia operation. During my period in charge the team enjoyed a string of good victories, including a 1–0 win over table-toppers Rangers at Ibrox. I was also in charge of the Hibs squad that won their one and only trophy in the three years I was assistant manager at the club. Now I'm the first to admit that the Tennent's Sixes may not constitute 'real' silverware, but in the ten years of the tournament, TV coverage, a £16,000 cheque to the winners and a packed SECC in Glasgow ensured that competition to win the trophy was fierce. I was confident going into the tournament at the end of January 1990 that we could do well given the quality squad I had chosen. I knew we had the best goalkeeper in 'The Goalie' and with naturally-gifted footballers such as John Collins, Mickey Weir, Paul Kane, Pat McGinlay and Brian Hamilton in our squad I was sure we had a great chance.

The tournament kicked off with group games on the Sunday and we qualified for the following day's semi-final, where we were drawn against our local rivals Hearts. Despite twenty minutes of end-to-end excitement, the game ended 1–1 and Hibs won a tense penalty shootout 2–1. In the final the boys didn't let me down and we beat St Mirren 2–0 where Paul Kane, in scoring the first goal, took his tally for the tournament to eight. Andy Goram was captain of the squad and winning his first medal at Hibs was a great excuse for Andy to take his team-mates for a night out in Glasgow to celebrate (not that Andy ever needed any excuses to hit the town). When Alex Miller returned following his operation his attitude towards me changed and I think he saw me as a serious threat for his job. It didn't help that in amongst all the media reporting of Hibs' financial problems the odd report appeared, saying that I might be replacing Miller as manager. At one point there was even talk of former Celtic manager Davie Hay and me forming a new management team, but at the end of the season I was told that I was no longer part of the management set up at Easter Road.

Whilst I was lucky to have had far more highs than lows, leaving Easter Road for the last time in May 1990 was without doubt the lowest point of my football career and one of the saddest days of my life. My good pal and ex-Hibs team-mate Jim Blyth resigned his scouting job, so disgusted was he with the way I had been treated, and wee Pete also left the club. In sharp contrast, Jimmy McLaughlan, who I had been friends with since our days at Tynecastle Boys' Club, was my best man at our wedding and who I had taken to Hibs, stayed in his part-time scouting job after I was sacked. The old saying is true, it's at times like these that you know who your true friends are.

Within a couple of weeks of my departure the then Hearts chairman Wallace Mercer announced his intention to buy Hibs for £6.2 million, with the avowed intention of merging Hibs with Hearts to create an 'Edinburgh United' team that would play from a new stadium on the west of the city. Fortunately the high profile 'Hands off Hibs' campaign stopped Mercer in his tracks and even managed to recruit many Hearts supporters who were equally outraged at Mercer's proposal. The 'Hands off Hibs' campaign also managed to oust David Duff as chairman and soon after Tom Farmer stepped in to rescue the club from the brink of extinction. It didn't come as a surprise to Hibs fans several years later when David Duff ended up in jail after he was convicted of swindling building societies out of hundreds of thousands of pounds, which earned him a two-year prison sentence. The summer of 1990 was not a happy one for Hibs fans and while they went to work saving their club, I endeavoured to find another job in football after four productive seasons at Easter Road.

Despite putting out the feelers to my extensive network of football contacts, I spent the 1990/91 season in the football wilderness, during which I kept myself busy singing for my supper at the karaoke night business Jim Blyth and I had started. Then at the beginning of the 1991/92 season I was approached by Mattie Hall, the chairman of Gala Fairydean, to take over as manager at the Dean. Gala were one of the top sides in the East of Scotland Seniors League, and a couple of seasons before I took over at Netherdale Jim Jeffries enjoyed several successful seasons in charge at Gala before he was lured away to manage Berwick Rangers before then moving to Falkirk and managing Hearts to Scottish Cup success in 1998. I asked Jim Blyth to join me as my assistant at Gala and we had a thoroughly enjoyable year in Galashiels. I was impressed with the overall standard of players at Gala, although I'm not sure what they thought of their new coach given that training nights would alternate each week depending on what karaoke gigs Jimmy and I had in our diary. They never complained about this and made the most of my unusual arrangement with Mattie Hall when I organised karaoke evenings for them to let their hair down.

In my one and only full season at Gala the team won a very competitive League Championship which was made all the sweeter when we clinched the title against our nearest challengers, Whitehill Welfare, after beating them 1–0 at their home ground in Rosewell. The following season Gala got off to a great start, winning the South of Scotland Qualifying Cup after defeating Civil Service Strollers 3–1 in the final. I was particularly pleased with that victory as I used the old Liverpool counter-attacking strategy to snatch two breakaway goals in the second half of the final. In truth, the Strollers were the better team on the day but my tactics worked a treat to enable Gala to win the match and the cup. By the time Gala's first round Scottish Cup tie arrived, Marion and I had returned to Cyprus and the Dean narrowly lost in a replay to Ross County in Dingwall. I have always been grateful to Mattie Hall for getting me back into football after a long year on the sidelines, and I still look for Gala Fairydean's results in the Sunday papers every weekend.

After two very enjoyable but unsuccessful years in Cyprus I returned to Scotland in the autumn of 1994 to join my old Hibs team-mate Allan McGraw as first team coach at Greenock Morton. Big Al was an institution at Morton, having been in the manager's seat since 1985 and he was also widely respected throughout Scottish football. When I arrived at Cappielow, Morton were battling to win promotion from the Second Division and I was impressed with many of the players Allan had acquired. Two young Scots, Derek Lilley and Derek McInnes, were the mainstays of the team. Lilley would subsequently move to Leeds United, and in 2004 was a member of the Livingston side that beat Hibs in the Scottish League Cup Final. Derek McInnes was transferred to Rangers in 1995 after Paul Gascoine recommended him to manager Walter Smith after Morton played Rangers at Ibrox in the second round of the League Cup.

When I arrived at Morton I quickly set about trying to help Allan win promotion from the Second Division, but as the season progressed it looked like Dumbarton, with Murdo McLeod in charge, were going to win the one automatic promotion spot available. In my view, the key to Morton subsequently winning that season's Scottish Second Division Championship was the signing of two young Finnish internationals, Marko Rajamaki and Janne Lindberg. Collectively they may have cost Morton £250,000 but they were quality footballers that made the difference between success and failure. Facts don't lie and three of the four players nominated for the Second Division Player of the Year that season were from Morton, with Derek McInnes topping the poll, closely followed by Derek Lilley and Marko Rajamaki.

As well as being part of a successful squad in my first season back coaching I thoroughly enjoyed working with Big Al. He was one of the few decent, trustworthy and honest people I encountered in football in the 1990s and we worked well together as a coaching team. The management team, players and fans were looking forward to playing in the First Division in 1995, but in all honesty I don't think anyone at the club believed that we would come as close as we did to making it into the SPL at our first attempt. I genuinely believe we would have won the First Division that year if we had not lost Derek McInnes to Rangers in October. After the League Cup match at Ibrox, which Rangers won 3–0, Walter Smith signed Derek, who was a life-long Rangers fan, for £260,000. It was too good an offer for Morton to turn down but after two other Morton midfield men got injured we didn't have enough experienced players in the squad to cope with Derek's loss.

However, it was gut-wrenching for everyone at Cappielow to lose out on second spot to Dundee United on goal difference, and they subsequently defeated Partick Thistle in the play-off to go up to the SPL the following season. The 1996/97 season in the First Division turned out to be a big disappointment for everyone at Morton and we finished in eighth place. It had been an extremely traumatic year for Allan McGraw, whose wife tragically died in 1996 after a long battle with cancer and Allan announced that 1996/97 would be his last season as manager. The Morton chairman John Wilson persuaded Allan to move upstairs and become General Manager at the club.

It was widely expected, given how well Allan and I had worked together, that I would take over from him as manager but the chairman had other ideas and when Allan vacated the manager's chair, Benny Rooney was appointed manager and I was released by Morton. It was not a decision everyone at Morton agreed with and my departure split the board down the middle.

For me it was a very sad and disappointing end to three very enjoyable years at Morton, that were not without a fair degree of success. As well as winning the Second Division title in my first season at the club we had got tantalisingly close to getting into the SPL the following season.

I was also delighted that I was able to take wee Pete, who by now was anything but 'wee', towering above me at over six feet, to Cappielow after things didn't work out for him in his two years with Kevin Keegan at Newcastle United. Pete proved himself to be a very versatile player for Morton, making seventy-six appearances in his four years at Cappielow. During Morton's first season back in the First Division, wee Pete enjoyed his most successful season at the club, which culminated in him winning the Morton fans' Player of the Year Award. I was proud as punch and delighted for Pete as he had worked really hard at his game since he was a youngster and managed to establish himself in a very good Morton side that came within a whisker of getting into the SPL. I left Cappielow down but not disheartened at the end of the 1996/97 season, little thinking that I would be back to manage The Ton four years later.

After my shock exit at Morton, Liverpool offered me a job scouting for them and I was delighted to be back working in football, especially at the club where I had enjoyed the best years of my playing days. Then in December 2000, totally out of the blue, I received a telephone call from Gordon MacDougall, the chairman of Cowdenbeath, asking me to take over the vacant manager's job. Craig Levein had left to take over at Hearts and MacDougall said he was keen to fill the manager's job quickly. The following day I was introduced as Cowdenbeath's new manager in a press conference at the stadium. Cowdenbeath's website reported at the time:

A press conference was held at Central Park (Monday 4 December) to announce the new man to succeed Craig Levein as the manager of the 'Blue Brazil'. Peter Cormack, a player with Hibernian, Nottingham Forest and Liverpool and a former Scottish international. Apart from his playing experience, Peter has an outstanding CV and has previously occupied managerial positions at Partick Thistle, Hibernian and Morton before plying his trade in Cyprus for several years.

I was quoted on the BBC website saying, 'We're sitting at the top of the league, thanks to hard work, good performances and good organisation, so the side will be left alone. I'm looking to get as much out of the players in the second half of the season and I've made it clear to them that they need to work hard and show the same commitment.' Club chairman Gordon MacDougall added, 'Peter has a lot of experience and we are delighted to get him.

Ten days later, after a couple of training sessions and no matches, I was telephoned by Gordon MacDougall who asked to meet me at a McDonald's restaurant near the Forth Road Bridge. When I arrived for the meeting MacDougall didn't dwell on the small talk and offered me a sum of money to leave the job he had just appointed me to. I was speechless at first, and then quickly became very angry, especially after he cited the reason for his decision was that I was making too many changes. I told him that the only change in my short time at the club was that I was taking training. There had been no games for me to pick a side, never mind make any changes. The whole thing was like a bad dream, only it was no dream. It was what had become of player power in Scottish football in the twenty-first century. In appointing me to the manager's job the Cowdenbeath board had overlooked Gary Kirk, player/assistant-coach to my predecessor, Craig Levein. True to my word, I wasn't about to make drastic changes and one of the first things I did following my appointment to the manager's job was to ask Kirk to continue as my number two. But the dummy was spat out of the pram and he refused. I hadn't even managed to consider who to approach to fill the vacancy when it became apparent that pressure was being put on MacDougall to get Gary Kirk installed as manager instead of me. If the club had thought Kirk was the best man for the job they should have appointed him instead of me. But they didn't. What they did instead was buckle under pressure rather than being back their original decision and stick to it. To my mind and those of many others, that decision as a disgrace.

I told MacDougall what I thought of his pathetic cash offer to buy my silence and much to his discomfort I forced him into making a decision. Unfortunately for me he decided that sacking me after ten days as manager and replacing me with Kirk was his best option.

The Scottish football world was as shocked as I was with the way Cowdenbeath handled the matter, and they were vilified in the Scottish media and criticised by their fans. The whole sorry saga reflected badly on the reputation of Scottish football and made Cowdenbeath look silly. I know that they are one of Scotland's many provincial clubs who have to manage their financial affairs on a shoestring budget, but the way the club treated me was an embarrassment to their fans and made them the laughing stock of Scottish football.

In not accepting MacDougall's money to keep these events quiet, I was determined to make sure people knew exactly what had gone on and a month later sports journalist Mike Aitken of *The Scotsman* published my side of the story in an article under the heading 'Cormack lifts the lid on ten days that shook his world'. It is worth repeating most of that article to give you the facts of what went on and also to let you see my mindset at the time.

The Scotsman 13 January 2001

> With nearly forty years of experience as a player and a coach behind him, Peter Cormack felt he'd been around the block often enough to understand the unwritten rules by which managers are judged.
>
> As a young footballer who honed his craft under Bill Shankly in the 70s – he went on to manage sides in places as far flung as Cyprus, Botswana and Renfrewshire – the Scot formed the opinion that most chairmen and directors behave like number crunchers.
>
> 'Management is usually about results,' observed Cormack. 'But my record at Cowdenbeath was a bit different. Played none, lost none. They didn't even give me a chance to fail.'
>
> Hired last month to succeed Craig Levein . . . Cormack suffered the indignity of being dismissed before the 'Blue Brazil' played a single game under his charge.
>
> Even the Brazil, who dance to a Samba beat and usher their managers in and out of the Maracana Stadium through a revolving door, might regard this kind of treatment as cavalier.

A month after the axe fell Cormack is no nearer to understanding the events which led to his departure but is philosophical enough to talk over the ten days which shook Central Park.

'The whole story started on the golf course at Gleneagles where I was playing golf with some business friends of mine. We'd just finished our round when my wife called and told me Craig Levein was the new Hearts manager. I thought the appointment was a surprise because it's a huge step from Central Park to Tynecastle. Anyway half an hour later I received a telephone call from Gordon MacDougall, the chairman of Cowdenbeath, who asked me what I was doing and if I'd be interested in the vacant manager's job.

'I went straight to Cowdenbeath from Gleneagles in my friend's Range Rover and Gordon told me I could have the job. He said we could go over everything at my house on the Sunday and warned me that my only problem might be with Gary Kirk (the assistant manager) who was peeved at not getting the job himself.

'I made it clear that my first thoughts were not to change anything. For a start, I didn't know the Third Division. So I said I would have a word with Gary and encourage him to stay. And that's exactly what happened.

'I said I didn't plan any changes, but I would look at ways of improving the side after the team won promotion.

'We didn't have a game on the Saturday and I took another training session that morning and went to watch Dumbarton v East Stirling in the afternoon and from there I took in Liverpool's next match at Anfield.

'Both Joe Royle and Steve Heighway got in touch to say they would do anything to help me and I returned to Scotland for another training session on the Monday.

'Afterwards I learnt from a player, who felt ashamed about

what was going on even though he had nothing personally to do with it, that things were happening behind my back. Gordon eventually telephoned me and we had that meeting in McDonald's near the Forth Bridge.

'He said that a lot of players were phoning up complaining about the changes. My response was, "I'm not having this." I said there were no problems in training and everyone had worked hard. To be honest, I could probably have handled what happened to me if the team had played five or six games and we'd lost four of them. But that wasn't the case.

'All that happened was the club enjoyed a spell of good publicity. Not only that, the reaction of the players was first rate – I didn't have any sense they were unhappy. If I'd felt that something was wrong then I would have sorted it out.

'When I asked him for an explanation of what was happening to me, he couldn't give me an answer. Even now I'm no closer to knowing what really went on. I'm not sure if the truth will come out.'

Although he can now look back now at what happened to him a month ago with a sense of detachment, Cormack doesn't try and disguise the hurt which consumed the family.

'My wife and I were devastated by what happened. I've had a few knocks in the past when I left Hibs and Morton, but never anything like this. It is easily my worst experience in football.

'I felt so disappointed about what they did to me because I knew everyone would want to know what I'd done wrong. If I'd taken a wee pay-off, kept my mouth shut and walked away people would have said there is more to this than meets the eye. So I told my solicitor what I intended to do and said my piece to the papers. Credit to the sportswriters, they were all very fair. But I didn't feel that Cowdenbeath left me any option.

'What left me feeling shattered was that there was no credible explanation for the decision to sack me. I've played it over and over in my head since then and asked myself if maybe I had too much ambition for the club.

'Cowdenbeath are one of the game's smaller outfits. After they appointed me, they got publicity worthy of a Premier League side. Did that alarm them? I don't know. They offered me money to go away and say that I had other commitments. But I wasn't prepared to do that. I told the chairman I would rather speak to the press and tell the truth.

'I'd been through hard times in football before, but I kept my own counsel and bit my tongue when I could have said quite a few things. It's not in my nature to slate anyone – if you look back at my career, that's not something I've done before.

'What happened to me at Cowdenbeath though was something else. I couldn't take the money and keep my mouth shut. I had to let people know how I felt. But you deal with things. Since then I've left the matter in the hands of my solicitors. Now I need to get on with the rest of my life.'

For all the pain he went through last month Cormack's still upbeat about the Beautiful Game. He was consoled by the phone calls of support he got from fellow managers such as Alex McLeish and Jim Leishman.

'Ninety per cent of the people in our sport are honest guys who won't cut you up. The Cowdenbeath experience left me scarred. But if I was asked to go back tomorrow I would, because I still love football.'

There is an old saying that there is no fool like an old fool and my love for football is so great that the Cowdenbeath saga did not put me off football management. In the summer of 2001 I got a telephone call from Douglas Rae asking if I was interested in taking over as manager at Morton. I had always got on well with Douglas during my first spell at Cappielow and he was one of the 'good guy' directors who wanted me to replace Allan McGraw as manager in 1997. At the end of the 2000/2001 season Morton had released all their playing staff and the club were threatened with liquidation. Morton were only saved from extinction after Douglas spearheaded a fans' consortium to run the club. However when they appointed me as manager in July 2001 Morton did not have one single player on their books. I quickly set to work contacting the extensive network of people that I knew in the game and calling in as many favours as I could. In a mad two-week spell I managed to sign several free agents, which included re-signing David McGregor who had been released by Morton at the end of the previous season and a former Cappielow legend, Warren Hawke, who had played for the club during my first spell as assistant manager.

My arm-twisting persuaded Livingston to loan Stewart Grecan and Hibs gave us Alan Reid, but my hardest task was getting clearance from Australia for Davie McPherson.

The former Rangers and Hearts man had moved to play Down Under for a couple of years but I had heard that Davie was keen to return to Scotland and still fancied playing. I tempted Davie by offering him the assistant manager role at Morton and whilst he was up for it Morton needed to clear diplomatic hurdles before he could arrive at Cappielow.

It had been a rollercoaster first couple of weeks in the Morton manager's job and I still don't know how I managed to get eleven players on the park for our first league match in Division Two against Stenhousemuir. By this time wee Pete was playing at Stenny and my cobbled-together Morton side managed to win our first league match but that was about as good as it got that season. Eight months into the Morton job I decided to call it a day, as the pressure of travelling back and forth from Edinburgh to Greenock and managing the club on a shoestring budget was beginning to affect my health.

Big Davie McPherson had made it clear, sometimes too clear for my liking, that he was ready to step into the manager's job but after thirteen games as caretaker-player/manger, Morton ended the season relegated to Division Three and Davie left the club.

I am delighted that Morton's fortunes have picked up since those crazy summer days in 2001 but that experience let me see how different football had become in the forty years I had been in the game.

Money has become the god, with television determining where the power lies and players, through their agents, demanding higher and higher wages. After a working life as player, coach and manager I guessed in March 2002 that my active involvement in the game had probably come to an end. Little did I think that a couple of years later I would be embracing football computer technology with my mate at Kevin Keegan's Soccer Circus. Fortunately it didn't involve working with any real-life clowns – I had come across enough of them in football by then to last a lifetime.

18

LIFE AFTER FOOTBALL

Whilst professional football was part of my life for forty years off and on and gave my family a very good living, I was never slow at trying my hand at other money-making ventures. As well as embarking on a failed career as a pop star, clothes designer and model at Liverpool, I had another unfortunate business experience whilst at Anfield.

After we bought our house at Ainsdale, the Liverpool lads put me in touch with a local carpet supplier who went by the name of Tony Carpets (typical Scouse humour). Marion and I became friendly with Tony and his wife, and after a couple of years at Anfield Tony contacted me with a business proposition. He had acquired an old cinema that he thought about converting into a carpet warehouse but approached me with the idea of turning the run-down cinema into a sports club featuring snooker, squash and badminton. I discussed it with a few of the Liverpool players and other friends and everyone thought it was a great idea.

Tony went away and got architects' drawings prepared and I approached the Liverpool chairman, John Smith, about providing a bar in the club. Just when it seemed that the venture was about to take off, one day when I was at training Marion left a telephone message for me at Melwood to say that two bailiffs were on their way there to serve me a writ. It transpired that, unbeknown to everyone, including Tony Carpets' wife and family, he was up to his eyes in debt and the architect had started legal proceedings to get payment for his work. Thankfully Chairman John Smith and everyone at Liverpool were sympathetic and very supportive. I don't think it was the first or last time a Liverpool player has been duped into a dodgy business venture. I had to write a cheque for £500 to cover the architect's fees and get the bailiffs off my back. Every time I see Duncan Bannatyne on TV I think of Tony Carpets and I'm sure if things had turned out differently, our sports club in Liverpool could have really taken off. But it was not to be, and Tony Carpets was scored off my Christmas card list after almost blackening my good name.

The venture with Tony taught me a lesson and I was very careful about my next business partner when the opportunity to try my hand at something else presented itself in 1990.

After my heartbreaking experience as assistant manager at Hibs, I decided to go back into the entertainment industry, this time with Jim Blyth, doing karaoke nights. I had attended a few karaoke evenings and thought, 'I can do that.' So when no football offers came in after I left Hibs in May 1990, Jim and I got together £12,000 for a state-of-the-art karaoke machine with three microphones. I had seen that most people were shy about singing on their own but would go on stage with a friend or in a group and the extra mics encouraged them all the more.

I'll always remember our first gig in the Tommy Younger pub in Leith Walk and after that we had bookings most nights of the week. The £12,000 loan was paid off in less than six months, and as well as compering the nights, I got to sing a few numbers as well. The karaoke nights were a far cry from the hotel entertainment night we enjoyed with Joe Royle and his family on holiday in Morocco back in the late 1970s. Marion, Donna Lee, wee Pete and I were so competitive on that holiday that the Royles nicknamed us 'The Von Trapp Family'. Well, by 1990 I decided to put my musical talents to good use and Jim and I had some great nights in the pubs and clubs of Edinburgh and the surrounding areas. The family also regularly took advantage of the karaoke machine and one New Year we sang and danced until dawn. The last thing I remember of the occasion is my mum coming downstairs at seven a.m. to get a drink to take her sleeping tablet and heading back off to bed with a bottle of alcopops. I'm sure she would have slept like a baby after taking that concoction.

The karaoke business continued even after Jim and I took over at Gala Fairydean and for most of the 1990s it gave us a very good income and loads of laughs. Although sometimes it was torture having to listen to well-oiled pub-goers who thought they were the dog's bollocks but sang like a castrated cats choir.

Then in 2000 I was approached by a firm of Edinburgh solicitors who asked me to front a series of sports functions. I had been dabbling at after-dinner speaking, and this led me to establish the Peter Cormack Sportsmans' Dinners. My old mate at Liverpool Tommy Smith came north for the first dinner at the Minto Hotel in Edinburgh in January 2001. I had no trouble selling the 200 tickets and Smithy went down a storm. The audience of young and old football fans loved Tommy's tales of his time at Anfield and they particularly enjoyed his legendary stories about Shanks. He had them eating out of his hands and I couldn't have chosen a better team-mate to launch my new business venture.

The dinners were also a great vehicle for raising funds for a local cancer charity and I subsequently organised dinners graced by footballing luminaries Nobby Stiles, Ron Yeats, Ian St John, Norman Hunter, Duncan McKenzie, Stevie Kindon, Alan Kennedy and Frank Worthington. All the ex-pros did me proud, although Frank lived up to his 'wild man' reputation when he took exception to a comment made by one of the other speakers. Fortunately I was sitting between them at the top table and was put in the unusual position of having to be peacemaker. I was able to placate Frank whilst a much-relieved ex-referee made a hasty exit, citing his early departure on another speaking engagement later that evening. It was the one and only time I had the pleasure of sending off a referee as payback for the six red cards I was on the end of in my playing career, not to mention the armed escort I received at Anorthosis.

Then in the summer of 2006 my ex-Liverpool team-mate Kevin Keegan contacted me to ask if I fancied working for him at his Soccer Circus business venture which he was opening at Braehead on the west side of Glasgow. A few years earlier Kevin mentioned to me that he had conceived the idea of a series of interactive football games that could be used for youngsters to practice their football skills and also double up as a leisure pursuit for kids' birthday parties and other special occasions. When he first mentioned it to me, Kevin was so convinced that he was onto a winner that he invested a fair amount of his own money into the project. After a possible site in Manchester fell through he identified the Braehead complex as ticking all the right boxes, with good transport links close to a football-loving constituency.

The Soccer Circus opened at Braehead at the end of September 2006 and I spent a couple of nights a week working there with Kevin and groups of young starry-eyed footballers of the future. I thoroughly enjoyed working again with youngsters and there is no doubt the interactive nature of the Circus appealed to the younger generation brought up on a staple diet of computer games and mobile telephones. The Soccer Circus is billed as '100 per cent football, 100 per cent fun' and there is no doubt it is that and if it helps improve young footballers' skills and encourages them to play the game then that can only be a good thing. Since 2006 two more Circuses have opened, one at Center Parcs in England and the third one appeared in Dubai in February 2010.

Nowadays, when I speak to anyone about football, not long into the conversation I am asked my views on the game today and in particular the huge salaries top players earn. More often than not this question is usually put to me in the form of a statement such as, 'Peter, do you not think it's ridiculous, the amount footballers get paid these days?' Well, my honest opinion is that if clubs are prepared to pay players astronomical sums to play in their side, then I say good luck to the players for making hay whilst the sun shines. Top footballers are no different to anyone at the top of their sporting profession – look at what golfers, racing drivers and tennis players earn in winnings and endorsements. Then, dare I say, look at the golden hellos, never mind the golden cheerios paid to the CEOs at banks on top of the huge annual salaries and bonuses they receive. At least footballers' wages are performance-related – you can't say that about bankers! You might not expect an ex-football pro to say anything else about the rich pickings on offer to players, but that's not to say that I think everything in today's football garden is rosy.

My biggest gripe about many of the players today is the impression they give that they are not enjoying themselves on the park. You'd think with the lifetime financial security most of the top players get from a couple of seasons in the game, never mind a full career, that they would be able to play with a smile on their faces. Maybe they just can't cope with the pressure, but you ask any top sportsman from whichever era and they would say that it's the pressure that drives you to succeed. I know that's how it was for me and my team-mates at every club I played for, but we still managed to have a laugh along the way.

Club tours were especially fun-filled, although on one occasion Marion didn't quite see the humorous side when I returned from a Liverpool tour of Germany. It must have been around the time I saw myself as a fashion trendsetter, and one evening on tour I turned up for dinner in cream flared trousers and matching cream jacket on top of a bright red shirt. As I strolled elegantly to the hotel restaurant past the swimming pool I was pounced upon by team-mates, obviously jealous of my trendy togs and thrown unceremoniously into the pool. I saw the funny side, but Marion was not laughing when I got home as she had only recently bought the suit from Austin Reed and it had shrank to half its original size. When I relayed Marion's displeasure to my Liverpool team-mates, Tommy Smith piped up, 'Why don't you bring it in and I'll give it to Tarby and he can pass it on to his wee pal Ronnie Corbett? It's bound to fit him.' Tommy always had an answer for everything.

I looked on every day at training as a bonus, never mind playing matches in front of tens of thousands of people. Today I hear players moan when kids ask them for their autograph and I tell them the time to grumble is when no one wants to know you. Football can be a very short career and players should appreciate and enjoy their time in the limelight, not complain about it.

The training players undergo nowadays has also changed dramatically from when I played. Whereas pre-season was about running the summer excesses out of your system until you were physically sick or physically exhausted, today sports science is applied to all aspects of football training. Tables with computers are dotted around training facilities, with players wired up to heart monitors and GPS tracking devices. If only the Hibs trainer Tom McNiven could have stuck a tracking device on Willie Hamilton his life would have been a lot easier but probably not as much fun as trying to work out where Willie had skived off to on our way back from training. As well as the new technology, players are devised personal training programmes, consult sports psychologists and dieticians which probably make today's footballers better athletes than in my day but the jury's out for me on whether or not players are more skilful and whether the game is better than it was in the 1960s, 70s and 80s.

Injuries have always been an occupational hazard to professional footballers and I had my fair share during my career. My first serious injury occurred at the start of my sixth season at Hibs, when I tore the ligaments in my ankle. As soon as the injury was diagnosed my ankle was encased in plaster and I was warned that I could be out for six weeks. Fortunately I was back playing after three weeks, but it was the start of mixed fortunes I was about to endure for the rest of my playing career. Not long thereafter I suffered swelling in my knee that stayed with me when I moved to England. The problem was the cartilage, and I quickly learnt that if I rested properly between games and protected it at training then I could get by in matches. That strategy didn't always work and at Forest, Liverpool and Bristol City there were times when I was out of action for several weeks at a time.

Like many players from that era I played in a lot of matches I probably shouldn't have after taking cortisone painkilling injections. Former team-mates of mine Allan McGraw and Tommy Smith have had their battles with those in authority since they stopped playing, about the problems they have encountered in later life because of the cortisone injections, but there were several reasons why players did this. The first was down to basic economics. Players' wages were structured around three components – a low basic salary, appearance money for playing and usually a decent win bonus. It invariably meant that if you were out injured your weekly wage packet would be a lot lighter than if you were playing in a winning team. It would be even worse if, as was normally the case, the team were playing more than one game in a week.

The second important reason players hated being out injured was the fear of not getting your place back in the side when you did get yourself fit. No more was this the case than at Liverpool, and to be honest I put off getting my knee operated on much longer than I should have because of the fierce competition for places in the Liverpool midfield. In early 1976 I had no choice once the doctors diagnosed internal bleeding on my knee, which required surgery and that put paid to the remainder of that season. By the time I returned to training at the start of the 1976/77 season Ray Kennedy had established himself in what had been my regular number five shirt and young guns Terry McDermott and Jimmy Case were also knocking at the door for a place in the Liverpool midfield. Whilst the knee op was a success I still had to be careful for the remainder of my career and there were several times at Bristol City and Hibs when I had to miss out on matches because of the knee ballooning up, particularly when pitches became dry and hard. Nowadays all the talk is about squad rotation where many regular first team players get rested to protect them from injury and overplaying. When I was playing, managers very rarely changed the team from one game to the next if everyone was fit. Managers would also put pressure on players to take risks with injuries and clubs were not as protective of players as they are nowadays. They tended to take the view back then that they had invested a lot of money in transfer fees and they frowned on not getting a return on their investment.

Today the opposite is the case and football clubs protect the investment they make in players and no expense is spared when it comes to looking after them when they are out injured. That has to be seen as a step forward. These days my knees still occasionally give me jip and I can be forgetful now and again – but then again, I'm no spring chicken, having celebrated my sixty-fifth birthday on 17 July 2011. Joking aside, I am convinced that years of heading footballs in games and at training is the root cause of my problem. However, the medical professionals say that it would be opening up a Pandora's Box to acknowledge this. This hasn't stopped many ex-professionals and their families challenging medical opinion. Back in the late 1990s, former Celtic players Billy McPhail and Jock Weir unsuccessfully pursued claims for compensation at an industrial tribunal and their case was highlighted in a *Frontline Scotland* TV programme on BBC Scotland a few years later. The best-known case was that of former West Brom and England international Jeff Astle who I played against in the early 1970s. Jeff's family took a case through the English courts after he died suddenly of degenerative brain disease in 2002. The coroner recorded death by industrial injury as a consequence of repeated minor trauma through heading the ball. I can understand why the medical profession is cautious, and unlike the United States where there have been extensive studies on the causes of brain damage to former boxers and American football players, not enough attention has been given to this issue in the UK. The ball manufacturers are very defensive on this issue, citing that these days footballs are much lighter, but I am convinced of the detrimental impact on the long-term health of footballers at all levels, professional and amateur but the Pandora's Box mentality prevails.

Amongst the charitable work I undertake these days, I especially enjoy helping Alzheimer Scotland and in particular their Football Reminiscence Project, along with former Hibs teammates Billy Hunter and Lawrie Reilly, who is still sprightly for his age. The project, managed by Martin Rothero and run with the Scottish Football Museum at Hampden, involves volunteers, many of whom are ex-players, meeting up with men who are suffering with dementia and we sit and blether about the good old days. I love the chat and it is amazing to hear the memories of games, players and incidents that come flooding back during these conversations. We all have a laugh and a joke about funny incidents that happened in games, and at the end of one of our meetings when the men were asked if they'd like to do it again, one old joker piped up, 'Aye, that would be braw but can we have a pie and Bovril instead of tea and biscuits next time?' That's another example of the older generation looking back fondly at their football memories.

Nowadays I fear for the future of many football clubs in Britain who are on a very slippery financial slope. The situation that arose at Rangers at the start of 2012 is a disaster, not just for than great club's players, staff and supporters – it was a wakeup call for everyone involved in football in the British Isles. Sir Alan Sugar recently revealed in a BBC 2 documentary that the cumulative debt of the twenty clubs in the English Premiership in 2011 was £3.3 billion. There is something clearly wrong when every club's annual expenditure is greater than its annual income – that is the economics of the madhouse and unsustainable in the long term. Michel Platini was on the programme talking about the new rules that FIFA intend to introduce, but I will believe that when I see it. Platini is well-intentioned, but I think the big clubs' tails are wagging the football authority dog. In Scotland the problems are even more acute. In simple terms, Scottish football club supporters are asked to pay far too much for the standard of football on offer. Like many football fans, I go to matches wanting to be entertained and enjoy good football from both teams. Very rarely are my expectations met. Ok, I hear you say, he's an ex-player who is setting his standards too high. Well, you might be right there, but what Scottish football needs to wake up to is that it's not just Peter Cormack who thinks that the quality of football played in the SPL is poor – the vast majority of fans who loyally attend games week-in and week-out think that's the case and they are voting with their feet (or their backsides in this era of all seated stadia).

Another forgettable SPL season passed in 2010/11 with Rangers pipping Celtic to the title by a single point and Hearts finishing a distant third, thirty points behind the Champions. I was lucky enough to get my first team debut for Hibs a few months after my sixteenth birthday. I was not an exception – in the 60s and 70s teenagers were quickly blooded in the first team at every club in Scotland if they had proved themselves in reserve matches. Now there is no reserve league to give youngsters that necessary experience and as a consequence very few teenagers are given a run-out in the first team.

It is much easier for clubs in Scotland to sign overseas players on the recommendation of agents or through their network of football contacts in here, there and everywhere. Like every football fan in Scotland, I savoured the class and skill of the likes of Henrik Larsson, Brian Laudrup and Gazza in the 1990s but sadly these days are long gone. The vast majority of the foreign imposters that have graced the Scottish game more recently are light-years apart from the world-class players at the top clubs in England and I firmly believe that they are holding back the development of young Scottish players. I'd love to see more Scottish clubs dispense with the services of the foreign legion in favour of grooming their own home-grown talent.

I genuinely believe that Scottish clubs have to take a step backward to the era when I started out in the game in order to go forward. Rather than waste money on overseas duds, they should nurture Scottish players. I don't know the statistics for the SPL but Sir Alan Sugar's football documentary reported that when the Premiership began in England in 1992 there were eleven foreign players in the twenty teams. In season 2009/10 there was over three hundred. England supporters dream every four years about winning the World Cup – you only have to look at those statistics to realise that their dream will remain just that for the foreseeable future. Still, they at least qualify for the Finals – Scotland fans' dream is simply to get past the qualifying group stage. The last time we were in a World Cup Finals seems an awful long time ago and qualifying for the next tournament in Brazil is going to be very tough, but let's hope having Wales in our group can invoke memories and summon up the spirit of the successful 1978 and 1986 World Cup qualifying campaigns.

It's a pretty bleak football picture and thankfully one that I do not have to worry about these days. The biggest challenge for Marion and me is deciding what we will do when our six lovely grandchildren visit. We are fortunate to be able to spend our leisure time with Donna Lee, her husband Lee and Reece, Ryan and Fraya and wee Pete and his wife Lee and their children Luke, Lois and Flynn. Six active and energetic grandchildren keep Marion and I on the go but it is great fun. They certainly ensure we sleep well after they've been for a visit. The other challenge Marion tasks herself with is deciding where we will go on holiday. Football was good to both of us and there are not many places we haven't visited together and these days we still enjoy holidaying abroad, especially with the family. I'm also fortunate to get invited along to the odd charity golf fundraiser by Jim Leishman or to Ray Clemence's annual event in Spain. These are great opportunities for meeting up with former teammates and rivals who are now just old friends. As you can imagine, the talk very rarely strays far from football and we are all experts with our own opinions on the game today. You'll not be surprised to hear that the consensus is that it's nothing like as good as it was in our day. Marion and I also regularly meet up with Neil and Mima Martin, who have been friends for over forty years and we always try to get down to Liverpool for the annual players reunion every December.

It is great catching up with old team-mates from the four years I spent at Anfield. The warmth and friendliness of the get-together is another great legacy left by Shanks and Bob Paisley. I often wonder what these wily old foxes would have made of the modern game with its foreign billionaire owners, football agents and player power. I'm pretty sure, like Sir Alex Ferguson, they would have adapted and put successful teams on the park week-in and week-out.

Recounting and re-living my football glory days for this auto-biography has reminded me of the great playing career I had at Hibs, Nottingham Forest, Liverpool and Bristol City in what I regard as the most exciting era in the history of British football. Of course I am unashamedly biased in that statement, but I also think the statistics bear me out. In the eleven seasons I played in England six different clubs won the First Division Championship, with Liverpool reigning supreme five times. On many occasions several clubs battled it out until the last game of the season. Contrast that to today's English Premiership, which is dominated by the four or five richest clubs with the remainder making up the numbers. Whilst Celtic and Rangers dominated the Scottish game in the 1960s there were dozens of excellent players at the other clubs, many of whom went down south to play in the English First Division or were snapped up by the Old Firm. I was lucky to play for the two greatest managers of that era – Jock Stein at Hibs and Bill Shankly at Liverpool – and both men shaped and defined my attitude to life just as much as they influenced my football career. I am eternally grateful to them and all the other managers I played under and team-mates I played with in my eighteen-year career.

This book is as much a tribute to them as it is a legacy of my life in football. My mum won my very first battle when her heart stopped when she was giving birth to me on 17 July 1946. Her survival was testament to her fighting spirit and she passed that on to me, putting me in good stead for the duration of my time in football. Thankfully my football highs greatly outnumbered the lows, and my journey from the Cowshed to the Kop has been as enjoyable as it was successful.

CAREER STATS

Hibernian FC

23 November 1962 debut vs Airdrie at Broomfield in Scottish
First Division aged 16 years 130 days.
Match result: Airdrie 2 vs Hibs 1.

In two spells at Hibs Peter played in 280 competitive matches
(including substitute appearances) and scored 100 goals.

202	Scottish league	77 goals
38	Scottish League Cup	10 goals
17	Scottish Cup	4 goals
13	Fairs Cup	3 goals
10	Summer Cup	6 goals

22 October 1980 Final competitive match as a player vs
Ayr United in Scottish League Cup Quarter Final.
Match result: Hibs 0 vs Ayr United 2.

Nottingham Forest FC

4 April 1970 debut vs West Bromwich Albion at
The Hawthorns in English First Division.
Match result: WBA 4 vs Nottingham Forest 0.

Between 4 April 1970 and 2 May 1972 Peter played in 86
competitive matches (including substitute appearances)
scoring 20 goals.

74	English First Division
5	English League Cup
5	FA Cup
2	Texaco Anglo-Scottish Cup

Liverpool FC

2 September 1972 Liverpool debut vs Derby County at
Baseball Ground in English First Division.
Result: Derby 2 vs Liverpool 1.

Between 2 September 1972 and 14 August 1976 Peter played
in 186 competitive games (including substitute appearances)
scoring 26 goals.

127	English First Division	21 goals
20	English League Cup	1 goal
15	UEFA Cup	1 goal
14	FA Cup	2 goals
4	European Cup	
4	European Cup Winners Cup	1 goal
2	Charity Shield	

Bristol City FC

13 November 1976 debut vs Tottenham Hotspur in English
First Division at White Hart Lane.
Match result: Spurs 0 vs Bristol City 1.

Between 13 November 1976 and 20 December 1979 Peter
played in 86 competitive matches (including substitute
appearances) and scored 19 goals.

67	English First Division	15 goals
5	FA Cup	1 goal
2	English League Cup	
12	Anglo Scottish Cup	3 goals

Partick Thistle FC

1 October 1983 Peter included himself in the thirteen-team
squad vs Brechin City at Glebe Park and came off the bench
for the last twenty minutes aged 37 years and 76 days.
Match result Brechin City 2 vs Partick Thistle 0.

This was Peter's only player-manager appearance in 3 years at
Firhill.

Scotland

25 June 1966 International debut v. Brazil in friendly at
Hampden Park.
Match result: Scotland 1 vs Brazil 1.

Peter gained nine full Scotland caps and made his final international appearance coming on as sub in a friendly match against Holland in Amsterdam on 1 December 1971 which the Dutch won 2–1.

Career Total

648 competitive matches 165 goals scored